Fat History

Fat History

Bodies and Beauty in the Modern West

With a New Preface

PETER N. STEARNS

NEW YORK UNIVERSITY PRESS

New York and London

NEW YORK UNIVERSITY PRESS
New York and London

Library of Congress Cataloging-in-Publication Data
Stearns, Peter N.
Fat history : bodies and beauty in the modern West / Peter N.
Stearns.
p. cm.
Includes bibliographical references and index.
Contents: The turning point—The medical path : physicians and
faddists—Fat as a turn-of-the-century target : why?—The
misogynist phase : 1920s–1960s—Stepping up the pace : old
motives, new methods—Fat city : American weight gains in the
twentieth century—The evolution of weight control in France—
The French regime—Atlantic crisscross : the Franco-American
contrasts—Conclusion : the fat's in the fire.
ISBN 0-8147-9824-1 (pbk. : alk. paper).
1. Weight loss—United States—History.   2. Weight loss—France—
History.   3. Body image—United States—History.   4. Body image—
France—History.   5. Fat—Social aspects—United States—History.
6. Fat—Social aspects—France—History.   I. Title.
RM222.2.S755   1997
613.2'509—dc21   96-45878
                        CIP

New York University Press books are printed on acid-free paper,
and their binding materials are chosen for strength and durability.

Manufactured in the United States of America

10 9 8 7 6 5 4 3 2 1

CONTENTS

NEW PREFACE

Research for this book was completed in the mid-1990s, and the book itself has been circulating for six years. In taking the opportunity to add some comments for this edition, a welcome occasion, there are two obvious targets. First, has the book's reception provoked any particular concerns? And second, more important: Have there been significant new trends since the 1990s? How do the book's findings stand up in light of the addition of a bit more contemporary history?

The Book's Reception

The book has, on the whole, fared well. Sales have been steady, and the book also has been cited in a persistent stream of media discussions, including radio and television shows about weight and diet trends. *Fat History* is not the only historical treatment of these issues, but it has become accepted as a standard. And interest and concern about weight, health, and the pressures and opportunities of appearance maintain an appetite for insights that the historical perspective readily provides. Adding a comparative approach to the history helps as well, offering some challenging vantage points on how and why Americans think and behave as they do (as well as why the French think and behave as they do).

Reviews of the book have been largely laudatory. The one partially critical comment that struck home was a lament that the book did not go far enough in providing support and guidance for people who suffered most from the intense pressures of the contemporary body image. The history of dieting and weight consciousness, in both France and the United States, certainly helps explain how troubled people could seize on demanding standards as a reason to reject normal eating, through anorexia nervosa or bulimia. It does not however focus on a condemnation of these standards, nor does it tell those suffering from or dealing with eating disorders what to do.

I sympathized with the criticism — and certainly with the pain eating disorders can cause — but ultimately I thought it was somewhat off the mark. First — and here I may be vulnerable — I do not think the historical record necessarily warrants a condemnatory approach. It is certainly true that the emergence of weight control standards has put pressure on people. This has undoubtedly encouraged eating disorders (though the best history of modern anorexia, by Joan Jacobs Blumberg, suggests the pattern began, chronologically, before the modern diet culture and therefore has more complex roots). It has also encouraged, particularly in the United States, widespread dissatisfaction with one's own body, which I find both odd and troubling. At the same time, modern historical conditions have also encouraged weight gains, thanks to more sedentary jobs, less walking, and the unprecedented abundance of food. Considerable weight gain has occurred even with the existence of highly touted slenderness standards. Some of these weight gains, in turn, have probably been harmful to health and quality of life. Here, the real question is not a criticism of the pressure slenderness standards apply (however harmful this pressure is to a minority), but a discussion of whether the standards, or something like them, should be revisited toward greater effectiveness. Maybe, given contemporary eating opportunities, we'd be worse off without them. It's a complicated situation, and the book's lack of crusading zeal reflects the complexity.

And there is a further point. This is a work of history — deliberately applied to a topic of pressing contemporary concern. As a historian deeply interested in the relationship of the past to the present, I think it's my job to analyze trends in a way that can promote understanding — in this case, of how contemporary diet pressures and weight patterns have emerged from developments over the past one hundred and twenty years, and what causes for these developments stand out. I do not think it's my job, directly, to add explicit recommendations about how this understanding should be used. I sincerely hope that a historical perspective helps readers step out of a purely contemporary box, to think about the factors that have accumulated to shape their thinking and behavior. They may well decide, as a result, to change attitudes a bit—to ease up, perhaps, on a slavish adherence to diet goals, to recognize the manipulation involved in presenting endless images of demanding slenderness. But they might also, after some thought, accept the historical vantage point but decide not to change at all. I truly believe that historical understanding is useful even if it does not lead to an explicit self-help message. I'm more interested in encouraging thoughtfulness than in telling people what to do. We have too many experts eager to sell advice, too few interested in helping us to gain perspective. But the tension between offering historical analysis and moving to explicit recommendations about current behavior is real, and some readers might prefer a different balance. At the least, the criticism helped me articulate my own thinking on the subject.

For me personally, the history of diet consciousness has suggested slightly more skepticism about extreme appearance demands and health claims, providing a bit more self-tolerance and additional sources of amusement about the foibles of contemporary life. But it has not convinced me to stop worrying at least a little.

I did write the book as part of a continued fascination with the subject of self-control and self-scrutiny in American life. In my judgment, modern Americans have developed a demanding set of personal standards, even while believing that their society is dominated by unbridled hedonism. Diet goals, and a sense of dissatisfaction with one's own body, form part of a larger pattern, all the more insidious in that we are largely unaware of the pressures involved. I do believe that it is in our interest, individually and politically, to gain better awareness of this aspect of contemporary reality. We are needlessly vulnerable to claims that we (or at least, those around us) lack character, that we have become endlessly self-indulgent, despite the fact that we have internalized a considerable array of self-regulatory criteria in what is, still, a rather moralistic society. Self-blame can also be a contemporary problem in that it distracts us from political and social factors that merit more concerted attention. Here, I do contend that there is a definite message in contemporary history.

But it is also true that while diet-consciousness promotes some arguably undesirable self-preoccupation, as against broader political concerns, our standards are looser in practice than in principle. The gap between profession and reality is greater than in some other areas of contemporary American moralism, such as smoking or germ-fighting. And the equation may have been changing a bit, which leads to the next challenge of updating my comments.

The Pendulum

One of the distinctive features of the book is its treatment of actual trends in weight, in the United States and France, along with the attention to the development and promotion of diet standards. The object, obviously, was to juxtapose ideals and realities, and the gap in the United States was an important finding.

But six years ago, interest in the standards themselves ran high. Concern about the unrealistic pressures, particularly on women and girls, helped the book fit into an active discourse. This concern persists, and I still get inquiries about how history can help us understand how the fashion industry and the medical profession combine, however innocently, to make women think ill of themselves and, in extremis, actually to become ill through disorders incurred in a tragic effort to achieve ideal slenderness. A fascinating issue of the journal *Social Forces*, in 1999, contained a number of articles contending that our diet culture continues to lead people astray and actually worsens health through oscillations, urging that fitness, not fatness, is the crucial point. And indeed, despite dire medical warnings, weight gains have not as yet actually generated deteriorations in mortality (though arguably they have constrained further progress, and their impact is limited partly because of new medicines against hypertension and diabetes).

On the whole, however, interests have shifted, and the part of the book that deals with actual weight trends and the growing gulf between recommendations and real American bodies now elicits the more frequent commentary. Three things, clearly, have happened to shift the balance of concern at least for the moment.

First, keepers of the flame long involved with promoting weight control have intensified their efforts. Health and insurance experts, in particular, continue their well-meaning campaign. This part of the formula, discussed in the book, persists with a vengeance.

Second, feminist analysis, though still relevant, has receded in vigor. An important source of attention to the manipulative and even destructive qualities of diet standards has partially lost its voice. Scholarly attention persists, as noted above, but the visibility of cautionary comments has diminished.

And third, American weight gains continue, providing substance for the growing literature on mounting obesity rates. There is new reality behind the shift in interest from the diet standards themselves, to the failure to live up to the standards.

Janus-faced, the book is relevant to both sets of interests. However, in offering an update, the change in opinion climate offers inescapable guidance. We need to talk particularly about real weight and the role of standards in an increasingly corpulent America.

There are two key questions, beyond briefly outlining the most recent trends. First, does the historical and comparative analysis the book offers still apply in explaining Franco-American differences and their roots in the past? And the answer is, yes, which means in my self-interested opinion that this book is still worth reading for the now as well as for the then. Second, are there signs that the American diet culture, developed over a century, is breaking up in favor of a new paradigm? And here the answer is, not proven; a lot of continuity remains, for certain, but there are some straws in the wind (as there always are) pointing toward change.

Fatter History and Its Causes

In the late 1990s and early 2000s, Americans, on average, continued the rapid weight gains that had begun to develop from the mid-1980s onward (and which are discussed in chapter 6, particularly on page 133). The idea of a significant break from the previous decades of noticeable but more moderate average weight increases becomes inescapable, as this new period now extends for almost two full decades. And this also means that the causes of this most recent set of trends, briefly discussed in chapter 6 and then later comparatively, require further expansion.

By 2002, the average American gained about 20 pounds between his or her twenties and his and her fifties; this was twice the rate in the 1970s. The percentage of obese and overweight rose to 62 percent, up from 48 percent in 1980 according to the Surgeon General's scathing calculation. Straight obesity rates had almost doubled in the same span.

Three factors, operating particularly vigorously in the United States throughout the twentieth century, certainly acquire growing salience in this current period. First, the commercial food industry, and particularly those devoted to snacks, gains a growing hold. In a sense, food consumerism, long at war with dieting from the alternating pages of early-twentieth-century women's magazines onward, wins. Americans begin to find it difficult to locate themselves at any distance from a snack supply. There is evidence also that the size of restaurant portions has increased as a relatively cheap way to entice customers. Second, the special case of children becomes even more significant, as childhood overweight expanded rapidly. (Some estimates held that the percentage of overweight children had tripled in twenty years.) Though warnings about children's weight gains begin to become common from the 1970s onward, as noted in the book, they simply have not matched parental sense that children's eating should be indulged or at least cannot be regulated. Worries about eating disorders contribute here as well; at least the darlings are not anorectic. Children were also affected by an expansion of video games and computer interests that often cut into physical activity. And third, of course, the minority population continues to expand, and with it the groups that never bought into the idea of American slenderness. Obesity increases were particularly marked among blacks and Hispanics. In other words, causes of American departures from diet ideals, discussed more fully in the chapters that follow, continued to prevail with accelerating impact.

But new factors added in, supplementing the prior inducements. These new factors are essential in explaining the dramatic departure from approved standards and prior behavior alike. The campaign against smoking must be considered. It kicked in during the 1980s and drew far more zealous response than dieting had achieved. Former smokers often ate more; and Americans proud of their nicotine self-control might ease up on their eating conscience. Formal, home-cooked dinners declined as wives worked more and older children went their separate ways. Fast food restaurants and supermarket prepared meals were the beneficiaries. Given well-established American traditions of hasty and fairly heedless eating, another finding explored extensively in *Fat History*, this new pattern unquestionably furthered weight gains. Finally, Americans from the mid-1980s onward began working longer hours to maintain incomes amid growing inequality and to meet the demands of profit-hungry superiors. More work and, often, less leisure easily created greater reliance on snacks as a source of comfort, often consumed in brief breaks or on the job itself. More work could also mean less parental time to supervise children's eating habits and more eagerness to tolerate food rewards that could relieve a sense of guilt about the lack of opportunity for more elaborate shared leisure. This factor eased in the late 1990s, with increased contact hours between parents and grade school children, but it was not entirely erased. A nation under increasing stress used food as solace.

Causation can be elusive, and of course it should be debated. The new factors combined with the longer-established vulnerabilities in American eating behavior. There is no contradiction with the analysis developed in *Fat History*, simply the need to recognize some additional promptings.

France Revisited

Comparison continues to help in sorting out the key components in the changes and continuities of recent behavior. *Fat History* argues that Americans long had more trouble than the French in living up to contemporary slenderness standards because of several durable differences in eating habits and eating goals, compounded by a greater American reluctance to discipline children in this regard. These differences continue to affect behavior.

But it is true that the international comparative picture became more complicated by the mid 1990s. Increases in obesity rates were noted in many countries, including even China and India, where the growth of an urban middle class introduced important new factors. These international trends highlighted the role of new food availability and food consumerism; the globalization of certain food outlets and habits, including fast foods; and the spread of more sedentary lifestyles, affecting children (video games and the internet) as well as adults. There was some global convergence around patterns that initially had been particularly visible in the United States.

France participated, and a new sense of a national problem developed. The average French person gained 1 percent in weight between 1997 and 2000. Obesity rates increased by 17 percent, to 9.6 percent of the total population. Obesity among children was particularly troubling, as rates increased by 50 to 100 percent, to 13 percent of the total. French commitment to disciplining children's eating was clearly relaxing in practice, or at least was inadequate against new pressures. As before, the less educated particularly suffered, their habits reflecting economic distress, including rising unemployment, combined with new eating patterns.

These changes were significant, and perhaps they predicted a future in which France and the United States would converge in corpulent consumerism. But key differences remained, and not only because the French had been thinner before the current craze took hold. Changes in average weight and in obesity percentages (including children) were more modest than in the United States. In another interesting contrast reflecting gendered aesthetics,

French women continued to keep their weight down, changing much less than men. And even as they warned about a new problem, the French persisted in cautioning against moralism in response.

But the critical difference was behavioral. At a rough approximation: the new pattern of French weight gain began a decade after the American intensification and then (late 1990s) proceeded at about 50 to 60 percent of the simultaneous American rate.

The new comparisons suggested the need for additional nuances in explanation. The impact of food affluence, hurried eating habits, shifts in women's role in meal preparation, and increasingly sedentary children now spread beyond the United States. But causation also underscores continuing differences. Along with the differentials explored in chapters 8 and 9, some of the factors that spurred additional American change operated differently in France.

Thus the American anti-smoking crusade had only modest echoes in France, which in turn reduced one of the sources of weight gains. More important, and truly striking, was the growing work gap. As Americans worked more — by 2002, recording the longest average hours in the industrial world, with on average the shortest vacations — the French tended to move down toward a 35-hour work week. There was simply less need for compensatory snacking, more interest in elaborating other forms of leisure and relaxation.

The main point is clear. Two countries that shared many cultural features, including a commitment to slenderness, had long varied in eating goals and habits, and several factors now maintained considerable variance. The comparative analysis explored more fully in the ensuing chapters provides the context for even more contemporary understanding. Again, cultural differences must be balanced against new parallels in weight trends. But they remained great enough that without too much hypocrisy, the French could still take national pride in their bodies, as they preened against their transatlantic cousins. As the *Nouvel Observateur* put it none too subtly in 2000, "America is nothing more than an immense eating machine."

Cultures and Prospects

And there is a final comparative point. Part of the Franco-American juxtapositions in *Fat History* distinguishes between the French aesthetic-health approach, and the American moralistic-health combination. Evidence suggests that the French approach continues to work better, whatever its greater shallowness in principle. To be sure, the French have added a new level of concern about weight gains, appending to older health and beauty arguments a warning about not falling into the American pattern of obesity. In the United States, a greater moralism persists, and it remains possible—a point discussed later in the book—that this moralism is actually counterproductive, in setting goals that are too high, with additional eating spurred by failure.

But is the moralistic culture itself cracking, adding to the behavioral change? Are Americans not only eating more, but getting comfortable with their larger bodies? Evidence is contradictory. Some fashion models are now fuller-figured. Some television shows feature paunchy actors, though mainly when working-class or ethnic settings are meant to be conveyed—so here the signals are not entirely clear. Going against this, however, is Betty Crocker, long a pastry symbol, was altered toward greater slenderness in 2000. The bare midriff look for young women puts a new premium on thinness. Diet advice and books still win wide attention, while pledges of weight loss still top the charts for New Year's resolutions. The heroic dieter, capable of casting off a hundred pounds or more, a staple of women's magazines a half-century ago, has returned in advertisements for a sandwich chain. A leading cola (140 calories per bottle) uses a tight-bellied teenage sex kitten as its ad symbol. And the spate of attacks on American obesity itself suggests the continued momentum against weight, with abundant aspersions on lack of willpower and character-eroding deficiencies in exercise. The culture built up for more than a century still has legs, though of course it might someday yield more fully to altered behavior.

Weight and dieting still exercise their fascination, which is why the analysis in *Fat History* warrants attention. The new twists, particularly in American weight gains and some new French concerns, add to the need to assess the causes of the gaps between ideals and reality—and also raise questions about the results. Are we even less enamored of our own bodies than we were a decade ago? The answer is, quite probably yes. Is our new behavior dangerous to our health? The dominant answer is, yes, though there are dissenting voices. What kinds of changes should we consider for altering behavior, or reducing self-distaste, or both? The answer is complex, but it can emerge only from considering our history.

PREFACE

Over the past century, a major addition has occurred in Western standards of beauty and morality: the need to stay thin, or at least to profess a desire to become thin. The results are wide-ranging, from a desperate quest for slimmer opera stars to a huge new commercial literature and product line designed to aid in the slimming. Representations of success change: in 1890 success was embodied in corpulence, failure in emaciation; by 1900 they were drawing even; and now success is thin. Even illness changes: nineteenth-century anorexics complained that eating hurt them, and neither they nor their doctors focused on thinness; twentieth-century anorexics talk about feeling fat and full, and everyone notes their extreme of slenderness. Most important — for the history of extremes such as anorexia has been studied more than the evolution of everyday anxieties and constraints — the list of things people worry about and the ways they evaluate (and often scorn) their own bodies have shifted dramatically in modern times. Intense beliefs in the disgusting inferiority of fat join more traditional revulsions against sexual deviations or uncontrolled drunkenness. Failure to live up to the new, standardized body image entails at least an appalling ugliness, at most a fundamentally flawed character.

But corpulence is a different target from some of the more traditional taboos in that it is so visible, particularly in an age where praise for slenderness is highlighted by increasingly revealing fashions. This is one of the reasons that the modern struggle against fat, in addition to being new and pervasive, cuts so deeply into many people's lives. One can conceal to some extent an inability to live up to society's emotional standards and even sexual demands, but fat cannot hide. Similarly, successful battles against fat can be different from struggles against other obsessions such as smoking or drinking, in that people have to eat; complete abstinence is impossible, so they must work out some kind of more subtle self-restraint.

This study traces a major new modern code as it formed and had its first effects. To be sure, the code built on some older elements, such as preachments of moderation and the Christian attack on gluttony as sin. But the full modern code, and the notion that even moderate fat was somehow disgraceful, were genuinely novel when contemporary slenderness standards began to emerge in the 1890s. A full century constitutes a fairly short time for the institution of such dramatic personal standards, so it is hardly surprising that this is also a history of hesitations and failures. Indeed, the new culture is still contested, particularly in the United States but even to an extent in Europe. Various organizations argue that fat is or should be beautiful, that fat people must be protected against cultural discrimination. Faced with evidence that the United States is not living up to French levels of thinness, a commentator urges that we revalue fat itself, to see in it an emblem of stability, of "loving ponderation," reminding us quite correctly that "in other ages, fat was beautiful." Different social groups and, in the United States, important racial cultures dispute the middle-class norms. It is particularly useful to undertake a history of the origins and evolution of a culture when its tentativeness and unevenness can also be noted.[1]

Dieting, weight consciousness and widespread hostility to obesity form one of the fundamental themes in modern life in countries like the United States and France. American women's magazines feature an average of one dieting article per issue, making the subject one of the ubiquitous staples of this genre. A near majority of American adults diet or profess to be about to diet. Under the spur of dramatic new body standards, the French on average have lost weight over the past quarter century. Yet few studies are available of this widespread phenomenon. The only substantial analysis derives from perceptive feminist complaints about the special impositions of dieting standards on women, but while this provides a legitimate angle of vision it is unduly narrow.[2] When and why did serious dieting concern begin? (Interestingly, some feminist studies mistake the basic chronology while missing the whole first phase of the modern trend; this helps explain why, despite much perceptive analysis, the studies skimp on the explanation by assuming a singular plot against women.) Was the American pattern of dieting the only one available to increasingly prosperous industrial societies? And why, given the tremendous attention devoted to dieting, have Americans encountered such mixed success in weight control? Decades of warring against fat have left us, on average, fatter than we used to be; here is another target for some serious thinking about a surprisingly meaty topic.

This book seeks to explore, through history and comparison, the meaning of fat and antifat in modern Western society, and particularly the United States and France. These two countries share the Western diet impulses of the past century, but they represent quite different poles within the common trajectory. I try to capture some of the charm of the topic in the many amusing programs and devices that have competed for attention in a weight-conscious century (dieting is not usually fun, but it can certainly be funny). I will even more consistently seek to understand, using a pervasive but seemingly humdrum topic to explore some surprisingly complex features of modern life. Fighting fat goes beyond fashion and even health. By delving into the larger meanings, we can better understand why many modern people worry as they do and even why such a gap may exist between slim ideals and bulging realities.

The study derives from several related premises. First and most obvious, anxiety about weight is so important in contemporary Western society that historical perspective is a vital part of our self-understanding. Concern about weight and dieting is not timeless; its origins are modern and can be quite precisely traced. It is also, at least in the form it took, not inevitable. Forces in the past created a need for change and formed a culture still very much in operation today. A large segment, possibly a majority, of contemporary American adults are concerned about their weight, many of them checking it regularly, some of them actually doing something

about it. Any phenomenon this widespread deserves historical treatment as something more than an antiquarian feature of the recent
past. Further, a serious history of fat and dieting is inextricably tied
to such established historical topics as gender, fashion, and body
imagery.

There are, to be sure, a few existing historical efforts, fewer,
however, than the importance of the subject warrants. I will use
prior histories gratefully, but while some of them offer useful detail
on the emergence of specific weight-watching organizations or
sequences of diet recipes, their analytical heft is inadequate.[3] In
the case of France, there is no explicit history at all, though studies
of fashion, appearances, and medical treatments of obesity are
helpful.[4]

Yet a comparative focus does far more then fill some unnecessary gaps in two nations' histories. It illumines crucial distinctions
in methods and meanings within a common modern process.
While many aspects of American and French dieting are similar
because of shared causation, crucial differences, ranging from timing to larger cultural purposes, developed in the twentieth century
as well. At first blush, the French seem to diet more straightfor-
wardly — that is, to control their weight without larger symbolic
baggage — than Americans do and do so more successfully. They
also snack less and eat more moderate portions in meals of a more
standard size.[5] So there is a challenging comparative difference
here, with France and the United States at opposite ends of the
modern spectrum. Only through a rather wide-ranging history can
we grasp how two different versions of a modern standard emerged,
and why Americans cannot readily imitate the French even when
they recognize that, in weight control and aesthetic self-esteem,
the French have surpassed them.[6]

At first glance, the relative French success may seem counterin-
tuitive, as many envious American travelers have noted. French
preoccupation with food might leave them more, not less vulnerable, to the perils of obesity. The French are both more slender and
more food conscious than their much more diet-prone but fatter
transatlantic counterparts. Both societies have seen some basic
changes in body perceptions over the past century as part of a

common Western experience with prosperity (contrasting, for example, with patterns in Russia, where explicit dieting is not a social norm). While the role of fat and slenderness in many cultures raises fascinating comparative issues — including cases where brides are deliberately fattened to increase their desirability — France and the United States, sharing key basic trends, offer more precise comparative targets and more revealing juxtapositions toward explaining what the modern mania is all about. For the two peoples' definition and implementation of change diverge considerably; even the amusing aspects vary, with the French more open to self-parody about food and Americans more susceptible to bizarre routines of self-denial.

Furthermore, the two countries have long been fascinated with each other's eating and with each other's bodies. American interest dates to the nineteenth century, when France came to symbolize fashion and stylish restaurant dining. This has continued even as American power has increased; French movie stars like Brigitte Bardot in the 1950s have recurrently symbolized the latest in bodies or bodily display. With greater knowledge has come complexity; impatience with French penchants for leisurely dining (a costly impatience in the case of the restaurant misplanning at the Euro-Disney, where it was assumed that the French would snack as quickly and often as Americans) combines with envious appreciation of French foods. French focus on American lifestyles is admittedly more recent. From 1900 onward, the United States was seen as a source of important advances in diet products and methods; this attachment intensified in the 1950s as American cultural presence became overwhelming. American models, widely discussed as well as photographed, surpass French stars as pervasive sources of body imagery. At the same time, diet methods constitute one of those areas where the French have prided themselves on resisting American errors. And a morbid fascination with American obesity has complicated the exchange as well; films like *L'Amérique Insolite* (*Unaccustomed America*) (1960) dwelt vividly on overweight Americans and on their fast, voluminous food consumption as they chowed down in diners and at picnics, a theme taken up again in *L'Amérique Interdite* (*Forbidden America*) (1982). The transatlantic fascination nourishes fat history in both countries, and both guides and sustains a comparison.

Finally, and here both countries participate, Western worries about weight and efforts to control eating represent a fascinating modern constraint in a period when liberation and individuality are often seen as hallmarks of a rebellion against Victorian restrictions. In fact, twentieth-century people unquestionably limit their eating or bemoan their inability to do so far more than their ancestors did. Part of this change results from more sedentary occupations and entertainment, more abundant food, and laborsaving devices such as automobiles. But part of the change, and certainly the extent of the concern, go beyond simple reactions to modern artifacts. In fact, eating restrictions are not the only constraints twentieth-century people place on themselves, even as they partially emancipate behaviors in other areas. At the same time, new constraints continue an older campaign to discipline the body, which has long been seen as a vital current in Western manners and definitions of respectability. Understanding the meanings of and reasons for the rise of our new disgust over fat clearly serves to add to our grasp of the complex evolution of contemporary values and the patterns of daily life.

By 1994 over 40 million Americans were involved in formal diet programs, with 45 percent of the population claiming dieter status of some sort, while between 12 and 40 percent of the French professed to be dieting. Diet products were gaining an ever increasing place on the food shelves. Awareness and concern about fat form one of the leading cultural symbols of the later twentieth century. Determining how this current began, what factors have sustained it, and what it means to people in advanced industrial societies gets at one of the staples of contemporary life, where professed ideals and individual behavior can clash in revealing ways.

Some conservative purists worry about the proliferation of historical topics that take us farther and farther afield from understanding the staples of history like power relationships, the activities of the state, and the role of great ideas. It is true that the development of new body imagery and new anxieties do not have much to do with political phenomena narrowly construed. Like all social conventions and regulations, however, body imagery is related to power, in this case in the increasing need of the powerful to regulate their fat as a demonstration of successful self-control and in the common scorn for individuals and lower-class groups who fail to measure up. And while not directly deriving from any particular Great Idea, hostility to fat is part of larger cultural shifts involving doctors and science, artistic standards, religious uncertainties, and, quite strikingly, an effort to establish a backhanded kind of ethical code in a period of rapidly changing values. They are not great ideas, to be sure, and indeed include a good bit of outright hokum in a field pervaded by faddists and exploiters, but ideas that came to form part of the modern mentality nevertheless.

And here, ultimately, is the main point. I began this study interested in dieting as a widespread human phenomenon and as an example of how modern people regulate themselves or are regulated, even while professing great personal freedom. It turns out, however, that explaining attitudes toward fat and the successes and failures of a culture of restraint involves probing various other aspects of modern life. I needed to explore basic responses to food, not surprisingly, and here French and American differences loom large; eating habits are cultural products, deeply rooted in social structures and systems of values.[7] Also, moral responses to a high consumption society and a need to compensate for the perils of indulgence figure in. Values associated with children and family play a role, helping to explain, for example, the American tension between feeding frenzies and diet ideals. Even politics prove relevant, as Americans commit to dieting (in comparison with the French) in part because of the meagerness of their political expression. Weight consciousness, like any seemingly prosaic topic that engages deep popular concern, provides a surprisingly wide window on what modern people are like and why they vary.

ACKNOWLEDGMENTS

Acknowledgments and a personal note: social historians who deal with what the French call the intimate side of the past face not only the challenge of demonstrating significance but also the necessity of acknowledging personal participation. The student of diplomatic alliances or crucial past elections may need to offer no disclaimers of involvement, but topics such as gender or emotion or body ideal inevitably include the researcher as participant. Several of the few histories and cultural studies of dieting already available emanate from individuals admittedly hostile to the modern weight regime, seeking liberation from its standards and greater tolerance for individuals (often including themselves) of more varied body type. I have no such specific stake, but I am involved with the topic as a recurrent, sometimes partly successful but never triumphant dieter, aware since boyhood that my form fell short of the contemporary ideal (which I unquestionably shared). I come to this topic neither with the superiority of slenderness achieved or the confidence of fatness defiant. Whether this involvement colors my treatment I cannot presume to say, but it unquestionably makes my travails part of my own history. While my appreciation for the topic stemmed from my wider interest in the constraints of modern life, it has surely been enhanced by my participation in some of its ambiguities.

I have benefited from lots of advice and assistance, and no small amount of solid research help. My thanks to my colleagues in the Center for Cultural Analysis at Carnegie Mellon University for various suggestions; I'm particularly indebted to Andrew Barnes,

Michael West, Barbara Freed, Steve Schlossman, Judith Modell, and Kenya Dworkin y Mendez. Mary Lou Roberts was exceptionally generous in guiding me to French materials. Susan B. Whitney added valuable suggestions on France. Noralee Frankel helped with materials as well, and Jill Fields and John Komlos offered a number of useful suggestions. Librarians at the Carnegie Mellon University Library, Alliance Française of Pittsburgh, the Musée Social, the Bibliothèque Marguerite Durand, and other centers in Paris were uniformly helpful. Special thanks to Mme. Geneviève Morley of the Bibliothèque historique de la Ville de Paris. Research assistants, providing ideas as well as data, included Liesl Miller, Tom Buchanan, Jason Andracki, Derek Davison, Kerri Ullacci, and Sung Ho Lee. Niko Pfund and Christine Wong at NYU Press supplied a variety of good ideas and assistance. As always I'm grateful to my family for interest and support, Carol Stearns was a model in many ways and Deborah Stearns offered a number of good ideas. Thanks also to Karen Callas for assistance with this manuscript. Bon appétit to all.

· I ·

American Fat

1 The Turning Point

Between 1890 and 1910, middle-class America began its ongoing battle against body fat. Never previously an item of systematic public concern, dieting or guilt about not dieting became an increasing staple of private life, along with a surprisingly strong current of disgust directed against people labeled obese. In contrast to patterns in the nineteenth century, when body styles, particularly but not exclusively for women, shifted faddishly every few decades, the growing passion for slimness set a framework that would last at least a century. To be sure, the slimness ideals would be occasionally modified in the twentieth century — women's breasts and hips were variable to a degree — but on the whole they not only persisted but intensified. The initial crusade against fat, shaping up around 1900, would seem tame by later twentieth-century standards, but it set the fundamental culture.

Historians have known about the turn away from plumpness for some time, though nonhistorical commentary often misses the point by confusing the intensification of dieting after World War II with the real origins of the phenomenon. The one good history of dieting identifies the turn-of-the-century change.[1] So do several studies of women's fashion history.[2] So does the exciting historical work on the nineteenth-century origins of modern eating disorders (about which we may know more than we know about changes in normal eating patterns in the same period).[3] Research of this sort not only must be acknowledged but also can be utilized to craft a fuller account of this quiet shift in American worries. For existing treatments fall short of a completely adequate account of the transi-

3

tion in several respects. Even Hillel Schwartz, the pioneer in exploring the American social history of dieting, oddly slights the initial turn to slimness in his haste to get into the crass commercial exploitations of the new standards in the later twentieth century. The result is, first, an incomplete grasp of the range of attacks on fat that began to emerge around 1900, not only in fashion or in specific slimming devices but in diverse public comment as well. A fuller history will admittedly confirm existing understanding of the chronology involved, but will add scope and significance to what was more than a cosmetic shift. Second and more important, existing accounts do not really explain the shift itself. Causation is lightly passed over with remarks about the triumph of the ideals of athleticism for women (which is rather a manifestation of the new trends than a full explanation) or with assumptions about commercial manipulations. Finally, because causation is not thoroughly understood, the dimensions of the change itself have been oddly downplayed. This contributes, in turn, to the general neglect of dieting by other social historians dealing with deep cultural change in the early twentieth century, a neglect that has limited the scope of otherwise exciting findings while trivializing diet history itself.

The fact is that the advent of systematic concern about dieting was an important change in middle-class life, particularly for women but across the gender divide as well. The paucity of social-historical treatment is surprising. Tracing what was to become such an abiding, daily preoccupation of millions of American people adds to our understanding of the changing experience of life in the twentieth century. There is every reason to explore this phenomenon as part of interpreting significant social change. Further, the growing attack on fat imposed decisive new constraints on American life in a period when, in many respects, increasing latitude and informality were gaining ground. Ultimately the history of dieting must be brought into conjunction with other areas where constraint was being reconsidered — emotion, sexuality, posture and dress, propriety of language, cleanliness — for a fuller picture of the dynamics of middle-class life over the past hundred years. Not surprisingly, the history of dieting reminds us of the need to go beyond simple generalizations about Victorian rigidities yielding (for better or worse) to tolerant permissiveness and individuality. In areas like the body, Americans imposed on themselves some novel and demanding strictures. A focused exploration of how this process got started is an essential first step. To be sure, an inquiry into dieting pulls away from conventional historical topics, at least initially. Dieting has little directly to do with politics, but after William Howard Taft, slimness did affect politics in the new constraints placed on the bodily desiderata of political candidates. New topics in social history often turn out to have broader implications, and amplifying the historical analysis of a widespread preoccupation, justifiable in terms of the pervasiveness of the phenomenon itself, will suggest a number of larger insights.

This section traces the advent of what would become a durable American diet craze, first by recapitulating relevant earlier developments in the nineteenth century, both those that foreshadowed dieting and those that the new attack on fat had to counter. The range of manifestations are charted next, again confirming familiar chronology but in more systematic fashion. Then causation is addressed, to repair a real analytical void. From this the analysis can be extended to assess what the change meant. The factors in the growing hostility to fat provide insight beyond explanation. More than justification for a subsequent century of anxious dieting, they entailed some necessary compensation for other developments in American life (beyond abundant food) in which the worry was perhaps as essential as the weight.

Before the Fat Focus

Thinness has long been an available ideal in Western culture. Western society produced no systematic encouragement of force-feeding, which some cultures introduced to create ideal plumpness in brides. Greek wisdom preached moderation (a notion Benjamin Franklin would reproduce in *Poor Richard's Almanac* in urging reason over appetite), but Christian revulsion against appetite was even more relevant. Though the Bible largely ignores fat or equates it approvingly with prosperity — the fat of the land — there are a few disparaging references. The images of saints were typically slender. Fasting was a virtue that could be carried to extremes by aspiring religious in the Middle Ages.[4] The Puritan version of Protestantism maintained this. The English Puritan Thomas Wright in 1630 defined the sin of gluttons, who "think, talk, and earnestly procure to have great cheer, dainty dishes; they eat more than nature requires; at the table they will have the best; and in fine, the easy rule to perceive them, is to note their care & anxiety to fare daintily, to feast often, and therein to delight much."[5] The few historians who have tackled the subject of dieting heretofore have properly noted that it built on long-standing beliefs and images that associated restraint in eating with holiness.

Christian-derived concern about the control of eating as a means of combating sin helps explain why food would be selected as a target of constraint in a society otherwise increasingly indulgent. Northern Christian societies, for example, had established the practice of depriving children of food as a punishment, long before systematic dieting or eating restraint emerged as goals. French peasants used this punishment into the twentieth century. Americans certainly could stress the ploy in the nineteenth century; in a famous instance, the president of Brown University (proud of his ability to avoid physical violence) deprived a stubborn young son of food for thirty-six hours until the boy bowed his will to his father. Many other cultures — including Christian Hispanics — view this use of food as a weapon against children as appalling. By the same token, the privileging of food as a method of control set a relevant framework for the culture of dieting that has emerged over the past century, though the culture by itself it did not create this framework.[6]

Concern with dieting took on new dimensions in the late eighteenth and early nineteenth centuries. It was at this point that the word "diet" began its evolution from its initial meaning in English, of a regimen specifying certain types of food to remedy illness, to its modern usage of losing weight.[7] Romanticism brought ideals of slender, ethereal beauty, though the same Byron who praised dieting also volubly liked voluptuousness in his women. In the 1830s, high fashion in New York briefly stressed a willowy look, with a hint of frailty, as standards of appearance began to be more important for respectable women. Harriet Beecher Stowe railed against the slenderness imagery of *Godey's Lady's Book,* the first popular woman's magazine, bemoaning the hostility to "opulence of physical proportions."[8] Some women began accordingly to eat more sparingly or to corset themselves, and an ideal of a slender waist (though with greater roundness above and below) persisted for young women. Unprecedented reports and apparently a rising incidence of anorexia nervosa soon after the mid-nineteenth century suggests that thinness was gaining enough new attention to motivate a durable form of female deviance, though it was the process of eating, not body shape, that ensnared anorexics at this point.[9] Fashion changes in the later 1850s, though short-lived, emphasized more natural clothing for women with fewer artificial restraints, which could combine with earlier hopes for thin-waistedness to create new interest in lightness. Insistence on secluding pregnant women in the interests of respectability, though inspired not by food concerns but by Victorian sexuality, might also have promoted a quest for slenderness particularly among women. More intense etiquette standards focused heavily on eating habits in the middle and upper classes, emphasizing proper implements along with avoiding slurping and gorging, yet another set of constraints that applied to food.[10]

During the mid-nineteenth century also, new nutrition crusaders began to win public attention. Growing concern about the body and what went into it paralleled the growth of new forms of food processing and a new if nervous commitment to a commercial market economy. At least in England, this derived from eighteenth-century medical concern about the effects of overeating on the liver and kidneys; here too diagnoses linked diseases to the more general increase in the consumption of goods. For the nineteenth-century United States, Stephen Nissenbaum has shown how crusaders like Sylvester Graham urged pure food, including avoiding fats and commercial baked goods, in a combination of health faddism and moral revulsion against the excesses of a market society. This linkage was crucial in the later development of modern dieting standards. Graham pushed vegetarianism along with sexual restraint in a crusade against overstimulation. Warnings against gluttony accompanied this message, though they were not the central point. Graham's message of simple foods, temperance, and chastity was widely disseminated in the 1840s, winning many converts, particularly among young, urban men. Other popular fads picked up at least part of the same message. Water cures, widely followed by wealthy women, added attention to careful and restrained nutrition, though again more in terms of the types of foods selected than through any particular focus on weight.[11]

Clearly, a substantial precedent existed for a crusade against fat, which helps explain the new movement that developed by the 1890s. But it is crucial to remember that this precedent in no sense created modern dieting. Specific dieting efforts were not reported in the United States, a few brief flurries in the 1830s aside. The word itself continued to refer to a general nutritional regimen, only adding the weight loss interest very gradually. This is why fad terms — like the English import "bantingism" or the American "fletcherism" — remained useful until about 1910, when diet as verb and noun gained its specific modern meaning. Religiously inspired fasting seems to have declined markedly in the United States (and England) during the nineteenth century, a shift of particular significance for women. New reports of anorexia nervosa may indeed have reflected the decline of this more traditional outlet for certain personality types. For middle-class Americans generally, interest in pure nutrition vastly exceeded any specific concern about weight control.

Most important, plumpness remained quite fashionable, particularly after the 1830s. Western art had long touted full figures — the work of Rubens is the most famous case in point — and nineteenth-century art on the whole maintained this tradition of beauty. Mature women were supposed to be fat. Elizabeth Cady Stanton was praised for her rotund features — "plump as a partridge" — because they were linked to successful motherhood.[12] Weight was seen as natural after frequent pregnancies during which women were urged to eat heartily. Leanness might be a virtue in the young, but it was a positive vice in the mature. Susan B. Anthony, accordingly, was criticized for her gauntness. Women on stage were supposed to be voluptuous, and if they used corsets, it was to accent their roundness. Between the 1860s and the 1880s, rotundity gained ground for men as well as women. European dress styles emphasized the "semblance of embonpoint," as a British observer noted among women in Boston in 1859. Portrait painters stressed buxom qualities. Doctors urged the importance of solid weight in their growing campaign against nervousness.[13] S. Weir Mitchell demonstrated how skinny forms correlated with discontented, nervous personalities. Actresses at all levels of the stage illustrated and promoted fashionable plumpness, adding bustles to a corseting designed to stress ample bosoms and derrieres. Costume, indeed, intended rather to rearrange fat than minimize it, while newspaper advertisements featured nostrums designed to help weight gain long before their columns opened up to diet products. A decent belly on a man denoted prosperity and sensible good health. As Mitchell noted, "A fat bank account tends to make a fat man"; "[p]lumpness, roundness, size . . . are rightly believed to indicate well-balanced health."[14] When even John L. Sullivan got stout, he could still be held up as a symbol of masculine strength and implicit sexuality, in contrast to skinny, effete dandies. "A little paunch above the belt was something to be proud of."[15] Even as some interest in dieting emerged in Europe amid medical advice concerning moderation, Americans persisted in maintaining their full-figure standards through the 1880s and beyond. The British Lillie Langtry, for example, was faulted for lacking "roundness of limb" because of too much exercise. As one fashionable woman later noted of the era (using a term that only later entered the popular vocabulary), "No one counted calories."[16] Touring European actresses who had begun to control their weight through dieting were greeted with some aesthetic skepticism. Individual Americans may have dieted, but there was no publicity and no general cultural support. Interest in exercise did begin to increase for both men and women, but it was not initially associated with slenderness.[17]

Dominant American food habits certainly supported the aesthetic and medical approval of corpulence. We return to American food traditions more fully later as part of a more elaborate analysis, but certain nineteenth-century patterns can be quickly established. Everyone who commented on American eating during the century noted its abundance. American foods, from strawberries to salmon, were bigger than their European counterparts, and the sheer quantity of offerings followed suit. This was a land of plenty, and meals demonstrated this directly, while Americans may have gained some cultural stake in using food to prove their national, as well as personal, material success. Upper-class meals (like those in Britain, but unlike the French) featured an amazing array of heavy courses, a pattern that extended into the twentieth century. Cookbooks and women's magazines emphasized baked goods with vast quantities of dough. Even the fastidious Ralph Waldo Emerson corresponded on the issue of eating pie, ultimately concluding that the pastry was fine if consumed for breakfast, as a preparation for the exertions of the day. *Godey's* began a regular cakes feature in the 1870s that seems in retrospect absolutely overwhelming. Apparently, women best demonstrated cooking prowess through this sweet, high-caloric offering. A single issue of this popular magazine might contain recipes for rice cake, sponge cake, Dundee cake, and Scotch marmalade cake, or butter pudding, Alderley pudding, ginger pudding, German fritters, Sally Lunn, soda scones, caramel custards, apple soufflé, and Italian rice pudding. The list seemed endless. Americans were also known for their rapid eating, as if maximal stuffing, not savoring quality, were the principal goal. Actual eating habits and recommended standards amply supported the approval of a certain girth in both male and female bodies; it would have been difficult to maintain a really ethereal ideal.[18]

In sum, important changes had to occur to generate the kind of concern with weight control and reduction that started to appear only in the 1890s. The concern not only reversed a generation-long plumpness fad. It did so with extraordinary durability and with a crusading zeal that would ultimately mark it as far more than surface fashion.

Signs of change began to emerge from several directions in the 1890s as the United States, after having clung to its customs of plenty and the corporal results, turned to a concern about fat a decade or so after a new sense of style had emerged in France and other parts of Western Europe. John L. Sullivan's unexpected boxing defeat in 1892, at the hands of a much trimmer "Gentleman Jim" Corbett, triggered widespread comments about the importance of slim efficiency over the kind of ill-discipline that a paunch suggested — an important reminder that the emergence of a new hostility to fat was not directly solely at women.

Overall, the revision of body imagery and the growing disgust directed against corpulence were concentrated in three sites where the modern American interest in dieting first developed consistent expression: shifts in fashion for women and men alike, a host of new fat-control devices, and the rise of public comment on fat. There was no carefully orchestrated general strategy and, as we will see, no dominant hortatory expertise; rather, these followed the new public passion, though they would later sustain and more fully shape this passion.

Fashion

Conflicting signals emerged from the world of fashion as the concern about fat began to emerge in the 1890s, which is not surprising given its previous delight in plumpness. Upper-class women were still trying to pad their clothes in 1895 to look more substantial than they were. Lillian Russell, a leading stage figure, maintained the association between heft and beauty well past 1900; as Clarence Day noted, "There was nothing wraithlike about Lillian Russell." But a British diet book initially written in 1863 began to acquire new popularity, going through twelve editions by 1902. William Banting described his battle against obesity, in which limiting starches and sugars allowed him to drop thirty-five pounds. It was the popularity of his emphasis on nutrition along with exercise that caused dieting to be called "bantering" or "bantingism" for a short time. British influence also emerged through the popularity of fashionably slender aristocrats and theater stars. On the east coast, portraits of women by Sargent stressed "pliant, willowy grace" as early as the 1870s.[19]

By 1900, with some recurrent exceptions for voluptuousness in theatrical women, the image of slenderness had largely triumphed. The ongoing impact of athleticism for women, a new concern about the sexuality of theatrical women (and their voluptuousness) related to the widely publicized antipornography crusades of Anthony Comstock, and new medical ideas that contradicted the association of moderate fat with good health all seemed to combine to produce a new fashion trend. Calisthenics groups spread among New York's fashionable upper class, and these were enhanced in the 1890s by the new bicycle craze. Shirt-waist blouses similarly emphasized natural, moderate curves. Audiences began to laugh at hefty chorus girls, which increased interest in slenderness among trend setters. The extremely thin Sarah Bernhardt, held to be ugly in her first American visit, was hailed for her beauty in 1900. Shortly thereafter George Ade wrote his popular musical comedy *The Slim Princess* for Elsie James, celebrating the end of the beefy Amazonian showgirl. By 1899 the *Denver Post* reported that New York society leaders had discovered that the secret of youth lay in watching one's diet.

Pornographic imagery shifted in precisely the same directions as high fashion. In the mid-nineteenth century, women in pornographic stories and pictures could come in all shapes — fat, saggy, lean, bouncy and so on. But by the 1890s, along with other changes in pornography including a new preference for Anglo-Saxons, slenderness predominated. "What perfection of form; firm bust; tiny waist; swelling hips; massive spherical posteriors; wee feet and hands." "Lucia was just a little above the middle height for girls . . . she was full [in her bosom] without being too plump. . . . She had a waist naturally small." Moderation in figure became a strikingly uniform requirement, with flexibility only for the buttocks.[20]

The mainstream image, of course, was most important. Between 1895 and 1914, *Life* magazine and other outlets featured the sketches of the Gibson Girl, who became a symbol of the newly fashionable body. Conceived by Charles Davis Gibson, the Gibson girl was tall, with long arms and legs and a definite air of athleticism. Her bosom and hips remained noticeable, but she was a distinctly thinner figure overall than any widely publicized female image in the United States since the 1830s, and the durable popularity of the sketch series literally knew no prior precedent. Slender women were in vogue to stay.[21]

A crucial locus of the new concern about fat in women's fashion involved the corset. From the 1870s onward, a new aesthetic fashion had attacked the wearing of corsets in favor of a more natural look. Feminists also belabored the constraints of corsets. Dresses, however, remained quite loose, so the result did not require slimness; further, the new style was not initially widely popular beyond the most fashionable upper class. By the 1890s, however, the uncorseted body became increasingly stylish among middle-class women, along with somewhat tighter clothing that now encouraged greater slenderness. Actual corsetless dresses arrived only in 1908, from a French designer, and the debate over foundation garments continued into the 1920s, with a lingerie makers' counterattack about the evils of corsetlessness in 1921. (New invocations of slenderness could require more rather than less corseting, as was indeed the case for some time.) At the high fashion level, however, the battle was essentially over by 1914. By this point magazines like *Vogue* had conceded, somewhat reluctantly, that "the mode of the corsetless figure is an established one," while a later article lamented modern woman's "absurd willingness to support her figure without external aid."

More subtly than the great corset controversy, growing utilization of standardized dress sizes for ready-to-wear women's clothing may have encouraged greater attention to slenderness. Ready-to-wear clothes had advanced in the middle-class market in the United States since the 1870s, but they were long ill-fitting. After 1900 sizing improved. This automatically drew greater attention to oddly shaped bodies. Standardization was not inherently supportive of thinness, but in a context in which fat was being attacked for other reasons, the advent of dress sizes (and the somewhat public store settings in which dresses were tried on) undoubtedly encouraged weight consciousness. This pressure continued throughout the first half of the century, with extreme sizes increasingly hard to find. Middle-class men, who accepted ready-to-wear clothing later and used tailors for suits through the 1930s, would face a similar situation in the ready-to-wear market by the 1950s.[22]

The rise of the new fashion standard, including its initial tentativeness, showed clearly in the leading periodical addressed to women around the turn of the century, the *Ladies Homes Journal*. Predictably, the first years of the magazine in the 1880s, though heavily focused on issues of style, reflected no concern about weight problems. Corset advertisements might suggest some interest, at least about allocating fat attractively; but even in explicit articles such as a "Letter to Homely Girls," weight issues did not surface. An inquiry about weight appeared in a catchall advice column in 1891: "Fanny M." was told that the plainest food was usually the most damaging; water and bread were both held to be fattening, "particularly water"; potatoes and all starchy vegetables should be avoided, but meat was fine — clearly, some of the new nutritional advice, such as Banting's, was circulating — exercise was vital and, in a theme that was to be a fundamental part of the looming crusade, "just remember that laziness and fat go hand in hand."[23] But this initial column, though interesting in reflecting reader concern and a few important beliefs, did not herald an imminent crusade. Most fashion discussion in the *Journal's* pages focused on quite different issues, such as dress lengths or skin conditions. Attention to overly thin women persisted; with the ongoing concern about excessive nervousness and frailty, too much activity and too little sleep demanded a fattening diet, for in its absence "good tissues cannot be built up." The *Journal* continued to respond to letters from "thin girls" into the twentieth century, sometimes implying that girldom was about equally divided between the too skinny and the too fat, with dissatisfaction with one's shape the only common quality.

Nevertheless, in keeping with the larger fashion trends, the pace and detail of comment about overweight began to step up from 1895 onward. A column called "Side-Talks with Girls" responded to letters from subscribers about fat on a regular basis. In 1896, "Phyllis and others" were urged to exercise and to avoid naps during the day while avoiding starches, sweets and coffee; the goal was "to reduce the flesh, to which you object." In 1897 "F. A. B. and others" learned that "extreme plumpness" could be defeated by exercise and "courage." European royalty was cited for examples of people who began to exercise regularly when stoutness threatened. "Constant work will . . . do more to reduce your flesh than anything else," though, again, sweets should be shunned. "Put in plain words that means if women were less lazy they would not grow so stout." An 1898 column, more diet-focused, suggested simply skipping a meal daily; lean meat and grapes were recommended, but oranges and lemons should not accompany a meat diet. By 1901, the *Journal* periodically carried explicit diet advice, though still often in response to reader letters. Mrs. Roper in 1901 again urged lean meat, this time along with coffee sipped slowly, with exercise in addition. A regular column on good health for girls, a subcategory of the "Pretty Girl Papers" authored by Emma Walker, often talked about how to "lose flesh." A specific letter in 1904 asked about honey, which was rated wholesome but fattening when eaten with bread, "consequently if you are very stout you should not eat it." Mrs. Walker even more summarily dismissed candy, "For any girl who desires to retain a slender and graceful figure, this is one of the first articles of diet that must be cut off." Plain old housework was touted as excellent exercise "for the girl who is too fat"; laziness and fat were again boon companions, with prosperity no excuse. Several pieces in 1905 attacked starches and sweets, though with concern for digestibility as well as fattiness. "Every fat girl whom I know is overfond of sweets and dainties." While exercise remained a staple suggestion, dietitians' recommendations and the plea to recognize the sheer amount consumed, particularly between meals, gained ground. And the warnings about fat intensified, adding health to beauty considerations. "Every pound of fat that is not needed for some purpose is a burden and should be disposed of as soon as possible." Fat women walked awkwardly ("I beg of you to avoid this") but also harmed their circulation and digestive systems. Parents, finally, began to be urged to control their children's eating, particularly in the sweets category, to help battle the American problem of overeating. " 'Three square meals a day' belong, I presume, to the dietetic sins of Americans; in large cities I see the ill-fed eating four meals a day — quite sufficient for a man under heavy labor — and these are mostly indolent people." Comments of this sort made it clear: a historic cycle of overindulgence must be redressed.[24]

By this point, clearly, an essentially modern approach to diet, health, and beauty had been reached. Weight control was vital except for those naturally thin. Dieters were even advised to place themselves under their physicians' care. To be sure, an accompanying, if no longer equal, attention given to excessive thinness and a lingering sense that plumpness and good humor were paired marked a transitional period. A few articles also concluded that slenderness might be "constitutional," with little to be done; the argument also occasionally applied to "obesity," though here the common judgment insisted on its "curability." And the standards for a fashionable form were somewhat lenient. Describing a "perfect woman" in an 1899 *Ladies Home Journal* article, Mr. and Mrs. Waxman noted the need to avoid angularity but also the importance of weight in proportion to height. The "perfectly formed" woman was between five feet three inches and five feet seven, weighing between 125 and 140 pounds. Bust should be twenty-eight to thirty-six inches, but hips about six to ten inches more than this, with a waist between twenty-two and twenty-eight inches — hardly the figure demands of a few decades hence. Most important, while the *Journal* was beginning to discuss dieting issues regularly, it was not featuring them as a primary promotional lure. Readers, more than authors and editors, seemed to be calling for attention to the problems of fat. The slick, commercialized fad diet approach that would later become a staple of women's magazine sales, was barely on the horizon, at least in the *Ladies Home Journal*, which prided itself on some self-restraint in advertising.[25]

While dieting concerns emerged as a growing feature of women's fashions, the same development, though differently packaged, began to occur on the men's side, as the 1892 critique of John L. Sullivan's lack of self-control had already suggested. Gender issues in the war against weight were to be vitally important, and they existed in the early skirmishes around 1900 without question. Men may have paid less attention to diet concerns, and they certainly were not called upon to be slender. But a new men's fashion arose, too, as implacably hostile to fat in principle as the growing appeals to female restraint in eating. Though some fashion histories have implied that women alone were squeezed by the new attacks on fat, if only because they alone had to preen for courtship and were somehow distinctively vulnerable to manipulation by mode, men's standards were thoroughly involved as well. The timing was identical, the use of shame and ridicule at least as great.

The focus for men centered on muscle development rather than appetite control. It was in the 1890s that Bernarr Macfadden began to give one-man bodybuilding shows. Once sickly, Macfadden had combined exercise and careful eating into personal physical success and to a lifelong career of role modeling. Macfadden took over the exercise magazine *Physical Culture* in 1899, boosting its subscription to 150,000 by 1906. Personal problems obscured Macfadden's reputation for a time, but the magazine underwent renewed expansion in the 1920s. It appealed particularly to middle-class men and preached an ardent message centered around new physical standards. Artificial gimmicks like corsetry were attacked in favor of an impassioned focus on control of gluttony and vigorous exercise. Advertisements stressed well-muscled men, nearly nude, with large but fat-free bodies. The middle-aged were particularly targeted, with slogans that made it clear that fat lay at the core of unnecessary aging: "early old age shows at the waistline"; "one must buy a new youth-giving belt." The new heroes, successful at work and demons with the ladies, were the antithesis of "fat and bald." Even earlier masculinity adepts were not exempt from new scrutiny. When Theodore Roosevelt died in 1919 at the age of sixty-two, *Physical Culture* mercilessly inquired, "Did Mr. Roosevelt's extra weight in any way lessen the length of his life?" Workout instructions had titles such as "The Regeneration of a 'Big Slob,'" with campaigns against the "fat look" and "young hippos." In not only Macfadden's magazines but others that featured male models, male appearance gained new attention and a good build, centered around control of weight, became central to men's fashion standards.[26]

Devices and Gimmicks

Along with changes in fashion and the unprecedented attention to exercise, the growing interest in weight control showed in an impressive scattering of commercial products, which could in turn disseminate the standards still more widely. Devices to reshape the body were not novel, of course. Corsets had long been used to accentuate female bosoms in relation to waist size. Nevertheless, an explicit line of products directed toward slimmer appearance showed up only after the slenderness fashions had already gained ground.

Reasonably precise chronology, a historian's nicety, is important to help set the stage for explanation. The few existing histories of dieting rely heavily on the idea of commercial exploitation driving otherwise intelligent Americans into frenzied purchasing in the vain hope of shedding pounds. We must return to this approach more systematically when we take up causation. The approach is not entirely wrong, to be sure, but it applies much more clearly to explaining why diet campaigns persisted and intensified in the 1920s and particularly after World War II than to accounting for the onset of new objections to fat. To be sure, certain devices like corsets may have been widely used for artificial slimness even before commercial exploitation turned in this direction; Macfadden's diatribes against men who relied on corsets suggests some closet battles against fat before commercial announcements surfaced. Nevertheless, commercial efforts did appear; they did illustrate and intensify the antifat campaign, spreading it to sectors beneath the high-fashion upper class; and they can be roughly pinpointed in time.

Advertisements for products that would help against weight began to spread about a decade after fashion dictates had suggested a new concern. Commerce in this area seems to have imitated life at first, rather than the other way around. The normally cautious *Ladies Home Journal* carried periodic notices — not just advertisements but columns — touting a few products as early as 1900. "Obesity is Curable without inquiry or dieting, or much expense," hailed Mrs. Warren. The magic? Drink a glass of Kissiengen water half an hour after each meal, and then the next day a similar glass of Vichy water. The two waters balanced acid and alkaline and acted directly on the fat, allowing a loss of two pounds per week. Tablets could replace the waters if these were unavailable. Mrs. Warren noted that thousands of readers should hail this formula "with delight," which "has been thoroughly tested and its efficacy proved." Along with recurrent corset ads, the *Journal* also carried notices for diet pamphlets by 1913. Susanna Cocroft, of Chicago, claimed to have helped 60,000 of the "most refined, intellectual women of America" to weigh exactly what they should weigh, at a cost of only a few minutes a day. She announced, "I have had a wonderful experience and I should like to tell you about it ." The accompanying picture showed a well-proportioned middle-aged woman who may well have fought through some weight in her time. Of course, Bernarr Macfadden pushed weight-control sessions as part of his lecture series, and after 1900 a number of physical culture parlors began to open in major American cities like New York, directed at clerks and other sedentary, middle-class men.[27]

But the most interesting commercial surge denoting the burgeoning diet craze showed up in daily newspapers, where advertising restrictions were lenient and where the tastes of a fairly diverse reading public might be mirrored. The *Pittsburgh Press*, a widely sold mass/middle-class paper in one of America's ten largest cities, carried literally no explicit diet-related ads from its inception in the 1870s until after 1900. At this point, however, a minor advertising flurry took shape. The product called Rengo, for example, first surfaced in 1908. Its advertisements noted how humiliating being overweight could prove at the hands of others; it urged readers to use Rengo "now" — "don't wait until you are a disgusting fright." A single month in 1910 saw relevant notices almost every other day. (Interestingly, the Rengo company also made "reducing corsets," apparently hoping to cash in on the slenderness craze from all directions.) Rengo, which one might purchase by mail or from druggists, was directed toward women and promised a weight loss of a pound a day: "You eat it like fruit or candy and easily reduce your fat a pound a day." Two days later, near a corset ad (La Grecque Belt) that promised to "cure too prominent abdomen and hips," while warning against the "patent medicine talk" of some corset advertisers, a column-like notice was headlined "No Need to be Fat: How to Reduce Flesh Easily in Natural Way without Drugs." The vendor claimed to have battled a growing double chin, enlarging hips, and bust for years. She had tried many things, including expensive rubber garments, to no avail. But then she had found a "simple, Harmless method that quickly took off the superfluous flesh without leaving any wrinkles or flabbiness." For a mere ten cents, she was willing to send a box of her remarkable discovery, not otherwise described, to anyone who is "fat, 'sloppy,' and overweight." To be sure, two columns away another magical product was touted for women who were too thin and run down — again, this was a transitional period, in which traditional concerns about undernutrition still figured strongly. But the war against fat was gaining the upper hand. The next day (March 6, 1910), a notice on the editorial page read "Fat is dangerous. It is unsightly, uncomfortable, spoils the figure, causing wrinkles, flabbiness and loss of vigor. Let me send you my Proof Treatment absolutely Free; you can safely reduce your fat a pound a day." This advertisement included before and after photographs along with testimonials from satisfied customers. Another pitch in the same paper, entitled "Cultivating Slimness," urged that "exercising or dieting are too slow" and Mamola Prescription Tablets would do the trick a lot more easily.[28]

A host of products and media began to form the profit-seeking caravan after 1900. Lillian Russell was granting newspaper interviews on diets by 1909, talking about how she did 250 roll-overs each morning in a frankly standoff battle against weight. This presaged the series of star diet advice to come in subsequent decades. Chittenden pills were widely advertised, capitalizing on the fame of a Yale scientist who studied calories and urged weight control. Health Vibrators hit the market in 1906. Reducing salons opened by 1914 (in Chicago) complete with even more widely touted equipment (Gardner Reducing Machines) to trim body fat. Public scales began to spread from 1891 onward and were widely used, though the public recording was embarrassing; scales for private homes first hit the market in 1913.[29]

And so the great commercial show had begun. Commercialized medicine or pseudomedicine had been part of the rise of consumerism in both Europe and the United States going back to the eighteenth century. What was novel was its application to the fat-control issue, where its established techniques of fantastic claims and sincere testimonials were now directed to what was clearly a growing public anxiety. Here, as with fashion, a trend was launched that would simply build momentum in succeeding decades.

In the Mind: New Perceptions of Fat

More interesting than fashion or commercialization of weight control is the growing belief that fat was bad, as reported in casual conversation. Evidence for a new set of perceptions is inherently scattered, but it accumulates from the 1890s onward and in many ways seems to predate a full commitment to new fashions and certainly the public openness to commercial appeals. Ideas may have preconditioned styles and advertising, though the decadal lag in advertising may also reflect the time taken to see ideas penetrate the lower reaches of the urban middle class from their possibly upper-class progenitors. What was happening was the creation of a new, quickly powerful stigma, reaching deeply into self-image and reactions to others alike.

Vocabulary began to suggest new concerns about fat by the last two decades of the nineteenth century. "Porky" had, in fact, come into use in the 1860s, "butterball" by 1879, "jumbo" in 1880. "Slob," interesting because of its particular applicability to overweight men, made its entry into the English language in the 1860s, transposing an Irish word for a certain kind of gooey mud. But the word had its debut in Britain (where a lord mayor of London was described as a "fat slob"), becoming significantly used in the United States only during the 1880s. Again, European interest in weight control preceded American. By 1910 the word began to appear in United States popular fiction, as in the phrase "you great fat slob" in the novel *Varmint*. Usage was picking up steadily by this point and would continue into the 1930s as "slob" entered normal vocabulary in the United States. Bernarr Macfadden was of course using "slob" as an epithet in his bodybuilding materials before World War I. The need for additional words to identify and reprove fat thus dates back before the clear incorporation of slenderness into fashion, suggesting a popular antipathy for fat that cannot simply be explained by style or commercial manipulations.[30]

Words were soon supplemented by more elaborate articulations. From *Living Age* in 1914: "Fat is now regarded as an indiscretion, and almost as a crime." From the *Philadelphia Cook Book*, authored first around 1900 and selling 152,000 copies by 1914: "An excess of flesh is to be looked upon as one of the most objectionable forms of disease." Edith Lowry, writing in 1920, claimed that as recently as 1900 a woman could "roll in fat and grow old in peace"; a decade later someone always seemed to be saying, "Why don't you reduce?" But new thinking was forming by 1900. Simon Patten in 1897 argued that the wealthy were killing themselves by overeating, their physical state, in fact, worse than that of the poor. David Graham Phillips's novel, *Susan Lenox: Her Fall and Rise*, in 1900 described the heroine as "sensuous, graceful, slender — the figure of girlhood in its perfection and of perfect womanhood too." This is, perhaps unsurprisingly, a translation of new fashions into moral approbation, though the equation of girlish shape with womanhood is a point requiring further attention. More important at this juncture are the lovely Susan's reactions to people more corpulent than she: "It was sheer horror that held Susan's gaze, upon Violet's incredible hips and thighs, violently obtruded by the close-reefed corset."

The Fat Man's Club of Connecticut was founded in 1866, as approval for a certain prosperous plumpness ran high; it closed in 1903. A 1907 play entitled *Nobody Loves a Fat Man* accompanied a growing number of jokes and cartoons directed against the fat — men particularly at first, including President Taft. In 1912 a young, upper-class girl, seeing a portrait of the once-fashionable Lillian Russell, asked with total naiveté, "Who is that fat lady?" Somehow, as her shocked mother realized, a new generation had been brought up not only with novel standards of physical beauty but with an awareness that overweight, when present, became the first characteristic to note.[31]

Even those who swam against the tide were uncomfortably aware of the new standards and of their own deficiency in failing to rise to the challenge. A pensive contributor's note in the *Atlantic Monthly* in 1907 suggested the omnipresence, if also the frequent ineffectiveness, of the new hostility to fat: A woman takes out a year-old dress and finds it no longer fits her. She reconciles herself to her new girth by evoking older standards of appearance; when she lived up to fashion a few years back, her face was pinched, but with fat the lines are eradicated and a greater contentment appears. Nevertheless, she knows what she should do, even though she also knows she will not. She should exercise; she used to ride her bicycle and go to the gymnasium faithfully. She should return to previous diet habits, eating bran, cabbage, and water instead of desserts and cocoa. Her fatigue and breathlessness result from her weight. Fat is itself "an ugly word," and euphemisms like plump and stout are scarcely more acceptable. Maturity tells her that she no longer has to worry about the matters that once concerned her, and she can accept reality. But placidity comes at a price; she can claim some serenity but must admit that it also attests how "I am proved both fat and old." The ubiquitousness of more rigorous weight standards even for people who continued to spread with age was one of the important results of the new perceptions of weight.[32] Growing concern about weight became a serious literary topic as well. Edith Wharton's Undine Spragg, in 1913's *The Custom of the Country*, contemplated her appearance. "Only one fact disturbed her: there was a hint of too much fullness in the curves of her neck and in the spring of her hips. She was tall enough to carry off a little extra weight, but excessive slimness was the fashion, and she shuddered at the thought that she might some day deviate from the perpendicular."[33]

World War I provided new opportunities to publicize the attack on fat, for healthy eating became part of a patriotic duty. "Any healthy, normal individual, who is now getting fat is unpatriotic." Military diet recommendations made it clear that weight control was not only essential to good looks, but was a basic ingredient of good health, even in coping with stress.[34]

What was happening between the 1880s and 1920 was a moral mobilization against fat among respectable Americans. Habits that had been dismissed or even praised were now condemned — quite analogously to the later campaign against smoking, with similar ethical overtones and efforts to stigmatize those who could not shape up. Children learned the new rules, whether or not they lived by them. The standards were powerful enough to justify interventions against others, as in the meddling promptings to reduce and the steady stream of bitter humor against the fat. Passion, and not just fashion, was involved. The public reproof of fat seems to have begun to take shape surprisingly early — hence the new and opprobrious slang words in advance of new diet fads and new products. Above all, it involved a level of revulsion and disgust that went well beyond stylistic considerations — the birth signs of the new stigma.[35] To be sure, earlier fashion periods had generated attacks on the nonstylish, but in the decades of stylish plumpness, calling someone "gaunt" for her thinness, while admittedly unpleasant, hardly carried the emotional load of the turn-of-the-century attacks on fat. Plays were not written to attack thinness; neologisms were not invented to heighten scorn. Both the timing and the emotional charge of the public perceptions of fat require further explanation and assessment. The perceptions did not spring simply from commercial manipulation. They also struck a surprisingly deep and intense chord, and this too would persist as in the familiar contemporary prejudices against the fat. Why did Americans start caring so much and with such revulsion against those who could not measure up to the new constraints?

2 The Medical Path: Physicians and Faddists

Doctors and medical advice participated in the growing campaign against fat right along with the pseudoscientific enthusiasts around the turn of the century. These groups and the arguments they adduced helped cause the new concern about overweight, as we will see. But doctors collectively also hesitated, reflecting common-sense cautions and more traditional standards. Often they seemed (like the commercial vendors of diet products or the authors in women's magazines) to be responding to public pressure at least as much as they were shaping it. Even the faddists found an audience not only through their ability to appeal to half-digested scientific innovations but also through public eagerness for remedies to a newly discovered problem. Examination of the medical and pseudomedical contributions to the new perception of fat adds some important ingredients, yet confirms the need to look more deeply for the fundamental dynamics of the process.

To put the case simply: health worries did not seem to cause the growing interest in weight control, among other things because they developed a bit late to serve as prime movers. They promoted and sustained it to some extent, but they also took from the more inchoate public concern the target and some of the moralistic vocabulary. In this regard, the campaign against fat differed greatly from the later attack on smoking, despite similar moral overtones, for with smoking, medical evidence clearly set the stage for the later popularization. In the case of fat, Americans assimilated a new understanding that overweight could be a health risk that on the whole simply substantiated and justified a belief that had already taken root. Popularized medical concerns about overweight begin to appear only after 1900. For their part, doctors shaped their own discussion through some of the popular prejudices, reflecting the power of these prejudices while extending them further. The relationship between American dieting and medicine thus shows a new body ideal extending into the health domain, where the power of the new standards was quickly demonstrated by patients demanding professional help. Soon, however, medical concern began to intensify, solidifying the anxiety about weight still further.

In the long run, of course, the concern about overweight dovetailed both with growing attention to health in American society and with the dramatic shift in disease patterns that was beginning to take shape around 1900. Between 1880 and 1920, infant mortality declined precipitously. The result was a population in which death, traditionally a scourge at both ends of the age scale, concentrated among older adults. This in turn meant that health issues increasingly focused on degenerative diseases rather than contagion. Not surprisingly, geriatric medicine began to emerge shortly before World War I, highlighting attention to problems of the heart and arteries. Contagious diseases afflicting adults also began to drop — the great influenza epidemic of 1919 was the last of its kind. Improved public sanitation joined with sulfa drugs, then penicillin and a growing array of inoculations, to attack traditional killers. As realization of degenerative problems spread, it meshed readily with growing attention to proper weight and nutrition. But while a generalized worry about health probably increased before 1900, along with the first largely professional-medical work on degenerative killers, the real surge of interest awaited the 1920s. It was at this point, for example, that taking blood pressure became a standard part of medical checkups. Prior to this point (and even beyond, in the case of infants), popular disease fears (for example, those focused in nineteenth-century fashion on tuberculosis) would prompt renewed appreciation of plumpness, not the new diet standards. It is important to dissociate the ultimate medical linkages of the antifat culture from its initial underpinnings.[1]

A Gradual Interest

Doctors did not become particularly troubled about weight as a factor in health until the 1890s. There was no medical conversion preceding the shift in public perception. Nutritional studies of various sorts were launched from the 1830s onward (and some tradition went back even further, to the Renaissance), with European research well in advance of American largely because of the familiar lag in American medical training until later in the nineteenth century and partly, perhaps, because American fashion also hesitated to embrace slenderness longer than its European counterpart. Even European work, however, moved toward a focus on weight only slowly. An 1850 article "on corpulence" in Britain refused to draw precise health conclusions or to set any particular weight standards. It was only in 1894 that a German doctor, Max Rubner, linked caloric output to organic metabolism, with no immediate effect on dietetics. Scattered articles on obesity, some of them issued in the United States, continued to refrain from general findings. Even the best American research hospitals like Massachusetts General or the New England Hospital for Women and Children, despite unusual interest in science and in record keeping, did not systematically list weights or weight changes of patients until the late 1880s. At the New England Hospital, very irregular records of weights began in 1874. In 1886 forms were introduced with spaces for pulse, temperature, respiratory rate, and weight, but the space for weight (and this one alone) was often left blank. While a first doctor's scale was produced in 1865, regular use of scales may have actually lagged behind the introduction of public scales in the 1890s. In the long run, weight anxieties linked up with a modern fetish for precise, standardized measurements, applying these to intimate aspects of the body then exposed to medical scrutiny, but it took a while for this to happen.[2]

Medical manuals by the 1870s did include discussions of nutritional issues. It was in the 1870s that the word calorie, previously introduced as a general heat measurement, began to be applied particularly to the assessment of the energy capacity in different foods, leading to Rubner's discovery. European research on carbohydrates and fats, and their role in producing heat, began to enter American materials, as did earlier German research on proteins. Until well after 1900, basic nutritional study centered in Europe, under the aegis of researchers like Karl van Noorden, who categorized different types of obesity.[3]

The bibliography of American works on diet, fat, and nutrition tells the story clearly. While a European momentum began to build by the mid-1880s, including regular articles in British journals on obesity and its treatment by the 1890s, Americans generated but a handful of scientific papers, mostly derivative from the transatlantic work, until 1900. Not until 1897 did any American essay deal with the implications of nutritional knowledge for medical practice or for evaluation of Americans' normal eating habits. From 1903 onward, in contrast, at least five American articles on feeding, weight reduction, and kindred topics, often with scientifically recommended diets, appeared in medical journals each year.[4]

Physicians' own recollections confirm a definite but slow transition. Articles as late as the 1930s routinely noted how American doctors turned to diet considerations very gradually. "The older members of the profession . . . can recall with feelings of humiliation the lack of interest in the subject of dietetics during the early years of their professional life. In those days drug therapy held the center of the stage [in dealing with disease], while dietary consideration received but scant attention." Again into the 1930s, medical articles on diet typically began with reference to older European work, such as that of the German Franz Moritz on the utility of weight-loss diets based on products like milk and bananas or the leadership of Carl Voit in providing guidelines for the dietary requirements for the normal adult.[5]

The fact was the American doctors, not scientifically trained for the most part, long maintained traditional beliefs that a certain amount of weight was useful in combatting the standard contagious diseases and that thinness was positively ill-advised. New information spread slowly, and as we will see, it was often greeted with considerable skepticism. Accusations of widespread ignorance of proper nutritional rules peppered doctors' comments about their colleagues.[6]

Nevertheless, two related factors pushed for change in American medicine, gradually making weight control an increasingly standard concern. First, as doctors began to realize that degenerative diseases required the same kind of attention previously given contagious diseases — a realization that began to be possible around 1900 given the reduction of infant mortality and the increasing pathological knowledge about the decay of organs in later adulthood — factors such as diet inevitably called for more attention. Most of the specific health warnings attached to campaigns against fat focused on the degenerative process for the heart, arteries, and the digestive organs. Second, the progress of nutritional research, from its European base, provided increasingly precise guidelines for assessing what healthy diets might consist of and what patients might be told.

The American pioneer in nutrition research was Wilbur Atwater of Wesleyan University. Relying on German findings and methods, Atwater was convinced that Americans had developed inefficient and unhealthy food habits due to the sheer agricultural abundance of the nation. Health — and also the lives of the poor, who overspent on food — could only benefit from a scientific approach to diet. Beginning in the 1880s, Atwater published a series of articles on nutrition, some of them in lay outlets, that began to popularize ideas of different types of food constituents — protein, carbohydrates, and the like — and the very notion that regulation of diet could improve health. Much of this research, carried on by others as well after 1890, focused not on weight control but on improving food quality and even quantity for the working class in the interests of healthier conditions and higher productivity. It was this aspect of Atwater's work that first captured the attention of the Department of Agriculture, which began to issue pamphlets on food values. Recommendations for daily calorie intake (Atwater suggested 3500 per day) were very high, even in comparison with contemporary European medical standards. But while the scientific nutrition movement failed in initial efforts to affect working-class eating habits, it was able, when suitably adapted, to address middle-class weight concerns by 1900. Russell Chittenden of Yale, for example, used Atwater's work around the turn of the century to formulate recommendations for calorie counting in relation to the energy an individual expended. Here was a scientific means of developing a pattern of weight control, or if necessary of weight reduction, in a period when fashion as well as health considerations were beginning to dictate new restraint.[7]

Even with a research base, itself conditioned on a growing understanding of the importance of degenerative and not simply contagious threats to health, many physicians held back in the decade after 1900. One distraction was a pronounced interest in labeling most obesity glandular or hereditary — interesting, maybe harmful, but irremediable. A category of "exogenous obesity" had been introduced in Europe, but many doctors found it a relatively modest grouping. "It cannot be denied . . . that there is a certain percentage of obesity cases . . . that may be definitely classed as clearly the result of over-eating or of sedentary habits. Even in these, however, it is doubtful if the patient's faulty habits are the primary cause or if there may not be some change in his intracellular chemistry . . . that produces an inordinate appetite that is beyond the power of the will to control." Dieting might help such people, according to this line of reasoning, but for most the newly popular diets were sheer torture. "Other pathological factors" accounted in truth for most obesity, and they were difficult if not impossible to manage. "In almost every fat child I have seen, the trouble has been due to endocrinal disturbance." Here again, diet advice was thought to be of little use. Furthermore, for many doctors, patients of the endogenous type "present[ed] no real problem" for they just needed to be set straight; nothing more should be necessary. Indeed, as we will see, doctors into the 1930s often found it difficult to take simple overweight seriously as a medical problem. The constitutionally obese were much more fascinating in a period in which endocrine research was advancing rapidly. These were people, it was commonly reported, who ate quite normally but gained weight even so; something metabolically was amiss.[8] Only in the 1940s was the endocrine approach to obesity definitively downplayed in favor of more general recognition of the eating issues associated with obesity. ("This once popular diagnosis is now realized to rest on very slender foundations.")[9] In the meantime, the idea of endocrine factors or heredity nay have distracted doctors from presenting a consistent front concerning the need for restraint in more standard cases of overweight; they might not, in fact, have been very interested.

Continued concern about underweight patients might have combined with the endocrine or heredity argument to produce considerable skepticism about dieting. "I feel sure that I have several times seen persons unknowingly starved to death under such circumstances, chiefly while under treatment for serious acute disease." The idea of restricting children's food, in a period when poverty so obviously caused malnutrition, could have seemed "always dangerous." Finally, as a deterrent to active intervention against overweight, there was simply the amount of professional dispute about what the problem was and how it should be tackled. "Another difficulty in getting strict observance to dietary rules and regular exercise, is the differences of physicians as to the importance of one or other limitation. Thus doubt comes into the mind of the patient, when notes are compared with a friend, who has another physician with different appreciation or outlook."[10]

Partly because of disputes, partly because of understandable traditionalism in an area where medical concern was quite new, many popularizing doctors, and doubtless many physicians in actual practice, continued to downplay the fat furor in the years after 1900. Maclay Lyon, a Kansas City doctor, wrote in 1910 about the folly of trying to change most people's eating habits. If they liked potatoes, let them eat potatoes. There was no ideal diet for everyone anyway. "Better admit to the patient: 'Eat what you want, what seems to agree; eat plenty, take good care of yourself, and we will worry along with the hope that Nature will step in and in some mysterious way bring you out of this and save my bacon by covering up my ignorance.'" Possibly, Dr. Lyon wrote, science would come up with clearer answers for a rational diet in future, but for the moment in his judgment most advice about cutting intake was arrant nonsense. In a more popularizing vein, Dr. Woods Hutchinson downplayed the importance of warring against fat to the readers of *Cosmopolitan* in 1910. Most fat was harmless and mainly (90 percent) hereditary anyway. Exercise should take care of the 10 percent that was really optional. The problem was mostly mental anyway, involving worries about beauty or "exciting ridicule." Proposed remedies were mostly frauds, and sometimes positively dangerous. Turkish baths and sweat-inducing rubber garments strained the heart or poisoned the body. A woman under 185 pounds had nothing to worry about, nor did a man under 250. Excessive obesity was bad, to be sure, burdening the bodily organs. But most fat people were "vigorous, efficient and successful individuals, who lead happy, healthy and useful lives." So they lived two years less — their deaths would be quick, which was all to the good. The moral? exercise with care, diet very little if at all, and don't make artificial problems for yourself.[11]

Competitive Fads

The cautious medical response to the rising anxiety about fat left the way open for a new series of pseudoscientific fads. Many of these built on earlier nutritional strategies, but they now added in weight control as well. The fads helped publicize the need to lose weight, just as they capitalized on existing concern. They complicated formal medical response further by lending an air of speciousness to the whole diet enterprise. A medical approach did develop during the decade after 1900, and it ultimately exceeded the faddist displays in influencing public belief. But the faddists had their role to play as well, particularly in the transition years at the turn of the century itself.

It was in 1905, for example, that the middle-class German immigrant Henry Lindlahr opened a clinic in Chicago, based on a European natural foods regimen. Lindlahr himself had lost over forty pounds in the 1890s. He became a full-fledged diet enthusiast; his son, trained as a doctor, expanded the clinic in the 1920s, developing the Catabolic diet whose popularity has recently been revived. Treating patients of both genders, but increasingly women, the focus often involved diabetics.

The most striking entrant to the new diet sweepstakes was one Horace Fletcher, an American who also excelled in associating himself with the growing, if inchoate, science of nutrition. Fletcher himself lost a great deal of weight in the late 1890s, and he hastened to advertise his resultant good health and gain public recognition from his understanding of how he managed his achievement. Writing widely in the *Ladies Home Journal, Good Health Magazine,* and other outlets, Fletcher advocated a new and precise science of chewing. "Thorough mastication," taking at least twenty careful, individually counted bites for each mouthful of food, would ease the task of a mechanism in the back of the mouth that performed a "filter function" crucial to digestion. Filter or no, the main point of "Fletcherized" chewing, as it was widely dubbed, was to make sure that no more food was taken in than was absolutely necessary to assuage real hunger. Food chewed so completely would lose taste (and probably bore the chewer) such that artificial appetite would be eliminated. Fletcher also appealed for a lowered consumption of meat and protein generally. Though advocates of all-meat diets still gained some attention, this appeal coincided with increasing nutritional arguments in favor of higher vegetable and carbohydrate intake "at the expense of more fatty foods."[12]

Fletcher did not really invent the idea of slow chewing. Nor were his claims to better health, and particularly better digestion, through nutrition novel. In this sense, Fletcher was simply the latest in a long line of nineteenth-century nutritional faddists, though his emphasis on controlling the quantity of food was more distinctive. Fletcher's wealth, as a retired businessman, facilitated his campaign, and he was also able to persuade other wealthy or influential individuals to advocate dieting. John D. Rockefeller, for example, though not a literal Fletcherite, in 1904 publicly announced his success in conquering a serious illness by losing weight. Fletcher also contributed funds to a number of nutrition laboratories in Britain and the United States. Docilely, a number of scientists soon announced their own conversion to thorough mastication, with resultant cures for headaches, colds, boils, and other disorders. A widely publicized dash up and down the 854 steps of the Washington Monument in 1902 gave Fletcher new American attention and drew the interest of the Yale physiologist

Russell Chittenden. Chittenden performed careful measurements on Fletcher and concluded that it was possible to maintain full functioning on far less food than had commonly been imagined. Specifically, Fletcher consumed less than half the amount of protein a day than experts such as Atwater had been recommending. Chittenden discovered that his own rheumatism virtually disappeared when he adopted Fletcher's plan; though he lost fourteen pounds, he felt stronger than ever. Fletcher's and Chittenden's work was taken up by a unit of the U.S. Army, which conducted an experiment in the Yale laboratories to prove that excellent physical fitness was compatible with small rations. (While Chittenden prudently dropped Fletcher's idea of a filter in the back of the mouth, he did analyze a package of Fletcher's stools, which were odorless because of thorough chewing, that Fletcher had mailed him.)[13]

Fletcher continued to lecture widely for several years, combining his advocacy with tales of physical prowess in Asia, charging through tropical jungles or braving immense blizzards in the Himalayas. A host of American and European celebrities subscribed to Fletcher's claims, including Henry James (for whom Fletcherism cured malaise and restored serenity) and his scientist brother William. Indeed, William James urged Harvard faculty and students to attend a Fletcher talk in 1905. Not only Fletcher but also Chittenden and other converts wrote regularly in both *Ladies Home Journal* and other fashionable outlets and the prestigious *Scientific American,* lending new vigor and apparent professionalism to the effort to persuade middle-class American to lose weight.

Fletcher himself saw dieting not simply as a health measure, but as a defense against the broader ills of urban life. In this, he formed a link with the older nutritional tradition, represented by earlier advocates like Sylvester Graham, who saw food choice as part of a wider attack on the perils of a modern economy. Fletcher's message, however, and certainly the echoes by scientists like Chittenden, shifted the emphasis more heavily toward health gains as the list of medical problems that weight loss and reduced protein intake could tackle expanded quite steadily.

Fletcherism affected virtually all fad diet advocates around 1900, but it did not gain complete monopoly. As Fletcherism began to fade (William James parted company in 1908, for example), Upton Sinclair parlayed his muckraking fame into an even more dramatic appeal for food restraint. Writing in *Cosmopolitan* and other outlets around 1910, Sinclair argued for long periods of total abstention from eating. Deeply interested in perfecting his health — maintaining the "glorious feeling" of perfect health — Sinclair had tried both Christian Science and Fletcherism. Most people, he was convinced, were sick; he himself had suffered from dyspepsia, headaches, and other ailments. Doctors had offered no solace, but Fletcher's work had turned his attention to his standard middle-class eating habits, which were by the same token bad. Fletcherism had weaned him from foods like fried chicken, but even with frequent chewing he still ate too much. His reading of Elie Metchnikoff's work (French research that warned of impure intestinal organisms) had informed him of the bacteria that unassimilated food would engender — six billion from one stint of desk work and overeating alone. So he fasted completely for several days, losing fifteen pounds and relying on raw vegetables and fruits when he did start eating again. He felt alert and healthy. Most Americans, he could now attest, ate too much: "Superfluous nutriment is taken into the system and ferments, and the body is filled with a greater quantity of poisonous matter than the organs of elimination can handle." The result: not only digestive problems, but clogged blood vessels, cirrhosis, and apoplexy.[14]

Sinclair's appeals for recurrent fasting won widespread approval. Many readers wrote to thank the author for a technique that restored their health as well. A follow-up piece in *Contemporary Review* provided attestations to the wonders of fasting, with claims of successful periods of denial lasting up to twenty-five days.[15]

The most popular single fad author in the diet field was John Harvey Kellogg, who took over an older nutritional sanitarium in Battle Creek, Michigan, begun in earlier religious-vegetarian crusades. Even more than Fletcher, Kellogg achieved scientific status as a nutritional expert. He helped popularize Fletcherism in 1902, inventing a "Chewing Song" for his patients to encourage their conversion. He also joined Metchnikoff's attack on poisonous intestinal bacteria. But vegetarianism was Kellogg's great crusade, with individualized diets of fruits and vegetables for each of his patients. While calorie reduction was not the main point, patients did, in fact, greatly curtail their normal intake along with "purifying" the products they consumed; calorie content was carefully checked. Research facilities allowed careful monitoring of weight, urine, blood pressure, and other characteristics of each sanitarium participant. While some patients rebelled against the diets of the "San," most proved willing to undertake massive changes in eating habits for the sake of better health. A British observer noted with astonishment that "an incredibly small number appeared to have any objections to or be affected in a deleterious manner by the great change." [16]

Diet faddists had a lasting influence. Physical education instructors could still be known to preach Fletcherism as late as the 1930s. Kellogg and Chittenden lived long lives, continuing to write on behalf of low-protein diets and overall restraint. Some medical doctors directly joined the faddist parade at its height. A New York doctor touted "Flavettes" as a diet tablet designed to curb the appetite, which "may be used in any condition where a diminution of any of the food intake is required," particularly though not exclusively in cases of obesity. Again, science was invoked in careful diagnoses of the contents of the pills and monitoring of results with patients, and astounding weight losses were reported. Miraculous improvements of blood pressure and other problems resulted, and the typical patients gratefully reported an unprecedented "feeling of well-being." Francis Humphris, of the American Electro-Therapeutic Association, advocated electrical stimulation, often in conjunction with other dieting techniques. "Very stout people" could lose as much as forty pounds a month under his regimen, which successfully countered the overeating and sedentary habits characteristic of middle age. Humphris pointed out the medical concomitants of much overweight: a heart and liver often enlarged and "infiltrated with fat," small lungs and attendant breathlessness, and adverse changes in the blood that "might occur to such an extent as to be visible to the naked eye." [17]

The heyday of this first round of extreme fads in diet began to draw to a close around 1910. The popularity of bizarre approaches, whether incredible feats of chewing or literally unbelievable claims of fasting, suggests a public eager for quick fixes to a suddenly acute weight problem and a scientific establishment not yet well formed to respond to new needs. Not surprisingly, many doctors reacted hostilely to diet faddism, resenting the competition but also quite plausibly noting the health risks involved. Dr. Lyon blasted Fletcher (carefully designated as "a layman") and Sinclair, saving his bitterest scorn for Chittenden, who as a scientist should know better; the idea of surviving while eating half a normal diet or fasting for eight or nine days was patently absurd. A Philadelphia doctor, David Edsall, blasted commercial sponsors, who were beginning to issue special low-fat foods, complete with unbelievable claims of nutritional benefit and weight-loss potential. According to Edsall, the products "have been used with an enormously exaggerated idea of their values, and have done a corresponding amount of harm." Commercial exploitation must be stopped and with it the ignorant credulity of too many physicians who accepted any myth without putting it to the test of science. Edsall and other debunkers insisted that too many clinical results were being adduced that were absolutely impossible. In the pages of the *Journal of the American Medical Association,* indeed, a tradition was being launched, which would extend through the 1930s, of vehemently and gleefully debunking one diet craze after another, calling on government prosecution and postal disbarment whenever possible.[18]

But the faddist phase, in addition to launching a host of milder and more clearly commercial product lines, helped persuade both doctors and the general public of the need for restraint in eating, at least in principle. The connection between weight reduction and better health seemed increasingly clear. Sober popularizations by doctors and others could distinguish by 1910 between the silliness of claims by people like Fletcher and the kernel of serious truth about a national health problem. Adults, so one article in *McClure's* noted, were not improving their health. The drop in contagious diseases almost exclusively benefited children. A Yale report was cited claiming that the death rate over fifty was actually rising. The villain? Poor eating habits: "Scientists now believe that nearly all the evils of middle life and old age are caused by unintelligent eating." The sedentary life of the successful business-man was a particular curse, with a disgusting list of visible symp-toms: "the protuberant abdomen, the pendant cheeks, the puffy eyes and the wrinkled neck which seem to have become the stigmata of a prosperous business career." Fortunately, science could not only identify the problem but also point to a solution, and diet heroes like Fletcher (commended for dropping from 207 pounds to a mere 163) deserved real credit for their contributions. Calories must be counted; meat, with its excessive protein, must be cut back. Chittenden, Kellogg, and the whole scientific and pseudoscientific panel seemed to unite in calling attention to eating restraint as a key to health.[19]

Growing Consensus

Indeed, it was the development of increasingly standard medical commentary on diet that helped displace the outright faddists, as doctors loosely assembled a common line of argument from about 1903 onward. By 1905, in fact, doctors were discussing issues of weight and reducing with increasing confidence. New York physi-cian John Wainwright noted that there was still no unanimity in the profession concerning the treatment of obesity. But he hailed the new knowledge that challenged existing theories of how to treat "corpulency," and he called for more practical work in the field. References to European work continued. Karl van Noorden was cited, though with disappointment that his diagnosis was not matched by clear guidelines as to how "superfluous flesh may be reduced." But his cautions about unduly rapid weight loss, his recommendations that any diet be tailored to individual situations, and his insistence that some traditional methods, like massage, were of dubious value were regarded as important. So was his recognition that a period of diet "followed by eleven months of self-indulgence" was "of little benefit." Van Noorden was also given credit for insisting on the treatment of obesity in combating several diseases, particularly those of the heart but also respiratory problems. Life insurance experience was also providing information about "how dangerous to life obesity is." Dr. Wainwright judged that cures in sanatoria seemed desirable where the need for weight reduction was particularly pressing; while warning against seizing on novelty for its own sake, he also had approving things to say about careful chewing and electrical treatments. He concluded by summing up available knowledge about what foods (along with regular exercise) were recommended, and what should be shunned, in diets directed against weight gain. A commonsense approach was beginning to be possible, along with a certain routine acceptance of the standard evaluation and treatment.[20]

Medical support for slenderness also gained ground. Another New York physician attacked any lingering idea that lean people must of necessity be underfed, although he added some stereotypes reminiscent of the transitional hesitations in fashion: "The appearance of the lean, it is true, may not always conform to our aesthetic sense, he may be easily effected [*sic*] by heat and cold and atmospheric changes in general, he may also be possessed of an irritable nature, but notwithstanding these apparent drawbacks and deficiencies, he may not only be hale and sound but may frequently display a degree of endurance and energy, not often met with in the over nourished individual." In fact, overfeeding was the real issue, as Chittenden had shown experimentally. "The dietary standards at present in vogue, especially in the cities, seem to be entirely too large." Health and functioning "are the better maintained, the more the sum of ingested assimilable nutrients is limited to the amount absolutely necessary to keep the body in metabolic balance." The author maintained that doctors must help their patients learn to count calories, that tables could be developed — and the author offered one — specifying appropriate weights according to age, height, and gender. At age thirty, for example, a man five feet nine inches tall should weigh 154 pounds; a woman five feet four, 124 pounds. The table allowed a ten-pound weight gain for men (nine pounds for women) during one's thirties, but called for some reduction thereafter (at age fifty, a man almost five feet eight should be back to about 156 pounds). And doctors should refrain from encouraging adults under "normal" weight to gain unless there was positive indication of some disease condition.[21]

As doctors began to comment adversely on normal American eating habits, so they became somewhat more comfortable in advising overweight individuals, not otherwise diseased, to shed some flesh. Granted, much obesity was hereditary or glandular. But doctors recognized that more cases than had once been realized resulted purely and simply from overeating ("In the great majority of cases, the cause is chiefly overeating"). And while treatment was often difficult because of patient resistance, it should be attempted: Doctors should carefully determine the causes of obesity and the condition of the heart and other organs. Patients should be weighed frequently — as often as once a week. Alcohol and starches should be cut from the diet, and in recalcitrant cases the frequency of meals must also be reduced. Patients needed guidance in learning what foods were best advised from a caloric standpoint, though no one regimen was indicated for overweight adults as a class. Regular exercise, walking or running, was also essential. Above all, doctors dealing with overweight could not simply diagnose physical symptoms; they must "study thoroughly the habits and mode of life of the patient" to see what combination of sedentary occupations and poor eating was involved and how radical must be the redress. In most cases, moderate exercise and exclusion of high calorie foods would do the trick; sometimes merely eliminating an extra sandwich or a glass of beer would "correct the evil." But other patients, particularly with a family history of obesity, required much closer regulation and supervision; cutting caloric intake from the normal 3000 per day to 2200 would generate a loss of over two pounds per week. Varied patient responses must also be considered. Some patients were so distressed by the loss of energy that extra weight produced that they would follow doctors' orders closely. But another group quickly relapsed, excusing themselves by the nuisance involved or by social or business pressures to eat heartily. "In this category I place especially young married women and club men of middle life." But whatever the difficulties, doctors should act, for certain facts were "now generally known and admitted." Rules should be set down to prevent further weight gain and if necessary to reduce to normal range. Again, standard nutritional advice was now available, arguing against the intake of too much sugar and starch. The approach was beginning to sound redundant ("I am conscious that in writing this article, I have not said much that is new"). But doctors still needed help in giving "sound, practical advice" to overweight patients; many were still embarrassed by lack of concrete guidelines. Hence the justification for repeating what by 1915 seemed to be "common sense views."[22]

Crucial to the growing acceptance of the need to deal with weight problems was the common recognition of adverse results of excess. "Accumulations of fat around the heart and intestines impede the actions of these organs. The ponderous body is sometimes too heavy for the legs; laziness results, leading occasionally to fatty degeneration of important muscles, including the heart." The counterindications of excess fat for diabetes were also widely noted. Doctors added, however, some more general considerations as they picked up messages about weight ideals from the culture around them. Hence "[t]he bodily weight should be reduced as soon as there is a surplus of fat, which is displeasing to the eye or mars the harmony of the body." Or, as another diet pitch put it: "To be thin is fashionable. Likewise, if not carried too far, it is conducive to comfort and longevity."[23]

Doctors still had to lament the recalcitrance of many patients. One wrote of a class of corpulent persons "who are very stout, yet are active and otherwise healthy." These were very hard to deal with, and often could at best be submitted to a regimen preventing the further accumulation of fat. Longings for institutionalization continued to surface, for it was difficult to keep patients to a diet at home given temptations and family pressures ("to be less strict than the physician has directed"). Patients must be determined, and people in their thirties were often particularly disobedient, but the health imperatives could not be ignored. Circulatory diseases including stress on the heart must be recognized, ideally by reducing weight "before any signs of failing compensation appear." Lowered blood pressure was a frequent benefit, and indicator, of successful weight loss, as doctors multiplied their case studies of the methods and health gains of weight reduction in adults. "It is not necessary to resort to bizarre, freak diets in order to accomplish a reduction in weight. . . . Rational measures, that follow known physiologic laws, consistently observed, are safer and, in the end, more effective." The medical approach, confident if undramatic, was secure.[24]

The elaboration and increasing routinization of doctors' approach to overweight was highlighted by the standard production of weight and calorie tables, which varied slightly according to which expert was involved, but which all recognized the need for reasonably precise measurements and controls. Dicta from insurance companies supported this approach and undoubtedly helped both doctors and the general public realize the health consequences of obesity. A life insurance examiners' manual as early as 1898 argued that anything more than 20 percent above standard weight tables must be deemed excessive. By 1912 the Actuarial Society of America, though through a rather flawed study, attempted conclusively to prove an exact correlation between the amount overweight and the risk of premature mortality. The development of growing nutritional expertise, including burgeoning home economics claims and the emergence of professional dietitians, on the whole supported the medical approach in arguing for a cautious and scientific approach to eating. In 1911, Henry Sherman, a Columbia University chemist involved in the expansion of home economics, published a more definitive statement of diet requirements, and this added both clarity and credibility to the medical offensive against fat. Sherman's book, *The Chemistry of Food and Nutrition*, avoided the faddist excesses of Chittenden by admitting a higher amount of daily protein while also supporting the general plea for reduced food consumption. The book rapidly became the standard reference in home economics courses. In 1914 Sherman used his prestige to urge that Americans halve their current consumption of meat.[25]

One final sign of the shift in medical opinion was very simple. Not only had doctors increasingly accepted the widespread hostility to fat and given it new medical justifications. They had also reversed their late nineteenth-century preferences when it came to exercise. Physical activity remained important, but the crucial emphasis now rested on restraint and good sense in eating. A Chicago doctor put the new priorities simply, if unwittingly: "The methods at our disposal for reducing obesity are chiefly dietetic. Second in importance is the regulation of the muscular exercise." Certainly the earlier belief that physical activity was alone sufficient for health, regardless of weight, was definitively buried.[26] This shift followed from the new experimental interest in nutrition and, probably, from the increasing demands of patients eager for direct attacks on their excess poundage. It set the stage for further attention to food restraint for people lacking the time or inclination to exercise, and it gave doctors a greater role (in guarding the weight charts and handing out diet sheets, all tidily measured in the best scientific-quantitative fashion) than they might have had in more generalized recommendations about exercise. While physical activity continued to be urged, the balance of attention shifted to food intake until late in the twentieth century.

Doctors and Causation

The evolution and dissemination of medical ideas about fat might suggest a broader pattern of "medicalization," by which doctors seized on new information and used it to browbeat an innocent public into novel anxieties the treatment of which, not surprisingly, extended physicians' power and profit. This is an interpretation that has been used, often with some exaggeration, concerning doctors' inroads in sexuality and birth control or even aspects of mental illness.[27] As doctors saw how monitoring weight could give them leverage over a host of lifestyle issues, some surely argued for reasons that were not purely scientific. Certainly the need to combat competition in the diet area — to label most of the faddists charlatans and quacks — built on a classic medicalization impulse to circle wagons around professional boundaries. And there is no question that, in turning to attacks on overeating, doctors began after 1900 to address a middle-class clientele that was potentially much more rewarding than the working-class groups to whom earlier nutritional advice had been directed. It was surely more satisfying and potentially more profitable to belabor middle-class excess (a favorite physicians' target, as Victorian sexual constraints demonstrated) than to continue to worry about the diet deficiencies of urban immigrants, the more common public health targets of the 1890s.[28]

Finally, the glee and, often, the imprecision with which doctors tossed around the word obesity, at least in their professional and popular articles, might suggest a characteristic ploy of medicalization. To be sure, doctors did not rush to call obesity a disease, as opposed to calling it a contributor to disease. But the term was deliberately extreme, even as it was applied to people who in laymen's terms might have been described as stout or plump. As body-weight tables developed, obesity gained more exact meanings, normally referring to people 20 percent or more above desired weight. It was true that earlier in the nineteenth century obesity had described extreme conditions; that it now might be applied to more modest and standard problems of overweight pointed to a bit of medical hyperbole designed to increase professional and public alarm. Though popular use of the word obese did, in fact, remain more restrained, doctors' labeling could well have had an effect within the medical community itself. From this point on, in medical writing and in much popular comment, extreme obesity was commonly used to illustrate the same term that was applied to people who were not drastically overweight. Thus articles on obesity frequently detailed elephantine 350 pounders, implying by the term a intimate connection with more normal, far less extreme weight problems. This conflation helped scare the normal overweight — I'm not just fat, I'm obese — and probably encouraged doctors themselves to think in urgent, hyperbolic terms.

On the whole, however, a medicalization model does not work well in explaining the initial stages of the campaign against fat and doctors' growing involvement in it. Rather, it applies to the intensification of efforts from 1920 onward. Medical views did change before 1920, and this was important in what doctors did with their patients and how they informed the general public. The changes added important motivations to the growing concern about weight control. It became harder and harder to believe that one could be fully healthy if significantly overweight. Calling this condition obesity in an appeal for treatment confirmed this diagnosis and helped call it to general attention.

Yet doctors moved into the diet area somewhat hesitantly; with some individual exceptions, they lagged a full decade behind fashion standards. Nor is there much evidence that health arguments really spurred the initial diet campaign (in contrast, for example, to matters of sexuality, where health beliefs loomed large in nineteenth-century discussions of the dangers of youthful excess).[29] Rather, they supplemented other reasoning. Doctors themselves, in touting the new wisdom about thinness and beauty, picked up at least as much from the general culture as they contributed to it during the transition years in medical discussions between 1895 and 1920.

Indeed, much of the causation of the growing medical concern about weight came from patient pressure, rather than the other way around. Of course, nutritional and actuarial discoveries played a role, and the increased attention to degenerative disease, particularly cardiovascular disease, might well have prompted physicians to reconsider fat in any event. But demands from middle-class clientele frequently played a prominent role. These reports escalated after 1920 to be sure, but patients' strivings for slenderness clearly began to affect doctors' thinking soon after 1900. It was not uncommon, for example, for doctors to discuss seeing patients who sought diet advice simply "because it is stylish to be thin." Some denigrated such types, as opposed to people who suffered physically from excessive fat, arguing a lack of sympathy for such patients. More neutrally, a doctor discussing the various reasons for treatment of overweight (which focused ultimately on possible injuries, diabetes, and circulatory disorders, along with insurance statistics on mortality) started out with "personal appearance and comfort": "Fashion and style have made the public 'weight conscious.' The modern desire, particularly of the female of the species, is slimness. It is undesirable to require special clothes, restrict social and recreational activities and be the target of jokes." Or more simply: "Overweight is one of the most common symptoms for which the practitioner is consulted. It is looked upon . . . as more or less of a joke." Given the pressures to seek remedy and the availability of all sorts of diets and drugs that might cause serious complications, doctors had no choice but to attend to their patients' demands, however marginally related to basic health. Or, as yet another nutritionist noted, "Overweight and methods of reducing have become questions of importance in professional circles, largely due, no doubt, to the fact that they have been given so much attention in nonprofessional circles. Whether this attention may be attributed to more interest and intelligence in matters pertaining to health, to fashion's decree or to other causes, the fact remains that discussion of these subjects has been widespread." The public press and advertising were widely cited as the basis for patients' appeals for medical help, which doctors must then attend to, aided by their own knowledge that overeating and overweight could be significant medical problems, fashion or no.[30]

Most important, aside from sheer absorption of public concern about overweight, was the link between the growing cultural hostility to fat and physicians' often-expressed moral disdain for their obese patients. This was a hostility, further, that steadily increased as the focus on hereditary or glandular overweight declined and as doctors acquired more experience with patients who simply could not stick to the diets that had been urged upon them. Some medical summaries shifted terminology, calling the overweight that resulted "simply" from excessive eating and inadequate exercise "indolence obesity." Patients suffering from this should shape up, and if they could not, a character deficiency was clearly indicated. "Since overweight is essentially an index of wrong living," thought physicians, a plump businessman was not an index of financial prosperity but rather a "sign of physical bankruptcy." Of course, in many obese individuals "the malady" was "a character defect, an evidence of lack of self-control." This was the group, so one physician argued, who followed one fad after another, never sticking to anything. The group might indeed be left to the faddists, so that doctors could "restrict our efforts to helping those who can appreciate the importance of adhering to dietary restrictions based upon accepted scientific principles."[31]

In sum, between 1900 and the 1920s doctors contributed to the growing awareness of overweight as a public and personal issue. They amplified the reasons for concern and provided support for careful nutritional solutions, based on growing attention to degenerative health problems and the scientific study of foods. At the same time, they joined in a campaign against fat that had already been launched, and they responded to popular anxiety, including attention-getting faddists, even as they further defined this anxiety. In the process, they echoed some of the disgust that the new popular perceptions of fat had involved, anchored by a revulsion against lack of self-control. They mirrored, and doubtless encouraged, the emotional or ethical side of the revulsion against overweight. Fat patients and their concerns, including their fashion concerns, could not be avoided. They might be helped. They were not, unless they quickly reformed, well liked.

3 Fat as a Turn-of-the-Century Target: Why?

What caused a growing number of Americans, in a growing number of fields from fashion to medicine to bodybuilding, to put fat in the fire around 1900? The explanation for a deep and durable revulsion against excessive weight has not been resolved in previous work, partly because it is inherently complex. Had an interest in dieting been a passing fad — like the preceding approval of plumpness, which developed in the 1860s — a brief reference to the whimsy of fashion might suffice. But the new anxieties about weight affected American consciousness more profoundly, which is why they have lasted for a full century and still burn bright. The inquiry into causation will not only help to explain the change, but also will produce fuller understanding of what the change was all about.

Organizing the Inquiry

The advent of a lasting hostility to fat involved a number of factors, and some of the most important ones operated beneath the surface. Two questions stand out: why the timing? and why the durability and intensity? After all, a previous disapproval of thinness had not led to constant preachments. There was aesthetic comment, a concern about health, but no passionate crusade. The turn against fat was another matter, involving an essentially moral condemnation virtually from the outset.

Part of the explanation for the campaign lies without question in preceding movements, going back to the image of thinness long associated with suffering Christianity and saintly virtue. A repository of public aesthetic memory was reengaged toward the end of the nineteenth century. Earlier nutritionist fads (like Sylvester Graham's), though not initially directed explicitly toward weight control, were revised and reworked, as some of the later faddists (like Kellogg) clearly demonstrated. Increasingly, demanding middle-class etiquette was applied to meals, which helped condition the American public to new self-control. Growing interest in athleticism (for both men and women, though in separate categories) had developed during the 1860s and 1870s. This, too, could have supported hostility to fat, though this was not chronologically an immediate effect. A leading historian of women's fashion does cite the final triumph of athleticism as the sole cause of the shift in styles, but in a passing reference that proves ultimately unsatisfactory.[1] Precedents set a stage for redefining the ideal body and help account for why food was singled out for new constraints, but they hardly explain why the redefinitions occurred when they did or why they took hold and endured.

The need to probe further than precedents can be readily demonstrated by suggesting a hypothetical scenario. If around the year 2000 American tastes suddenly turned toward greater plumpness, excoriating weight control as not only a commercial but also an aesthetic and medical nightmare (a shift that might certainly be welcome to aging baby boomers), and if flab remained fashionable for many decades, an explanation that merely cited precedent would immediately seem unsatisfactory. Despite nods to the earlier aesthetic traditions of Raphael and Rubens, and to the theatrical preferences of the American public before 1890, analysts would inevitably claim the need to find more, to seek more subtle and varied factors for a cause.

The desultory search for the cause of the antifat crusade has been undeniably complicated by the gender factor. Much of the identification of the 1890s as a turning point for fat has occurred in the context of women's fashion history (and some of the work involved is very good indeed). Because Victorian women were undeniably put upon by men in certain ways, particularly in their removal from economic production and substantial confinement to a domestic sphere, it has been easy to assume that fashion dictates simply enforced the prevailing gender imbalance. Women were asked to be thin so that they could be even further treated as aesthetic objects; slenderness seemed to reinforce the image of frailty, from romantic yearnings over sickly maidens to the more full-blown incorporation of thinness into fashion at the century's end. A recent survey of the history of anorexia relies on this framework almost exclusively to explain the change in fashion, along with some seemingly haphazard decisions by aristocratic Europeans (the empress of Austria, empress Eugénie of France) to alter their image. This explanatory line may have some merit. It may even help explain timing: new insistence on aesthetic effort might give women a new, more sexual domestic role as their functions as housewives and, particularly, as mothers were declining, given changes in domestic appliances and birthrates. But while standards of slenderness were particularly marked for women, the larger shift against fat was not simply a women's issue. Men received a great deal of comment, and most of the new slang, like "slob," referred to them particularly. Nor were most middle-class women (perhaps in contrast to some European aristocrats) mere pedestal people, open to such facile manipulation. The overall change, by applying to both genders and, indeed, in its timing, despite some earlier interest in small-waisted young women, requires a broader and more serious explanatory effort.[2]

The other major existing thrust in explaining the turn against fat, particularly among popularizing diet historians, emphasizes commercial manipulation. Hillel Schwartz and several more recent authors see a profit-hungry business community, in league with faddists and some doctors, masterminding the tremendous surge of diet concern in the twentieth century.[3] Their explanation, while not offered very formally, is oversimple in principle and erroneous in empirical fact. Social historians inevitably debate the relationship between formal establishments — whether political, religious, or commercial — and a wider public, and sometimes they conclude that top-down manipulation is the only accurate explanatory approach. More commonly, however, they find that an interactive relationship between manipulators and manipulatees alone explains why a major cultural or behavioral change occurs. Even studies of advertising note the limited range of innovation open to actual commercial pioneers, given stubborn popular tastes.[4] To dismiss, then, the growing anxiety about fat as the result of profiteering from above is implausible. It does not explain why middle-class people in various venues from fashion showrooms to doctors' offices bought into the appeal.

The explanation is also empirically dubious. Of course, some manipulation was involved in the early diet craze. Fashion designers sold goods that touted slenderness (though why they were able to do so might remain unclear). Even more obviously, faddists like Fletcher and Macfadden gained gratifying fame and some money in pushing the importance of eliminating body fat. That these figures, and the publicity campaigns and advertising usage that surrounded them, presaged the wider commercial exploitation of diet interests is unquestionable. They must be granted a role in causation. But that they played a primary role is almost certainly incorrect. Hostility to fat was beginning to develop at least five to ten years before any major faddist broke into widespread attention. The faddists would not have gained such quick and extensive publicity if the interest was not already present. Later on in the twentieth century — in the 1920s and particularly after World War II — commercial exploitation unquestionably played a major part in drumming home the diet message. Schwartz and his colleagues are on sounder ground in focusing on its later manifestations. Even here, however, a recognition that a revulsion against fat predated widespread success in commercial dieting cautions against pushing the top-down exploitation too unilaterally — a point to which we must return.

Two elements of the turn-of-the-century causation are, in sum, already established, but their significance must be qualified. Aesthetic, religious, and athletic precedents for hostility to fat helped shape the cultural turn, as did the fairly prompt insertion of talented commercial hucksters.

Two other, fairly obvious, ingredients can be added. First, the very multifacetedness of the antifat campaign helps explain its rapid momentum. By the early 1900s, doctors could cite fashion standards, fashion writers could cite health concerns, both groups could point to the popularity of Fletcherism, while advocates of physical fitness could cite and be cited by all the other groups. The various strands involved in the first gathering of diet consciousness, supplemented by earlier precedent and by advertising manipulation, fed (if the term may be used) each other. We have suggested that, along with new science, the prior commitment of fashion standards directly explains growing medical interest, which then served to support further fashion claims. Logically, the existence of a complex skein does not quite explain the phenomenon in the first place — some other factor must make up the first yarn — but the skein certainly began to play a causal role quite quickly.

The final factor that commands attention is the simple change in American living and working patterns — particularly important in the middle class, which first turned against fat — that was becoming increasingly visible toward the end of the nineteenth century. With the growth of white collar jobs and the introduction of some laborsaving devices that altered household work, more and more Americans were becoming more sedentary. Streetcars, then the automobile, even began to reduce walking for the middle class. Weight might easily go up in this setting unless fat was newly and vigorously stigmatized. As we will see, there was some evidence that American weight was increasing even as the hostility to fat took over perception and ideal. Oddly, very few observers directly commented on the need to diet to counteract a more sedentary life, though references to exercise and, even more interestingly, frequent attacks on laziness might well have expressed this obliquely. Whether fully conscious or not, however, the need to reach for new standards simply to maintain existing weight may well have entered public and personal awareness, motivating the new denouncers of fat and conditioning a wider public to accept their message.

Here, then is a package of causes for the antifat campaign. Armed with a few precedents, the American middle class was roused by standard setters in fashion (particularly important for women, already won over to the importance of style) and by doctors (themselves informed by advances in nutritional science and by the change in disease patterns). The amalgam was quickly heightened by self-interested promoters (who utilized new scientific findings and antifat precedent). And it was assembled and received in a context of increasingly sedentary lifestyles, which spurred a public not keenly interested in trend setting to pay attention simply in the interests of maintaining normal weight and appearance.

Without question, this mix of factors was deeply involved in motivating and shaping the campaign. Powerful as this mix was, however, it does not quite explain why perceptions about fat began to change as early as they did — the varied evidence comes from the mid-1890s — nor why concern about fat so quickly involved an intense level of disgust. Deeper causation was involved, combined with more specific factors. To be sure, this causation was not usually consciously understood by the middle-class public or even most of the leaders in the diet effort. The causation must be evoked by correlating the campaign against fat with major contemporary developments in American society, both obvious links and those revealed in scattered references. Through this exploration of broader social and cultural context an understanding emerges of the insistence on self-control, the accusations of laziness associated with overweight, and the revulsion against those who could not shape up. The results of this second level of analysis are suggestive and, I will argue, highly probable, even though they cannot be definitively proved in the same sense that new discoveries about calories or fashion's concessions to greater athleticism can be invoked.

Why were the 1890s the inception point of such a durable new culture rather than the 1870s, when an office-bound middle class might have begun to worry about extra pounds, or the 1920s, when the automobile was more firmly established as an alternative to walking long distances? Why was fat quickly addressed not simply as an important issue of health and appearance, but as an intense moral concern, with revulsion and accusations of bad character (along with a host of new epithets) directed against the flabby recalcitrants? Why did American diet faddism so quickly pick up extremists, people like Fletcher or Upton Sinclair who urged extreme self-punishment (days of fasting or hours of monotonous chewing) as a weapon in the new battle against weight? Here, the point is not that a lot of Americans bought into these extremes, for there is no evidence of this, but that they seemed symbolically attracted to such excesses of denial.

The growing insistence on proper weight control as a sign of good character, as well as a proof of health-consciousness and style, was the first of several new constraints the American middle class placed on itself in the first part of the twentieth century. As diet consciousness spread even further after World War I, it would be joined by newly rigorous injunctions against homosexuality and by a series of redefinitions of appropriate emotional style directed against certain kind of intensities — including a freedom of emotional and physical expression among male friends — that had been approved, even welcomed in the nineteenth century.[5] Of course, new latitudes developed at the same time, for example, in the area of heterosexual contact.[6] But this was precisely the point. Constraint, including the new constraints urged on eating and body shape, was reinvented to match — indeed, to compensate for — new areas of greater freedom. The introduction of weight standards was a vital, early part of this broader shift. Sometimes the connections were quite direct, as in the growing belief that slenderness was sexy — remember, the fictional heroine Susan Lenox in the David Graham Phillips novel was "sensuous, graceful, slender" — after a long period in which plumpness had as ardently been associated with sexual attractiveness. These are the complex links that must now be explored in the second part of this causation analysis.

Underlying the shifts in fashion and perception was a complex reaction to growing consumerism. Just as the increase of commercial exchange early in the nineteenth century had provoked a wave of nutritional purism, highlighted by the work and popularity of people like Sylvester Graham who sought in healthy food an antidote to market corruption, so by the century's end a growing commitment to acquisitiveness generated an even more widespread and durable zeal for attacking fat as a symbol of moral probity. Increasing interest in acquiring consumer products and expressing oneself through such acquisition was not, of course, a sudden development. From the early nineteenth century, popularity of purchased clothing had already established the importance of fashion well beyond the urban upper class. At the same time, growing consumerism almost invariably sparks moral protest. In Europe, as we will see, the existence of strong precapitalist social classes encouraged outright statements of hostility to the new economic and social order, directed against the frivolousness of consumer interests, the defiance of proper social hierarchy, and (often) the special vulnerability of women.[7] Statements of this sort were not unknown in the United States, but they were more difficult to formulate amid a more fully capitalist social structure. For a time, religious jeremiads helped express anxieties about consumerism. Well into the 1830s, traditionalist mainstream Calvinist groups maintained dire warnings about life's seriousness and the hollowness of worldly distractions, even as consumer activity in fact picked up. As a Presbyterian sermon directed at young seminary students put it: "In your intercourse with society, be careful to exemplify the seriousness and simple dignity of the Christian. . . . Avoid everything like even an approximation of lightness in your speech, or levity in your deportment." Gaiety and frivolity were transient, inevitably punished by the terrors of impending death. Unless devotion to Christ commanded life, reinforced by fear and guilt, inner peace was impossible, for the knowledge of everlasting torment "was sufficient to destroy all . . . enjoyment." Not surprisingly, these sentiments were often connected with the burgeoning temperance movement, the first indication of how concern about worldly pleasures could join with new efforts at personal denial.[8]

But the major Protestant denominations seemed to relax their condemnation of life's material pleasures by midcentury, certainly by the 1870s. Advocacy of a vengeful God and references to eternal damnation were specifically reproved, often after some bitter internal quarrels in individual churches during the 1830s and 1840s. To be sure, the temperance movement persisted, and Presbyterian ministers were capable, with real foresight, of connecting it with wider restraint. One minister in 1853 condemned any temperance advocate who so focused on alcohol that he granted himself latitude in every other sphere: "by the parade of his luxury, in eating, drinking, and dressing, and almost every indulgence of the flesh." And, of course, conventional sentiments about otherworldly goals persisted. "Man should aspire to more durable riches than those this world can offer." Even in the 1870s fashion might be attacked. "If we spent more time of Sabbath mornings in preparation of the heart than in the adornment of the person, might we not be better able to worship God in the beauty of holiness?"[9] Greater tolerance gained ground nevertheless, particularly after about 1875. The *Presbyterian Banner*, a religious weekly, began at this point to praise the pleasure to be gained from good music and appropriate novels — even tales of romance. "For the average man or woman a true love-story never loses its charm." Women who ignored fashion might now be condemned. "If a woman has no natural taste in dress, she must be a little deficient in her appreciation of the beautiful. . . . Indifference, and consequent inattention to dress, often shows pedantry, self-righteousness, or indolence, and whilst extolled by the severe utilitarian as a virtue, may frequently be noted as a defect." At this point indeed, the paper began taking fashion advertisements, and even launched a regular column on fashion and "the further importations of French Costumes." Happiness now demonstrated true religious spirit, as against "the accumulated mould of sourness." "When the angels have enlarged and purified your own heart, . . . they will thus secure to you the full unabridged edition of happiness in this world, as well as in world no. 2." "Enjoy the present . . . the blessings of this day if God sends them."[10]

This was a major shift: the most logical cultural reaction to consumerism for the American middle class, reliance on traditional religious sternness, lost considerable force in the final third of the nineteenth century, despite the new vigor of temperance movements and new attacks on public discussion of sexuality through the Comstock laws. This set the stage for expressing a new, compensatory need to maintain moral anxiety and the potential for virtue — in this case, through attacks on fat — even for people who enjoyed an escalation of consumerism in other aspects of their lives.

Certainly consumerism itself burgeoned at the end of the century. Attractive products expanded beyond fashionable clothing to include a growing range of home furnishings, including the ubiquitous imported oriental rugs, and brand-new products like bicycles. Advertisements changed, shifting from dry, informational headings to more emotional appeals, evoking better ways of life through particular products. Silk goods, still described in terms of price and utility in newspaper product lists in the 1890s, by 1900 were touted as "alluring," "bewitching" — "to feel young and carefree, buy our silk." Time spent shopping, particularly in the increasingly attractive department stores, demonstrated the heightened function of consumerism in middle-class leisure life. The object of shopping, including window-shopping, was less community socialization of the sort associated with market shopping in earlier periods of urban development, and more the fascinated enjoyment, real or imagined, of goods themselves. The development of kleptomania in the final decades of the nineteenth century, in the United States as in Western Europe, constituted an extreme of the new levels of attachment to the process of acquisition. A deviant minority of people, disproportionately women, became attached to grasping things they did not need as a solace for other limitations or discontents in life. More prosaically but equally revealingly, Christmas gift-giving habits changed in a consumerist direction. By the 1890s Americans began to exchange purchased gifts rather than simple homemade items, a transition of particular relevance to childhood. The new middle-class habit of allowances for children, again an innovation of the 1890s, was designed among other things to train youngsters in consumer spending and to use the allures of modest purchasing as a childhood reward. Explicit employment of purchased items for emotional guidance and motivation also increased, again as a staple of middle-class childhood. By the 1880s girls could purchase an array of expensive dolls, complete with elaborate clothing and paraphernalia such as caskets and mourning garb designed to train in the proper expressions of Victorian grief. Boys could enjoy a growing array of military toys, including model soldiers. Children of both genders purchased a expanding range of age-specific reading, increasingly free from overriding adult supervision. In virtually every aspect of middle-class life, from allocation of leisure time to the definition of childhood, the pace of consumerism stepped up measurably shortly before 1900.[11]

What was happening was a major redefinition of modern consumerism from its more tentative origins in the late eighteenth to early nineteenth centuries. The array of goods expanded greatly beyond clothing and household items. Leisure time itself became commercialized with the growth of professional sports, bicycle excursions, and popular theater. Advertising shifted to more overtly sensual appeals, while becoming more ubiquitous and more abundantly illustrated. Consumerism began to take a new place in establishing personal meanings, as people window-shopped to create fantasies for themselves, urged consumer training on their children, began even to surround infants with store-bought items. Small wonder that holidays became occasions to express special consumer zeal or that disappointed consumerism — a belief that the family had not achieved a rich enough living standard — began to figure in the growing rate of American divorces (another problem area noted for the first time in the 1890s).[12]

Yet this turn to greater personal indulgence did not come easily. Even as religious criticism of consumerism declined, many Americans quietly worried that they were losing precious moral fiber — or, rather, that they must invent new areas of discipline to compensate for those that were crumbling. This unease was compounded by obvious changes in the context of middle-class work. Corporate management and professional bureaucracies were replacing the entrepreneurship and competitive individualism that had previously described business or the law. Hours of work were declining. The link between work and classic middle-class values was loosening. Indeed one motivation for the burst of new consumerism was the need for a compensatory outlet. Yet this could merely compound the moral dilemma, in joining indulgence with a relaxation of zeal. But the combination seemed inexorable, and insofar as it stemmed from changes in business, it was hard to attack directly. Of course, there were critics of this vast expansion of consumer culture. Thorsten Veblen's blast against the new leisure class came out in 1899 and was widely publicized. On the whole, however, there was much less coherent attack on consumerism in the United States than in European countries, if only because the dictates of commerce seemed hard to assail.[13]

What was needed was a more subtle set of moral compensations. Consumerism itself was adjusted and modified in ways to allow many middle-class Americans to believe that they could indulge while retaining their ethical commitments through concomitant personal restraint and self-improvement. Cultural historians like Jackson Lears have already identified one of these channels of consumerist redemption in the quest for health that was joined to mass advertising by 1910. Moralists, including ministers, who worried about the increasing ease of urban civilization — as the *Atlantic Monthly* put it in 1909, "The world is by degrees getting ready to lie abed all day and transmit its business" — could join doctors in urging consumers to emphasize products that would improve their health. Foods could be advertised in terms of their nutritional value. Wider movements such as muscular Christianity and the YMCA arose to emphasize vitality in a society worried about drowning in abundance. Recovering naturalness, even amid a host of new and artificial needs, might control consumerism without clashing with it openly.[14] Dominance over the body through deliberate self-sacrifice was the most important expression of this new moral approach.

Well before 1910, the popular concern about dieting focused and personalized this middle-class need for a demanding compensation for changing personal behaviors. People could indulge their taste for fashion and other products with a realization that, if they disciplined their bodies through an attack on fat, they could preserve or even enhance their health and also establish their moral credentials. The widespread association of fat with laziness, so vivid in fashion and medical commentary alike, directly translated the desire to use disciplined eating as a moral tool in a society where growing consumer tastes and more abundant leisure time seemed to contradict the work ethic of the Victorian middle class. By extension, an appropriately slender figure could denote the kind of firm character, capable of self-control, that one would seek in a good worker in an age of growing indulgence; ready employability and weight management could be conflated. This connection had begun to take shape among psychologists and educators who promoted athleticism and muscularity as proofs against moral as well as physical indolence. A good body, defined now by self-restraint, was a vital sign of moral quality. Pronouncements by experts like G. Stanley Hall — interestingly, focused mainly on males — pointed to these links by the 1890s. By 1900, the body's testimony to character was explicitly being extended to control of weight. Doctors' comments, beyond designating problems due to laziness, frequently noted the relationship between fat and "the changes in the mode of living that characterize present-day urban existence." While their references partly pointed to more sedentary work, they also invoked the more general changes in values that could sap moral fiber. This evaluation could easily be associated with the growing medical belief that exercise alone was not enough to control weight; real abstinence was essential. "Those who wish to get rid of accumulated body fat must eat fewer calories" over a long period of time. Here, then, in the association of an eating regimen with antidotes to the generalized problems of consumerist excess, was a crucial source both of the moral qualities and of the intensity of the growing hostility to excessive weight.[15]

Dieting was ideally suited to an American need for an implicit but vigorous moral counterweight to growing consumer indulgence. It picked up on earlier efforts to use purity in food to balance increasing commercialization in the larger society, like the Sylvester Graham approach or the nutritional concerns raised in eighteenth-century England as a means of curtailing appetite as a moral antidote to the first wave of modern consumerism.[16] Here is where earlier religious precedent really counted, as it was secularized to respond to a new kind of values dilemma. Dieting was also rigorously individual, though socially enforced. It was a personal responsibility, requiring worry about one's own weight and, as we will see, no small amount of self-loathing when personal discipline failed. It suited a society in which political expressions of social issues were fairly restrained — in contrast to Europe, no big political movements built up against consumerism in the turn-of-the-century United States — and in which individual responsibility to live up to opportunity was unusually highly emphasized.[17]

Some individuals articulated the association between dieting and moral concern about consumerism quite directly. Faddists like Fletcher talked about the need for food restraint in an atmosphere of growing, potentially insidious abundance. More elaborately, Simon N. Patten, a distinguished and widely read economist at the Wharton School at the University of Pennsylvania, explicitly associated his assessments of "the economy of abundance" with a necessary control in the intake of food and drink. Patten fashioned himself as an advocate of the morally administered modern economy. Abundance was good — in his popularized publications, he hailed the benefits that could come from the "age of surplus," — but the reduction of poverty also required restraint. Consumerism must not build on "crude appetites," and the key to this control involved a new level of moderation in eating. Old wants must be suppressed in favor of new; Patten sought to adapt Darwin, arguing that in modern society restraint was the key to assuring the survival of the fittest as moral rather than physical qualities gained priority. Patten wrote repeatedly against gluttony in the later 1890s, before turning to more general assessments of the modern age, basing his approach not on personal health or style but on the "steady improvement of appetite control."[18]

Patten was singular, to be sure, and although widely known, he did not launch a larger school in his image. His work did articulate, however, the larger concern about using diet as moral ballast for growing consumerism. A person who sacrificed at the table or systematically worried about weight might more freely indulge in other new tastes, convinced that some suffering and guilt sufficed to compensate for open enjoyments in the glittering arenas of acquisition. Here, identical in time, vocabulary, and concepts with those used in the discussions of weight, was the crucial connection between vital changes in American society and installation of a new perception of the body and its control. This explains why dieting emerged when it did in the United States, but above all why it was immediately loaded with ethical connotations — and why it served as a latter-day testimony to personal discipline and an abhorrence of laziness.

The need for the new counterweight to consumerism resulted not only from increases in acquisition, from Christmas presents to window-shopping to the growth of leisure pursuits, but also from a decline of disciplinary alternatives beyond the waning religious jeremiads. As we have seen, nutritional fads had earlier been available to match advances in commercial capitalism, though they included no specific attack on fat. Yet the earlier versions of these fads had invariably been coupled with other efforts at repression, including temperance injunctions against drinking alcohol and insistence on restraint of sexual activity. Sylvester Graham, for example, was even better known for his crusades against sexual excess than for his pleas for purer foods, and in his own mind and the minds of his followers, these campaigns were logically linked.[19] This linkage was far more difficult by 1900. Diet advocates, whether faddists or sober medical writers, might include warnings about excessive drinking either from moral concern about indulgence or from the simple acknowledgment of the caloric content of alcoholic beverages. But they could no longer readily join the attack on weight with warnings about sexuality. This meant, in turn, that the zeal directed against fat had to sustain moral qualities that previously were more widely distributed in injunctions about bodily functions.

For, in fact, middle-class sexuality was changing rather rapidly, if quietly, around 1900 in ways that could add some need for moral expiation to the more obvious burdens of consumerism. In certain respects, of course, Victorian sexual prudishness seemed to increase in the later nineteenth century. Campaigns against pornography and open advocacy of birth control gained ground under such figures as Anthony Comstock. In reality, however, sexual interest was increasing in the middle class, which was both encouraged by and reflected in the new dissociation between diet advice and sexual restraint. Medical horror stories about the dangers of inappropriate sexuality receded. The Mosher survey of the 1890s revealed a growing interest in sexual pleasure among upper middle class women, particularly those born after 1870. Birth-control needs still required recurrent abstinence, but use of artificial devices undoubtedly gained ground. And the birthrate itself plummeted to new lows.[20]

Both these developments — the increase in sexual pleasure seeking and the reduction in conceptions — carried the seeds of potential guilt. Victorian sexual standards were not so relaxed that new indulgence could win acceptance without some pangs of conscience. And the avoidance of more traditional levels of childbearing, however justified by enhanced attention to each individual child and the larger economic requirements of middle-class consumer standards, carried its own moral cost. Concerns might apply to men and women alike, who could see dieting as a new, corrective bodily discipline. But while the first phase of American battles against fat drew both genders, it was obvious that the connection with sexual guilt related most directly to women.[21]

Indeed, a key symptom of anxiety in these areas was the beginning of a growing attack on Victorian standards of motherhood. Around 1900, discussions of motherhood in middle-class publications began to be couched in terms of problems, in contrast to the paeans of praise for pure, self-sacrificing mothers that had been staples of Victorian family literature. Women's magazines carried articles on new tensions between mothers and daughters, blaming mothers for failing to understand modern aspirations. Advice manuals criticized excessive maternal demands, talking about "the unnatural burden of filial obligations and scruples imposed by some mothers" as a major cause of conflict within families. Feminists like Charlotte Perkins Gilman also questioned maternal adequacy. As Gilman wrote in 1903, "The terror of the mother lest her child should love some other person better than herself shows that she is afraid of comparison." This was just the beginning of salvos against maternalism that escalated after 1920, as family experts joined general commentators in attacking mothers' emotional impulses. Even in its early stages, however, the questioning of motherhood reflected a rethinking of old standards related to the declining birthrate and the incipient tendency to think of women and their family functions more in terms of sexuality, less in terms of care of children.[22]

This rethinking, in turn, readily linked to the new impulse to insist on slenderness, particularly as it was directed toward and accepted by women past the first blush of youth. The clearest single revision of image generated by the turn-of-the-century diet standards applied to middle-aged women whose full figures now testified not to successful child rearing and maternal maturity but to an inability to maintain proper shape.[23] For women concerned, however unconsciously, about an untraditional interest in sex and reluctant to imitate their own mothers' level of childbearing, injunctions to discipline the body by keeping slim even into middle age may have seemed a welcome form of compensatory discipline. Correspondingly, the growing association of slenderness with sexiness, applied far more to women than to men in the new fashion standards, directly associated a somewhat punitive approach to eating with access to the heights of sensual pleasure. When not only fashion gurus but even doctors commented on the importance of reducing fat in the interests of female beauty, it is fair to assume that something more than random aesthetics was involved. As turn-of-the-century moralists spoke of being shocked by indecent modern costumes like shorter skirts, the need to impose or demonstrate compensatory restraint in the body itself could be intense. As with consumerism, weight discipline helped balance out sexual indulgence, but in this case the requirements bore disproportionately on women.

Controlling appetite has been a significant component of appropriate moral and religious behavior at many points in human history and in diverse cultures. It is clearly a significant reaction, though by no means a constant across time and place. As religious discipline declined for many middle-class Americans, even devoted churchgoers, restraint in eating and its inescapable manifestation of slenderness took on independent moral functions, denoting good character to those who might through diet salve their consciences, made somewhat uneasy by growing consumerist and sexual pleasure. Fat became a secular sin and an obvious one at that. A few people, indeed, were drawn to worship at the temple of fat-free bodies, like the devoted male bodybuilders. More people used the attack on weight not as a religion but as a discipline that had definite moralizing overtones. Successful war on fat meant painful but rewarding control, the same kind of struggle that battles with sin had always entailed. Unsuccessful control of fat meant guilt and worry, which themselves could be morally useful in persuading people that they were paying a price for indulgence even though they had not gained the heights of purity. As with sin, the perception of fat left room for those who wanted to believe in predestination; hence the frequent public as well as medical enthusiasms for ideas of hereditary or glandular fat, disgusting but inescapable. As with sin, the fight against fat left ample room for those who advocated magic formulas that might remove the problem through some simple procedure or product — an indulgence to combat indulgence, so to speak. And as with sin, the increasingly intense disapproval of fat, laced with moral and emotional overtones, divided middle-class humankind between the saved and the lost, the thin and the obese, with a host of anxious strugglers uncomfortably in between. Fat and guilt became inextricably intertwined in a society that needed new guilt to balance its new appetites and that saw fat as a visible reminder of the dark side of a consumer society.

The concern about weight was in this sense a clear cultural construct, prepared by earlier nutritional interests and certainly supported by science, but by no means some inevitable consequence of fashion or even a more sedentary style of life. Its timing and fervor owed much to the need for a target to balance changes in consumerist and sexual standards and a perceived challenge to the middle-class work ethic. The religious qualities of dieting, in an otherwise increasingly secular context, followed from its service as moral discipline. Here was the reason the new culture first emerged in the 1890s as consumerist expressions multiplied and, above all, the reason this culture so quickly gained intensity and extreme, if symbolic, illustrations in self-denial.[24] Only in the United States did the use of dieting to demonstrate character in an indulgent age take such intense form, from the early references to the moral failings of the fat to an ongoing fascination with dramatic struggles with weight that evoked the battles against sin of an earlier day.

Toward Fat's Future

The factors that caused the initial surge of diet concern also shaped much of the subsequent development of American anxieties about weight. The causes would only amplify with time, fed in addition by the established perceptions available from the turn-of-the-century transition. A need to compensate for sedentary work, growing medical awareness of fat's dangers, an aesthetic of slenderness, and use of weight standards to legitimate an increasingly consumerist, sexually open society all continued; there was no fundamental subsequent break. Indeed, even as commercial exploitation of dieting increased toward the middle of the century, the moral service component expanded as well. Of course, there was an important subsequent history, with some significant new features. But the basic framework persisted, shaped by the powerful culture that had emerged by 1920. Without obviating the need for explicit historical treatment of the ensuing seventy-five years, some initial signposts can guide the analysis toward better understanding of the complex mix of causes that had set up the framework in the first place, making the need to control fat no mere fashion or medical fad but rather a cherished, if anxiety-causing value in American culture. A powerful continuity described this aspect of American daily life: intensification rather than change predominated once the diet wheel was set in motion.

For there was no need for dramatic new causes. The basic aesthetic and medical standards had already been set, they would just receive new specifics. Though dieting and weight watching would become more visible in American society in later decades, that visibility merely accelerated an ongoing trend. Not only were middle-class people being *told* to worry about their weight by 1910, they *were* worrying. And they were concerned not only with weight itself but with its symbolic message of laziness and moral failure. The pressure middle-class patients put on doctors to come up with useful advice reflected the level of concern. Worry would escalate, but it did not have to be newly created. The first two decades of American anxiety about fat had engendered a powerful culture that would itself be the primary force behind further developments.

This means, of course, that later commercialization of diet products, which unquestionably soared well beyond the bounds of pre-World War I hucksterism, built on well-established cultural standards within the American middle class. Commercialization exploited the nervousness about weight, but it did not create it. That dieting became part of consumerism was ironic, to be sure, as a hostility to fat that was intended to compensate for consumer passions increasingly pushed people to buy new things. But even the hucksters realized the moral force behind dieting as they continued to call for weight reduction as a sign of discipline and good character. They might promise to make reduction easy or they might appeal to real self-sacrifice — a call not unknown to religion itself, as people seek different paths away from sin and toward salvation, but they often revealed their understanding that dieting meant more in the American context than simply creating a pleasing body.

Above all, the ongoing passion for weight control continued to demonstrate its moral service in an indulgent society. The tendency to intensify the standards — to make the weight charts tougher, to make the female waist ever slimmer, to present ever more ubiquitous male and female models of slenderness — reflected a need for stringency as consumerism gained ground. Diet concern increased after 1920 because of new commercial pressures and new medical knowledge, but also because there was more to atone for by personal denial or self-criticism. Escalation, in other words, reflected the growing power of the forces that had created hostility to body fat in the first place. This helps account for the somewhat cyclical quality in the prioritization of weight concerns. When acquisitiveness pushed ahead, as in the 1920s and late 1940s to 1950s, cautions on weight notched up as well. At other points, the culture relaxed a bit without fundamentally yielding. It is not surprising that the most pressing attention turned elsewhere in the 1930s when outright hunger demanded redress, though diet publicity continued. It is probably more revealing that the diet craze also receded a bit in the 1980s, amid stagnation in the middle-class standard of living. New criticisms of the pressure to lose weight surfaced even though no novel medical or aesthetic discoveries supported such a relaxation. More to the point, as we will detail more fully in chapter 6, Americans increased the pace at which they actually gained weight. Amid all the various factors, the initial cultural force stands out: when consumerism stalemated thanks to new money worries, the need to display guilt and discipline eased just a bit, continuing the moral correlation.

· II ·

Intensification of the Culture, 1920–1990s: Expiation and Its Limits

4 The Misogynist Phase: 1920s–1960s

Because the basic dimensions of hostility to fat and their complex cultural roots were well established before 1920 in the United States, one need not linger over every detail to trace subsequent developments. Dieting became part of American faddism, which means the significance of fundamental features is not matched by the gyrations of specific diet formulas and products. The interest in dieting fairly steadily accelerated, which also provides new opportunities to follow its impact in individuals' lives. The link with a need for discipline and guilt persisted and clearly intensified along with heightened consumerism, accounting for some of the tone of the diet literature of the midcentury decades. None of this was automatic, but it can be portrayed with some efficiency.

Nevertheless, there were some striking new developments. The most important was the gap that opened up between a persistent, widely articulated set of cultural standards and the actual eating and weight patterns of the American public. Before tackling this huge anomaly, however, we need to treat some special features of the ongoing culture, beginning with the several decades in which, despite relatively gender-free origins, it turned to focus primarily, and often very nastily, on American women.

What happened here — in the most familiar aspect of modern weight attitudes — was in many ways rather simple, but it had vital repercussions. With dieting established as a moral category, available to compensate for real or imagined indulgence in other facets of American society, it could be ratcheted up to attach additional moral issues posed by particular segments of the population. Greater license for women (as consumers and in other respects) called down a heightened need for compensation by people implicitly hostile to women but also by many women themselves. The result was a frenzy of diet materials explicitly directed at women in the decades after 1920 as overt attention to weight became a new gender divide in a period when gender distinctions of other sorts were diminishing. This was not the only result to be noted in the intensification of weight control, despite the understandable feminist focus that has been placed on the topic. Men participated, a bit less stridently, in the ongoing culture as well, particularly after 1950, when the basic patterns became less gendered once again. But the use of dieting to monitor women in response to new developments after World War I was an undeniably important innovation in the standards applied to weight, extending as it did the service of these standards in moral compensation. For a generation, at least, weight morality bore disproportionately on women precisely because of their growing independence, or seeming independence, from other standards.

Ladies First

In 1921 the first Miss America stood 5 feet, one inch tall, with a twenty-five inch waist and a weight of 108 pounds. Sixty years later her counterparts were at least five inches taller, but their waists were three inches smaller and their weight was only slightly heavier. Here is a snapshot of a familiar phenomenon: the aesthetic standards for women in twentieth-century America have become progressively more stringent, with particular emphasis on weight control and slenderness, while men have not been subjected to pressures of comparable intensity. Female pathology, in the form of eating disorders, has incorporated the gender imbalance, with anorectic girls tragically adhering to weight-control signals sent to their gender and age group; men are largely exempt. Women dominate the formal dieting field. By the early 1970s, 72 percent of all dieters were women. Most diet books, and the majority of commercial programs such as Weight Watchers and Jenny Craig, have been directed primarily toward women. The cultural insistence on slenderness has been a major facet of women's lives for many decades.[1]

These familiar findings about gender imbalance have been subjected to important interpretations, with dieting seen as a major constraint on female independence. Naomi Wolf has noted how dieting potentially fills women's time and attention, keeping them busy and hence distracted from other interests more disruptive to the established gender order. Wolf goes on to pinpoint particular feminine styles, noting the weakness inherent in the 1920s flapper look but the fuller, more voluptuous figures permitted in the 1950s when maternalism was more in vogue. (The appearance of the first sweater girl, Lana Turner, actually dates to 1937.) Two psychologists, Rosalyn Meadows and Lillie Weiss, have seen profound sexual implications in the dieting imperative for women; both sexuality and eating pose dilemmas about indulgence versus repression, and both may involve fundamental tensions between women's contemporary struggle for personal identity and their concomitant search for reassuring love. Marcia Millman contrasted the immense self-doubt of fat women with much greater latitude in the definition of fat for men, and lesser male sensitivity when a fat label applied, though she granted that male pressure was increasing. The understanding that dieting standards lodge deeply in women's culture is thus abundantly present, even if no one interpretation has predominated. Although prosaic factors need not be entirely dismissed — American women may have had more weight problems than men in the twentieth century in at least some measurable respects, which would help explain why their need for restraint was particularly emphasized — the clear differentiation between men and women in the weight-control arena has underlying significance. Public insistence on women's obligations toward slenderness, and considerable internalization of these same norms on the part of endlessly dieting women, link to wider shifts in gender relations in recent decades.[2]

Yet, despite Naomi Wolf's bows in this direction, this gender differentiation has not been analyzed historically. Indeed, some accounts, like the sexuality-diet linkage of Meadows and Weiss, fail to recognize how early in the twentieth century women's preoccupation with dieting began and err in their cyclical explanations (first sexual constraint, then eating) in consequence. For our purposes, the key point is the expansion of the gender component following 1920, thirty years after the modern hostility to fat first began to be established. The differential focus on women must not be exaggerated; its full reign lasted only until the 1950s, though important aftereffects persist to the present day. During its peak currency, the effort to constrain women's bodies heightened the moralistic component of American diet culture, building gender-specific preachments from the surrogate ethics already established.

The rising concentration on overweight women constituted a departure from the substantial gender neutrality of the first generation of American concern about dieting. To be sure, the concern had showed up quickly in women's fashions and magazines (though the latter were read by men as well). But all the early heroes of dieting — from William Banting on through Lindlahr, Macfadden, and Fletcher — were men. Women began to find voice only with actresses like Lillian Russell, who gave interviews in her later years about her struggles against fat, and Susanna Cocroft of Chicago and her line of products. Early antiobesity insults like "slob" were, as we have seen, more male than female, and Fletcher's most prominent followers were all men. Men left fewer diaries than women did, so we have less direct evidence of how widely they internalized the new injunctions. But they joined early weight-control clubs and bought various new products, including vibrators.[3] Among sober doctors and pseudoscientific faddists, the target of growing concern about fat had little initial gender specificity. Fletcher wrote in women's magazines but also general periodicals, while the audiences for his speeches seemed to be disproportionately male. Findings about "how dangerous to life obesity is" were directed at contemporary Americans whose habits were slothful, without gender distinction. Weight tables, newly popularized by insurance companies as well as physicians, obviously set standards for both sexes, and the small weight gain allowed during middle age was if anything slightly more generous for women; thus a man could gain one-fifteenth additional weight during his thirties, while women were allowed over one-fourteenth. Obesity, not gender, was the target, and what specificity there was aimed at social class, at middle-class excess, without regard to sex. Plump businessmen were as often invoked as bad examples as were overindulgent housewives.[4]

Only one point in the medical approach before 1920 suggested gender differentiation. Doctors did sometimes argue that middle-aged women were more likely to gain weight than men, either because they were more idle or because they simply had lower "oxidizing power." This finding was not too prominent, though it does recall the kind of gender distinctions doctors had made in dealing with neurasthenia two decades earlier when middle-class men were admired for overwork while their wives, suffering the same disease, were blasted for laziness and indulgence.[5] Along with the greater emphasis on slenderness in fashion and some unkind remarks about fat women in outlets like the *Ladies' Home Journal*, a basis for later distinctions could be discerned.

But it was only in the 1920s that the more familiar gender contours surrounding dieting fully developed, only then that the attacks on weight focused particularly on women's guilt. Demanding bodybuilding imagery surrounded men still, to be sure, as Charles Atlas began his popular muscularity campaign in 1926. The lanky thinness of film stars could make men uncomfortable, just as their female counterparts set impossible standards for average women. Though men talked far less about their battles with fat, we need not assume that these did not occur. Even as they increased, distinctions by gender did not obscure some common pressure to restrain appetite, some common experience of embarrassment when restraint did not succeed and the spread of middle age obscured once-youthful looks.

In the culture at large, however, gender distinctions began to emerge in a variety of locales. One revealing arena was childhood, as envisaged by popular medical writers and child-rearing experts. Initial concerns about undue weight had not focused on children, where the key problems long seemed to be inadequate nutrition rather than excess. Nevertheless, some attention began to be devoted to childhood problems of overweight by the 1920s, and the trickle of concern expanded with time, save during the Depression when malnutrition again monopolized the relevant experts. In turn, when overweight children were discussed from the 1920s until the 1970s, the focus was almost invariably on girls. Boys were either not mentioned or were excused on grounds of explicitly distinctive behaviors such as sports activities where a hefty build could be an advantage. While this gender differentiation was most marked in mainstream child-rearing manuals and popular family magazines, it also showed up in formal medical journals to some extent.

Thus an article on obesity in the *Women's Home Companion* in 1920 quite simply noted, "The situation is more serious for girls, than for boys. The latter usually have better opportunities to be normally active, and also they are not as much disturbed about their appearance as the members of the opposite sex." True to this declaration, the article went on to describe a dieting family in which only the women were watching their weight. And to demonstrate further that obesity was a female issue, the only pictures accompanying the article featured an overweight girl.[6]

In contrast, articles dealing with problems of underweight tended to use boys as illustrations. Two *Good Housekeeping* pieces in the 1930s, by a woman doctor, entitled "When a Child is Thin" and "Thin Child," referred only to boys, while a medical journal in the same period detailed two parents' battles with their underweight boy in an attempt to build him up. Recipes provided were explicitly directed to fattening up one's skinny son.[7] The dominant male body builder from 1926 to the 1940s, Charles Atlas, endlessly advertised in boys' comic books, emphasized not his weight loss, like Bernarr Macfadden, but his progress to muscular maturity from a bullied youth as a "ninety-eight-pound weakling."

While one aberrant *Parents' Magazine* piece in the 1940s focused evenhandedly on the weight problems of both sexes (arguing, however that both under- and overweight conditions were purely glandular in origin), materials issued by the Child Study Association featured a couple seeking help for their daughter, whose drastic weight increase led to teasing by her peers. In contrast, a doctor urged parents not to give a second thought if their son proved "stocky" since his natural activity would rid him of fat by the age of ten or eleven. Boys' healthy appetites should never be curbed. Here, as generally, words like "stocky" and "husky" were used to describe overweight boys, while their female counterparts were termed "obese." And this was no mere popularized advice: diary evidence suggests that mothers were being told largely to dismiss boys' problems with excessive weight ("not serious" was what one doctor termed an eight-year-old boy's extra twenty pounds) while concerns about appearance and acceptance prompted much different responses for girls.[8]

During the 1950s, the journal *Pediatrics* began to discuss children's weight problems without gender-specific pronouns, treating obesity issues as an aspect of childhood rather than girlhood. But the popular literature lagged behind. A book entitled *Feeding the Family* dealt only with women when it came to obesity, providing information about "girls desiring to keep from gaining too much weight." The same book discussed underweight boys ("The Reluctant Eater"). Child-rearing experts warned that even chubby boys might be poorly nourished (ignoring the fat itself), while addressing their sisters directly: "Your doctor and your mother can help, but you're the only one who can really do this. It's up to you to make up your own mind. You can go on being a fat girl, or you can follow the diet and get down to a normal weight that's healthy and attractive." As late as 1971, while signaling some improvement in gender balance, an expert urged that although being overweight was a problem among teenage boys, a full 80 percent of their sisters suffered from the disability. Only with the later 1960s did popularized comment on children's nutritional issues begin to catch up with expert realization that gender was not a major factor and that excessive weight was a concern for many children of both sexes. By this point, scientific research (which increasingly called attention to childhood as a source of obesity problems) and a new political climate (in which sexism was explicitly identified) doubtless conjoined. Boys and girls began to be treated evenly in the popular child-rearing manuals. In the meantime, however, two generations of Americans had grown up amid cultural signals that markedly differentiated the genders where fat was concerned.[9]

During the mid-twentieth century, the identification of girls with obesity was clearly double-edged. On the one hand, it partly reflected a public sense that appearance was more important for females than for males and that slenderness was a vital part of female appearance. On the other hand, it also promoted an increasing disparagement of overweight girls and a tendency to see their inability to reduce as a definite character flaw. Greater tolerance for boys similarly both mirrored and encouraged more latitude in style. The specific tendency to use male examples for malnutrition — during the Depression, for example — suggested particular revulsion against nutritional causes for unnecessary male weakness, just as the tendency to dismiss overweight as a temporary boyhood condition reflected an unexamined belief that males were naturally more athletic and therefore needed less personal discipline in this area. At a time when school sports for boys were gaining further in popularity and when some beefiness could be positively desirable, particularly in a budding football player, the tolerance for male fat and tendency to describe it euphemistically were supported from yet another angle. The bodies of boys and girls had different purposes, in childhood and also in prospective adulthood, and the degree of rigor to be applied varied in consequence. A hint that girls more often suffered emotional problems of the sort that led to overeating was also present.

Again, distinctions should not be exaggerated. Fat boys could be singled out in other settings, despite their absence from nutritional advice literature. The popular fiction series of the period, the Hardy boys, featured a chum named Chet, clearly plump and equally clearly a slightly comic figure compared to his lean, athletic colleagues. But the stereotypes emerging in the advice literature could clearly be replicated, perhaps to some extent initiated, in children's values. Heavy girls were teased, called "fatty" by the boys; schoolyard verse, such as "fatty, fatty two by four, couldn't get in the bathroom door," was usually gendered, as obviously was the subtle satire, "here comes the bride, big fat and wide." Here is one reason girls often initiated their own dieting, sometimes excessive, as they neared their teens, just as mothers spontaneously began to insist that their daughters lose weight while largely ignoring this issue in their sons. The culture became deeply ingrained, with apparent expert sanction lurking in the background.[10]

Not surprisingly, gender distinctions concerning fat among adults increased in the same period. Emily Post's etiquette books into the 1940s noted fat as a drawback for women ("it is hard for an overweight woman to be dignified"), while saying nothing about men. Doctors, who had been fairly gender neutral in obesity comments around 1900, save in noting that women might suffer more than men, began to turn nastier in public statements in the 1920s. The subject of fat itself remained touchy for physicians, who were not always sure they could do much about it and who were sensibly antagonistic to faddists. Nevertheless, it was revealing that explicit caution about the subject tended to turn against women. Particularly annoying were the women who crowded into doctors' offices clamoring for remedies simply "because it is stylish to be thin." Some doctors attacked the motivation outright, contrasting these superficial women with patients who suffered physically from excessive fat; referring to the fashion conscious, one doctor said, "We have not a great deal of sympathy for these people." Slightly more moderately, a colleague commented on how fashion and style had made the public "weight conscious." "The modern desire, particularly of the female of the species, is slimness. It is undesirable to require special clothes, restrict social and recreational activities and be the target of jokes." But again, many doctors could not prevent a sneer: "Over weight [*sic*] is one of the most common symptoms for which the practitioner is consulted. It is looked upon . . . as more or less of a joke." Yet even while belittling the motives of style-conscious women, doctors themselves took a dislike to female fat. "Overweight is also a mar to beauty. . . . An excess of fat destroys grace and delicacy. A fat face has a monstrous uniformity. No theatrical producer would hire a plump actress to mirror the real depths of the human soul."[11]

Doctors, in other words, echoed the growing public belief that not only was fat ugly, but fat women were particularly flawed. Their willingness to associate obesity with women was partly due to the patients who brought their weight problems for medical treatment. Men did not seek help as often. Doctors' open disgust at fat women was their own contribution, but it could, subtly or not so subtly, spur their female patients to further concern. And while understandable, given the fashion-driven sources of women's weight anxieties, the doctors' preoccupation with women and obesity was in one obvious sense odd. All the insurance data, regularly and prominently circulated from about 1910 onward, showed that overweight was a health problem regardless of gender. Mortality figures for the obese were clearly high, and to the extent that weight particularly burdened the heart and arteries, men might be held more at risk than women since women were living longer. These connections, which began to become familiar in the 1960s and 1970s with a more gender-free attention to the dangers of fat, were simply not made for the roughly forty years after World War I, despite routine bows in that direction by popular medical articles about the relationship between weight control and good health. In the interim, doctors both reflected a gender distortion regarding fat and promoted it. Women worried more openly about fat; doctors saw that more women worried about fat; so doctors' comments, associating women, fat, and weakness, tended to encourage women to worry more.

A 1923 article by a woman doctor, Ruth Wadsworth, captured the dilemma early on, while demonstrating the power doctors might assert even when seeming to dismiss female frivolity. Wadsworth maintained that women sought to lose weight if only because of a "revolution in clothes." In the old days, it was easy to use costume to disguise the body; bustles or "plumpers" could mask unwonted thinness. But close-fitting or revealing clothes — which after all, the author valiantly insisted, represented "freedom" instead of bondage and ease instead of burden — made concealment impossible. Women were moved by vanity, to be sure, but also by a desire to be more physically effective, less breathless and passive. Yet they hesitated to consult doctors who might not yet be fully in tune with the new health standards or who might prove simply dismissive of the dictates of style. Women expected to be "pooh-poohed or scolded" because they had no specific disease or complaint to which to point. The result? More guilt and worry, and perhaps a turn to some ineffective commercial product. Yet, Wadsworth concluded, doctors really did have the science necessary to treat unwanted pounds, and they knew the advantages of moderate weight despite the fact that they could not quite agree on precise standards. They offered, through scientific principles of nutrition, what women needed, even if the precipitating motive was nothing more than a desire to fit into that "new evening gown." In presenting science claims while also scoffing at yet another example of women's whimsies, doctors such as Wadsworth undoubtedly built a powerful role in helping to define the new constraints on the female body. The very fact that middle-class women consulted doctors more often than men did, which subjected them to routine office weigh-ins, supported the doctors' growing role as arbiters of weight and related moral discipline.

Medical concern about women and fat spilled over into growing efforts to restrict weight gains among women who were pregnant. Here was a clear combination of genuine scientific belief and the sheer ability to regulate through monthly consultations. From the 1930s until the 1970s, obstetricians often applied pressure in this area, perhaps more than was medically justified, though this is a disputed territory even now. Experts like Alan Guttmacher urged weight gains limited to twenty pounds, which compelled some dieting among pregnant women. And while the experts referred to legitimate issues like blood pressure and dangerous clumsiness, they also offered revealing asides about the need to limit intake "for vanity's sake alone," while implying that greater weight gains were somehow pathological. Though through a mixture of motives, doctors again encouraged women to see that excessive weight was not only a medical issue but a matter of self-respect as well.[12]

The gendered approach to fat moved beyond child-rearing literature and doctors' offices. It was in the 1920s that the word "broad" came into use as a derogatory term for women in American English. The term was first noted as a New York expression around 1911 and may not have originated as a physical description. For a brief time it enjoyed a dual career, referring to prostitutes and other women of loose morals as well as serving as an unflattering label for women generally. Gradually the latter meaning triumphed, and while not explicitly tied to the new sensitivity to female fat, the term certainly evoked some of the same critique: women's shape, unless carefully disciplined, was now suspect. Terms for fat men, like "slob," did not spill over to become generic, at least in common usage.[13]

Explicit advice to adults about dieting mirrored the growing gender disparity between the 1920s and the 1960s in several ways. First, it was disproportionately addressed to women. Diet cookbooks, to be sure, were for "people," as administered through wives as cooks, but the arguments and most of the explicit diet recommendations in books and magazine articles assumed a female audience. Clubs and summer camps formed for overweight girls, not children in general. Men's magazines like *Esquire*, which came into existence in this period, did not discuss dieting (though fashion advertisements assumed slenderness); the contrast with the ubiquity of the subject in women's outlets, including periodicals directed toward teenage girls, was striking. For every occasional reference that targeted men, there were scores that focused on women alone.[14]

Second, diet discussions for women almost invariably emphasized aesthetic factors. Health, if mentioned as well, was a bit player in the drama of fat. Thus a popular book in 1959 cited three reasons for strict dieting that seem ridiculously redundant save for the need to drive home the imperative of fashion: (1) so women can fit into current styles, particularly now that bathing suits are increasingly skimpy; (2) it is "desirable to avoid inordinate curves and shapes and protuberances, which do not look well in the more revealing garments"; and (3) fat is aesthetically unpleasant. Later, to be sure, physical problems were noted, including fatigue, diabetes, and cirrhosis of the liver, but the woman-centered appearance criteria clearly predominated. Sexual arguments figured strongly, but with the familiar gender bias: men disdained intercourse with overweight wives, and this could have emotional side effects on women beyond endangering the marriage. "Where there was once delicacy there is now grossness. What was graceful has become plodding. . . . An obese woman in a messy house is not the average man's ideal of marriage." Other female-centered spurs to dieting were added, including the reluctance of fat women to engage in social activities or go shopping.[15]

Most striking was the sheer disdain for fat women that infused popular reading matter by the 1940s and 1950s. It was revealing enough that a whole diet industry arose on the basis of a female audience and that most arguments for diet products focused on

women's criteria of appearance and social acceptance. More note-
worthy still was the conjuncture of commercial diet pitches with a
moral mockery of the women for whom they were intended. Disgust had been suggested in the first decades of the dieting craze,
before 1920, but it had rarely been gender specific. Now, as the
level of revulsion accumulated in literature aimed at the very
groups being insulted, women were the clear targets. Thus fat
women were "lazy and undisciplined. They prefer[red] lying in
bed a bit longer to actually planning, preparing and consuming a
[sensible] breakfast meal." The fat woman would become evasive:
"She accuses her husband of being supercritical, which makes her
too nervous to plan menus or shop properly (she would be a lot
more nervous if she knew her husband is running around with
his slim secretary because his wife is so fat and unattractive)."
"Psychiatrists have exposed the fat person for what she really is —
miserable, self indulgent and lacking in self control." And bluntly,
in another book directed toward women and arguing that normal
women should be able to maintain an acceptable appearance and
keep their need to be loved within bounds, "[b]eing fat is a sickness"; a fat woman's body (with fat men implicitly exempt?) was "a
physical nonentity," an object of ridicule, a sign of self-hate and
social failure, a woman's "resignation from society." "Are you aware
that fatness has destroyed your sex appeal and made you look older,
somewhat like a buffoon whom people are inclined not to take
seriously in any area or on any level?"[16]

The phenomenon of middle-class women reading materials that
soundly criticized them was not new, of course. The secular theme
of audience masochism (which may have replaced religious attacks
on sin, only now for a more specifically female clientele) began
with Victorian periodicals in the mid-nineteenth century, in which
women readers were chastised for shameful neglect of their children and other faults.[17] But the transposing the theme of this
literature onto obesity was a phenomenon of the mid-twentieth
century, and with it came an unprecedented venom for the targets
of the material. Fat women, distinguished at once from men and
from normality, were told that they ate too much because of self-
hate, in terms designed to push this same self-hatred to ever greater

intensity. Surely an odd pattern, though one repeated frequently during the peak decades of the war against fat women and one that echoes still today.

Both the timing and the vicious intensity of the focus on female obesity invite analysis. After an initial period in which concern about overweight developed without tremendous gender imbalance, fat became a disproportionate ingredient in attacks on women and in women's self-perceptions. Female as well as male experts, ordinary middle-class women who bought diet products and sought doctors' advice, even an increasing array of pubescent girls agreed that obesity was a particularly female issue, to be fought as a matter of simple decency or to be lamented as a badge of irretrievable personal shame. Many fat women felt such shame and self-doubt that they never dated, trying to hide at home as much as possible.

Other signs of the new pressure on women to be slender during the decades after 1920 may be familiar enough. Disney, ever alert to sales appeal, adopted an impossibly willowy form for heroines in the 1930s with Cinderella and maintained this style through Pocahontas in 1995, adding only a more visible bust. Barbie, that unusually slim and unusually popular doll, was born in 1959, and while Ken was no fitness slouch, it was Barbie who more obviously set standards, if only because boys ignored both characters. Comic strip women like Mary Worth, once a plump elderly matron, slimmed down markedly in the 1960s even as they refused to change in other respects. The signals were ubiquitous, for virtually all female age groups.

The varied attacks on female fat were not particularly introspective. It seemed so obvious that fat women were ugly that no explanation for criticism seemed necessary. This means that, while the causes of this new culture must be sought, they must be suggested from correlative developments in American gender patterns; like the basic context for the initial attack on fat bodies, they cannot be conclusively proved. Here, of course, the timing of the turn against women's real or imagined obesity is particularly revealing, in providing a corrective as women made gains in other respects. In turn, the corrective element, the imposition of a new constraint even as old ones loosened, helps explain the odd, often nasty intensity with which the novel campaign was conducted by men and women alike and the extent to which its message seemed to be accepted by much of the female audience as they strove to diet or withdrew in obese shame. The moral test inherent in modern American dieting now found extended applicability to women.

Uppity, Indulgent Broads and a Need for Guilt

The disproportionate imposition of weight-control standards on women occurred at precisely the point that many older gender distinctions were eroding. The timing of the heightened insistence on this differentiation between men and women (if not the intensity, which must be explained on other bases) clearly suggests that a substitution was in the works. Middle-class women were no longer described, as they had been in the nineteenth century, as polar opposites to men in emotional reactions. Child rearing literature and work advice alike noted the need for both sexes to restrain anger without arguing that men were naturally aggressive but women by nature anger free; the same merger, at least in articulated standards, held true for proclivities to fear or to jealousy.[18] But while this Victorian staple was eroding as men and women mixed socially and professionally in new ways, the process created a need to state new criteria that would clarify that women still were not men and still were not equal. The notion that they had a special weight problem was an obvious gender-defining substitute, and its salience in the standards urged on children suggests an implicit realization that it was important to establish this differential worry early on.

The impulse to develop new gender differentials as previous ones declined (not a law of history, to be sure, but plausible given the importance of gender in Victorian culture) does not explain why weight became the target. Here, a second correlation came into play, within a setting in which overweight had already been identified as a moral problem — slenderness as a sign of modern virtue. The attack on female fat conjoined with the ongoing reduction of motherhood as a physical task and as a cultural emblem for women. There is no question that this reduction coalesced in the 1920s, building on the more scattered signals from previous decades. The decade saw a new low in middle-class birth rates, combined with a growing acceptance of artificial birth-control devices by married women and a more open sexuality by younger women and wives alike. The cultural prestige of motherhood dropped as well, continuing the trend of the early 1900s, as Victorian paeans of praise for self-sacrificing mothers began to sound increasingly, even embarrassingly, antiquated except on Mother's Day (newly created as a once-a-year license for emotional nostalgia). Salvos against maternalism escalated after 1920 as family experts joined general commentators in attacking mothers' emotional impulses. Social workers excoriated maternal sentimentality, contrasting their scientific approach to problems of children. "It is high time that we seriously consider facts, not fictitious heart throbs." Led by John Watson, behaviorists attacked mothers' cloying affections; Watson himself offered a chapter on "The Dangers of Too Much Mother Love"; maternal control would "transform a healthy child into a whining, dependent 'Mother's boy.'" Other experts criticized mothers for inadequate as well as excessive care, the idea of some automatic maternal genius disappeared from the literature. "There are other women, often very fond of children, who are conspicuously lacking" in the knack of managing children properly.[19] Even as attacks against excessive mothering moderated by the late 1930s, maternal instincts continued to be hedged with warnings in the family advice manuals.

Here was a cultural sea change that made rigorous dieting a natural for women. As presented by experts, at least, women's family roles began to shift from maternal primacy to shared sexuality. The same decade that saw the pronounced turn away from Victorian maternalism, the 1920s, also saw a new breed of marriage experts begin a long campaign to persuade middle-class people that most martial problems began in bed. Slenderness, enforced now in principle not only on young women but also on the middle-aged, dramatized the growing aversion to maternal delights; women, even in maturity, should not look like they had borne children. Rigorous discipline of women's bodies helped men and women alike gain some confidence that declining maternal functions did not leave women free for every form of indulgence. They might be, even should be, newly sexy, but this sexuality was precisely the reason that they should impose constraint on their appetites in other respects. Sluttish girls were commonly depicted as ill-disciplined both in sexual behavior and in eating habits, their fat bodies a visible symbol of deeper disgrace. The notion that a sexy woman was a slender woman — a visible nonmother — contrary to standards in many cultures including those of the United States just a half century before, surely rested in part in the need to demonstrate that severity or guilt, or both, did not disappear from woman's lot, but merely transferred from across-the-board sexual restraint to control of eating. The flapper costume of the 1920s stated the connection explicitly; it was all right to reveal a good bit of body if the body was rigorously disciplined, almost boyish. Revealing bathing suits from the 1940s onward encouraged more bust, but maintained the requirement for disciplined eating. Women themselves, as they become sexual partners as least as much as they were mothers, may well have welcomed this opportunity to demonstrate their capacity for control and self-punishment. The intensity of seemingly aesthetic goals, in redefining female beauty, followed from the need for new ways to moralize women through constraint. To be sure, the emphasis on dieting persisted even as maternalism regained a bit more popularity in the late 1940s and 1950s, but the basic psychocultural source remained valid.[20]

The need to impose rigor to compensate for the decline in women's moral primacy and growing sexual awareness added to the basic interest in dieting as a counterweight to consumer indulgence. As consumers, too, women were identified by society and themselves as primary participants, so the chance to show punitive discipline, or guilt, had gender implications in this regard as well. Women's obvious consumer interests operated in a cultural context still capable of recalling the results of Eve's appetites. Here, women themselves could have found perverse comfort in subscribing to rigorous standards in order to repay their new latitudes in other lifestyle areas. It was in the 1920s that middle- and lower-class women began to indulge widely in new beauty products like cosmetics, and rigorous concomitant standards, like special dieting or the new obligation to shave underarm and leg hair, could make modern beauty seem a moral imperative, not a female frivolity. Dieting and guilt provided moral counterweights for a gender undergoing rapid change and for men who might otherwise have turned against developments that, by Victorian standards, constituted growing license.

The final ingredient for the imposition of new anxieties about weight on women involved power as well as moral balance. Along with anxieties and hostilities resulting from the decline of motherhood, power considerations explain the intensity of the concern about women's weight from the 1920s onward and the clear efforts to use weight as a tool for discipline or attack. For the contrast between women's growing power at work and in public life (if still in an inferior position for the most part) with an emphasis on a slenderness that could connote greater physical frailty was both striking and deliberate. Newly enfranchised women must be told to curb their appetites and reduce, quite literally, their physical presence. In this sense, the attack on size related to a growing tendency to refer to women in diminutive and dismissive terms. Thus the *Ladies Home Journal* had launched a marriage advice column in 1910 entitled "The Little Woman and the Busy Man." Stories referred to women as cute, childish creatures. A short piece called "When I Love Him," published in 1915, features a husband insisting that his wife put her rubbers on: "'What do I care what a little chit like you thinks? You put those rubbers on!'. . . . I poke out my feet and laugh [she had them on already, despite her protests]. I love to have him pretend to beat me." This was part of the process by which the Victorian angel in the house was transformed into the girlish flapper figure of the 1920s — often referred to as "girlie" by her husband.[21]

Music of the period picked up the same diminutive themes, sometimes tying them directly to dieting. Al Dubin and Harry Warren's "Keep Young and Beautiful" from the 1930s, talking of "what's cute about cutie," urged the "duty" of slimness "if you want to be loved"; "if you're wise, exercise all the fat off, take it off, over here, over there." Rodgers and Hammerstein picked up the theme after World War II, writing of "honeybun's" "hundred and one pounds of fun," while another 1950s tune about "the girl that I marry" insisted not only that she be "as soft and as pink as a nursery" but also "a doll I can carry, the girl that I marry will be." Thinking of wives or sweethearts simultaneously as small and as immature and encouraging them to think this way themselves fit the framework of weight control and served to reduce the threats attached to women's gains in other areas.

The African American Alternative: Power and Size

The explanation of the new constraint in women's bodies as moral response to new indulgence and new power is class- and race-specific; it was a new fact of life for the white middle class. The explanation gains credence, through exploring the clear difference between African American and mainstream white, middle-class culture in the area of weight control and the reasons for this difference. The culture of dieting did not win a substantial black audience precisely because the ethical demands for it were absent.

The simple fact was that, individual exceptions aside, the preoccupation with weight and dieting did not catch on among African American women, either as a matter of practice or in the cultural signals generated. The pages of *Ebony* magazine from 1943 onward (particularly until the 1980s) were singularly spare in their treatment of weight problems, compared to their middle-class white counterparts. This was not because of a neglect of beauty needs: *Ebony* widely discussed beauty aids of other sorts, including (in the 1950s especially) hair straighteners and skin whiteners. A few diet articles appeared, particularly after 1970, both in the form of general nutritional suggestions and case studies of individuals who had lost a great deal of weight (a common theme in predominantly white magazines in the 1950s), but the pattern was sporadic at best, in contrast to how dieting had the become a staple in white journals during the same years.

Further, the articles and ancillary materials that did surface maintained a distinctive tone in a number of respects. References to religion were abundant. Religiosity could involve appeals to prayer as a basis for weight control, but it also embodied a sense the God determined what size a person should be. "God don't make no mistakes," was, one way or another, a common sentiment. "Whatever you have, you must make the most of it. You cannot go back to God and say 'Excuse me, I'd like. . . .' " Dieting was an unnecessary attack on the Lord's standards. Despite its target audience of relatively privileged, light-skinned blacks, *Ebony* also reflected considerable belief that black people had enough to worry about without adding weight to the list ("You never know why you're being discriminated against . . . whether it's because of being black or obese or what"), with a sense that weight loss would not make much difference in the treatment received in the long run.[22]

Most striking, however, aside from the infrequency of diet discussions, was *Ebony's* definite openness to women who were above officially recommended weight. This showed in weight standards that defined "obesity" more loosely (about 50 percent more loosely) than official government publications in the same years. It showed in the black models and entertainers, who were decidedly heavier than white models (who also figured prominently in *Ebony's* pages, particularly before 1960). It showed in decisions to include "full-figured" women in *Ebony's* troupe of models, which toured the nation frequently. Michelle Zeno, for example, carried 193 pounds on her 5 feet 10 inches when she joined the *Ebony* group. Arguing, "I come from large people," Zeno also noted how most African American women in her audiences related easily to her looks, explicitly rejecting pressure from her agent to lose a great deal of weight, "You have to feel beautiful, just as beautiful as the next person." *Ebony* also embraced articles that counterattacked the national slimness trends. While this material surfaced particularly in the 1980s and early 1990s, when a number of periodicals were featuring more assertive heavy women ("Fat people of America, unite. . . . Speak up for your rights. Live for today and stop putting things off for a thinner tomorrow"), *Ebony* registered comments even at the height of the diet craze of the 1970s. A 1978 article,

"Big Can Be Beautiful," noted "[t]he days are past when the 'big woman' was synonymous with ugly woman, plain woman, or unattractive woman," and urged that black women should reject the "think thin fad" companies, while learning to dress to highlight their best features. Furthermore, through the whole period, *Ebony* recurrently noted how much black men appreciated some real heft in a woman. "I've never been attracted to thin or even average-size sisters. I need a woman I can hold on to. Truth be told, my ideal woman is a size 20," reported a graduate of the University of the District of Columbia. "The only thing a thin woman can do for me is introduce me to a woman of size." Men's aesthetic judgments often mirrored those of the woman themselves, in a clearly distinctive subculture concerning body standards.[23]

Quite simply, as a medical report suggested, "the social environment of Black women is less negative about obesity than might be commonly assumed based on data for White women." This distinction has continued among adolescent American girls to the present time. Size and attractiveness were not routinely contrasted, nor were size and self-esteem, and slenderness was likely to be criticized. African American teenagers worried far less about their bodies than did their generally more anxious white counterparts. They also smoked less, in contrast to white girls, who used smoking for weight control. Among blacks generally, large women were held to be more stable emotionally and less preoccupied with superficial issues. Again, male reactions reflected distinctive female standards. "Before I got married, I dated a number of small women and their appearance often dominated their life. . . . I remember planning a trip to the Bahamas with one young lady and in the two-week period before we left, I saw the craziest person I've ever seen in my life trying to starve herself to lose weight. Things like that rob everyday pleasures of their joy. With my wife, it's not like that. When we go to the islands, we go to enjoy the whole experience — the beach, the food, each other."[24]

Why was African American culture, even in the middle class, so different from white where women's weight was concerned? A number of factors contributed, of course, including religious convictions and the priority of dealing with issues of race rather than size. Black outlook preserved standards of appearance that had been more general in the United States a hundred years before, but they may also have reflected some particular food preferences of this racial group, some perhaps going back to Africa itself where, Ali Mazrui has rather proudly noted, the efforts to constrain women through white dieting standards have never taken hold. It is possible that an association of fat women with beauty and power persisted from African culture, helping black Americans ignore white middle-class standards; the Yoruba, for example, seem to equate female size with pride in property. More prosaically, greater concern with sheer plenty (with cheap calories, given their greater poverty) has obviously preoccupied twentieth-century blacks, and this constraint could even affect black middle-class outlook.[25]

Above all, however, the African American tolerance, even embrace, of large women reflects the distinctive power position women have held in African American families and the family economy. Unlike their white counterparts, most black women have always worked, even when married; and in some physical labor, size was a positive advantage, associated with strength, not fat. Even during Reconstruction the demands of work, plus inherited African notions of beauty that showed in dress habits, prompted esteem for full-figured women, in contrast to the corseting of the women in the white planter class. African Americans of the period often used descriptions like "fine large portly looking woman" or "rather chunky and good looking," and small women seemed to have more difficulty achieving the status accorded their larger sisters. One petite women, called "runty" by her siblings, complained that people often did not recognize her as an adult even after she married and had a child. Even in the nineteenth century, then, the bases of beauty were distinctive, just as women's other obligations were distinctive, in this vital American subculture.

More than whites, it can be suggested, black women were in a position to set their own beauty standards, for men were as likely to be thought of as sex objects as women; men, clearly, often bought into the same definitions in finding big women particularly attractive. And more than with whites, the fact and cultural prestige of motherhood persisted among black families; indeed, matriarchal structures may have intensified after the late 1950s amid the employment crisis of black males. African American birthrates remained higher; there was less reason to apologize for a decline of maternity through body restraint. In sum, weight control could not be made to serve the same purposes of subordination and apologetic compensation for women in the African American community as it came to do amid the white middle class. The key causes of dominant body imagery were different, indeed in some respects reversed.[26]

Assessment

Among middle-class whites, the campaign against female fat from the 1920s onward clearly reflected a pervasive need to use the earlier established bias against weight to maintain some basic Victorian values that were difficult to jettison entirely, even as specific targets changed. Victorian gender standards, emphasizing massive differentiations between men and women from roles through sexuality and emotion to basic morality, plus a commitment to female frailty, had been vigorously inculcated. Some of them (such as the greater irrationality of women) built on older Western beliefs, which may have helped them solidify; but even newer, purely Victorian items (like women's sexual innocence or greater natural morality) had powerful resonance.

Generations raised between 1870 and 1920 progressively shook off many Victorian beliefs. They changed their minds about women and sexual pleasure. They modified insistence that women confine themselves to the home. They increasingly discussed emotional problems of childhood rather than distinctive goals for boys and for girls. And, of course, they more readily embraced leisure pursuits and rampant consumerism. The notion of a substantial shift in norms in the decades around 1900 is well established.[27] But a shift of this sort would be neither complete nor without cost. Even aside from reactionaries — and both religious and Klan revivals in the 1920s reflected a desire to cling to older values outright[28] — middle-class America, consciously or unconsciously, needed some links with the past. Thus new advice about sexuality, though genuinely un-Victorian, preserved the notion that women were more sexually passive than men, while translating an older belief that men must practice unusual sexual restraint into a new insistence that men were responsible for holding themselves back in the interests of stimulating women through foreplay. The package was very novel, but the contents included reformulations of Victorian conventions. Other new formulations that began in the 1920s and then persisted served similar functions in providing replacement gender differentiations. Thus the increasing fierceness of male athleticism, expressed particularly in the rise of football as a national passion, could make women (particularly if fashionably thin) seem frail by contrast, even as they wielded political rights and participated in other public leisure.[29]

The attack on women's weight served the same transitional goals, preserving gender distinctions in new ways that allowed women new consumer, work, and sexual behaviors. While not arguing that women were naturally more moral than men, the multifaceted pressure to diet did ask women to discipline themselves in ways men might more readily ignore as a means of proving their worth. It allowed new indulgence in consumer and sexual pleasures by using anxiety about weight as a counterbalance; restraint was not jettisoned, just relocated in the intense effort to infuse female fat with guilt. While no longer directly contending that women were weak, the insistence on slimness limited the capacity to impose physically. Attractive women must be relatively slight. Here African Americans, less involved with Victorianism and so not needing of a subtle restatement, clarified by contrast; "big mama" was an approved and obviously powerful image. The intense pressure on white women to reduce or apologize served, like Victorian culture, as a means of insisting on constraint, and whether some of the American women involved realized this or not, their counterparts in other cultures could see the pattern clearly enough: "Witness the amount of effort a young woman in western societies has to put in to look attractive enough to hook eligible young men. One gets the feeling they are on constant self display . . . [having to] diet to stay trim. . . . [Weight control] is one of the humiliations western women have to go through."[30]

Like Victorianism, however, the new standards imposed on women's weight had some compensations; it is as important for this mid-twentieth-century period as for the nineteenth century not to oversimplify, and some of the feminist critique in this respect has gone too far. Achievement of something like the desired weight might boost self-confidence and attract envy and sexual interest, while also providing a sense of moral superiority within the family. Slenderness achieved could be a source of quiet arrogance ("no longer pitying the obese, but censuring them") regarding other women or one's own spouse. Precisely because it was difficult for women to be responsible for the family's food while also keeping thin, success could bolster pride and family status just as, in theory, sexual purity had done in the nineteenth century. Many women became family weight monitors, criticizing their slovenly husbands and spurring children, particularly daughters, to new levels of restraint. By the 1970s some women were complaining, in fact, that their mothers' carping had driven them to excessive eating simply in defiance, while a sober scholarly study documented how women often overregulated children's eating patterns, leaving them without sufficient internal controls once on their own. Here, like the impositions of Victorian morality, was a complex theme, but one that illustrated how authority could flow from compliance with the new cultural norms.[31]

For there was no question that the standards hit home. The number of women dieters steadily increased, reaching many millions a year by the 1950s. Weight goals became a standard expression of women's personal ideals, a perennial focus of New Year's resolutions as well as a ubiquitous staple in the popular magazines. Writing to the "Dear Abby" newspaper column in 1994, a woman urged the desirability of enjoying the moment — not waiting until one was rich enough or exactly the right weight — sensible advice, but revealingly reflecting a routine association of weight standards with a much more traditional measure of the highest reaches of personal success. Men, it seems safe to say, would not usually pair thinness with wealth as a life goal, at least in a public forum. American women's weight-control passions inspired similar developments in Europe after World War II, where formal dieting became associated with femininity American-style. And in the United

States, the norms applied to women, from pre-adolescence onward, became steadily more demanding, and, for some, more personally daunting.[32]

Conclusion

The use from the 1920s onward of hostility to fat as a special means of discipline and self-discipline for women began to moderate between the 1950s and the 1970s in response to changes in women's aspirations and behaviors. Many segments of American society grew somewhat more accustomed to relatively open female sexuality, while women as targets for their uneasiness about consumerism may also have eased as men, too, became visible in the marketplace — yuppiedom was, after all, an ungendered commitment to high consumer standards. While women's new work roles caused concern, they may have lessened the role of weight control as a vehicle in weakening women in relation to men. The need to use fat as a symbol of bad character persisted, but its service as a substitute for older, Victorian gender differentiations and versions of female weakness diminished as Victorianism itself more fully receded. Pressures on women continued, and even increased, but as part of a general, not a gendered campaign — though women admittedly provided a historically sensitized audience.

Thus men became increasingly open about their concern for weight, and strictures on women persisted but were less distinctive. This was the point at which the special focus on fat girls receded in favor of attention to children generally in the childrearing literature. Even before this, as the next chapter will show, it is a mistake to focus too heavily on the female portion of the antifat campaign, for men were involved both in growing pressures to stay trim and in the need for a cultural compensation for concerns about indulgence in other respects.

Yet the virtual half century of vigorous attention to women's weight, and the developments for which it intended to compensate, continued to leave a mark into the 1990s. Adolescent white girls unquestionably worry about weight more than boys do, maintaining an imbalance in aesthetics and in advice about dealing with children's bodies that went back to the 1920s. Women continue to dominate the weight salons, and most advertising for diet products is still directed at them as well. They read about fat far more commonly than men do. Men persist in attacks on heavy spouses where women, though not silent, remain more reticent. Thus a complaint against a 200-pound woman in a letter to Ann Landers noted, "Sally is . . . depriving me of great sex," echoing the assumption that female fat and sex are antithetical and that a proper woman keeps herself up to standard. New enthusiasm for women's dieting has even intensified in certain groups. It was in the late 1970s and 1980s that fundamentalist Christian groups began to issue books promoting rigorous weight loss among women. With a general commitment to women's inferiority in the family, the pressure to diet served these groups as a means of cultural control, as it had in the general white middle class in previous decades. Even as the gendered quality of the campaign against fat lessened, in favor of a more uniform pressure to expiate through slenderness or guilt, women faced unusual rigor if they tried to live up to the body image suggested for them or unusual anxiety, even self-loathing, if they failed to try.[33]

5 Stepping up the Pace: Old Motives, New Methods

The most important development in the campaign against fat from the 1920s onward involved its sheer intensification. Special features of the constraints on women were significant in this larger context, for there was no question that the campaign — and even more, its reception — were gendered. But men were included as well, particularly from the 1950s onward, and the belaboring of feminine fat must be seen as part of this accelerating effort among middle-class Americans generally. After a few comments on the male battle against fat, we must then convey the overall process of intensification and the reasons for it. As American affluence increased following World War II, the ethical imperatives of appetite restraint increased as well. Fuller awareness of health factors entered in, along with a more abundant array of commercial gimmickry, but the most fundamental development was the elaboration of the linkage between dieting and moral compensation. The availability of an established cultural vocabulary to demonstrate virtue amid indulgence showed through clearly as the need increased. The fight for slimness involved beauty and longevity, but it continued to serve as a proof of good character in an age of obvious indulgence.

Fat Men, Too

Attention to male standards continued between 1920 and the late 1940s, even as women received the most biting commentary. Men's magazines did not contain extensive diet columns, to be sure, but they featured slender male models and a variety of advertisements for relevant products. *Esquire,* for example, the first fashionable modern men's magazine, founded in 1933, regularly carried notices for products like the Weil belt, which girdled and thinned the male waist (purportedly up to eight inches) while providing massage action that quickly removed actual fat (providing a "real" reduction in waist size of three inches in ten days). Illustrations included claims of a loss of fifty pounds and contrasting pictures of middle-aged to elderly men in slob-before and success-after poses. After World War II, *Esquire* added other items to its advertisement list, including electrical massage outfits attested to by leading athletes and businessmen. The magazine also put out a cookbook with a calorie counter section.[1]

Women's magazines also carried features on men, and there is no reason to assume that men did not take notice (either directly or through beneficently nagging wives). A typical comment in the *Ladies' Home Journal* involved a young man whose boyhood had been tormented by overeating.[2] Admittedly appearance did not yet matter much in his tender years, but the boy was subjected to merciless teasing from his peers: "it wasn't fun to have the other boys giggle at the sight of me and call 'Q-ball' and 'Fatso.' " Later, of course, girls ignored him, while his siblings pitied him. The story, like those involving women, ended happily, as the man saw the light of dieting and took more than eleven inches from his waist and hips. Men could also easily pick up weight warnings and diet information from general periodicals. Health publications carried diet advice and weight tables from the 1920s onward. General news magazines offered a spate of information in the 1940s and 1950s. Special books, like the series offering a "Fat Boy" diet, sold hundreds of thousands of copies in the years following World War II. In a weight-conscious culture, it did not require the redundancy of the women's magazines for men to hear the message and to be properly abashed about their own bodies when the pounds began to add up. Even changing styles affected men. Beachwear became more revealing as the concealing top gave way to a manly bare chest and belly. Tapered suits replaced the double-breasted look of the interwar years, making paunches harder to conceal. Intensification, in sum, unquestionably affected men.

To be sure, aesthetic pressure was long less great on males than on females. The amazing fascination of women's magazines with the subject of diet and the moral derelictions of fat found no full echo in what men read. Men were less often told that their love life hinged on slimness than women were, in part because the culture probably did allow somewhat greater latitude. Women depended more on looks to catch a mate. It was no accident that the extreme women's expression of the diet imperative, anorexia nervosa, was rare among men, though in some settings, like the military, overweight men drew more adverse comment than did women. In two areas, however, men may have received more rigorous warnings than women did during the midcentury decades. The first involved peer teasing. Boys reported a great deal of pressure from schoolmates, particularly if their weight impeded athletic ability. "I remember sitting down, eating my packed lunch, and hearing the voices mock me for my size. I never sat in the cafeteria after that incident." "I remember the days of childhood when the schoolyard slang — 'Lardass' — produced unseen emotional scars. I had wept often over the pain inflicted by those who would be my friends if I were thin." ("Lardass," indeed, seems to have become a very common epithet in American schoolyards in the 1940s and 1950s.) "Once I was even spat on by one of these students." "You know, Michael, you waddle when you run." The quiet self-hate that this atmosphere could engender might rival the more widely discussed self-loathing of fat girls.[3]

The second source of warning about fat was medical, directed at both males and females but with special salience for men, who began to learn of their unusual vulnerability to the diseases of heart and arteries to which fat made them subject. A full history of men's health anxieties has yet to be written. One authority argues that it was in the 1950s that men grew afraid of heart attacks, trying to change a variety of behaviors in an effort to save themselves. It was in 1963, for example, that the "Fat Boy" cookbook series issued a polyunsaturated version, to help cope with cholesterol's role in male heart disease.[4] It is likely, however, that real concern developed earlier. It was soon after 1900 that the concept of blood pressure reached public awareness, with appropriate warnings soon attached. Relatedly, the sphygmomanometer was invented in 1896, and its increasing use for measuring blood pressure in routine medical checkups brought home to middle-class Americans the important mystery of internal conditions within their bodies. Attention to inner, organic degeneration increased as well as common contagious diseases came under greater control, particularly after the influenza epidemic of 1919. While phobias about germs persisted, the growing significance of degenerative diseases won public notice. Not coincidentally, efforts to popularize fundraising for and awareness of cancer gained ground rapidly in the 1920s and 1930s, generating the first instance of a successful public campaign over a degenerative ailment. In sum, with the widespread awareness of the nervous pressures of modern society as a backdrop, practical changes in medical routines and disease patterns, supported by wide public discussions, set the stage for a much more specific use of health as a measurement of body standards; and men learned quickly that they had more to worry about under this heading than women did.[5]

Indeed, the diet books for men that began to emerge in the 1950s, headed by Elmer Wheeler's various works, developed a distinctively masculine set of weight-loss stories. The audience for these works was immediate and huge — Wheeler drew over 90,000 responses to an offer of a slide rule for weight. In these male accounts, the aesthetic values touted for women were absent, or at least muted. Rather, emphasis was placed on the competitive atmosphere among men; the fatty who lost his weight, who began to draw admiring glances from women, was going to score points on his buddies. "Fat Men Can't Win" was a representative title in this genre. Dieting became a chance to display male character and independent initiative. Most male diet heroes proudly cited their ability to control their own weight without help from psychiatrists or, sometimes, from physicians. While wives might serve as goads and nags, the results of male dieting would renew male power in a marriage. Kay Barth gained new initiative over his wife, as his diet allowed him to undertake hikes and explorations that she shied away from save under his prodding. Wheeler amazed his wife in bed; whereas when he was fat he could hardly stay awake, now it's she who loses sleep thanks to his sexual prowess.[6]

Again, men carried their concern about fat distinctively. They joined weight control organizations far less commonly. They almost certainly talked less about their anxieties. They may have minimized open expressions of concern, just as some women exaggerated their own worries; the gender cultures were different. Also, men did have, in hulking football stars or bodybuilders, an alternative male model of a sort unavailable to fashionable white women. But the general pressure to keep reasonably trim, and the moral evaluation that underlay it, bore on them as well, which is why the general process of intensification must be discussed from the standpoint of the American middle-class as a whole and not simply its hard-pressed female members. In the 1950s a television Superman played by George Reeves could look a bit paunchy without seeming contradiction — an impossibility two decades later, when actors who played Superman had to have flat, muscular stomachs to match their ability to withstand bullets.

By the 1970s, indeed, it was generally acknowledged that men's eagerness to lose weight began to match that of women; what distinctions had previously existed began to dissipate, save in the precise modes of expression.[7] Male worries about appearance, and the resultant need for slenderness, increased, along with ever-wider publicity about the perils of cholesterol for men. Growing employment in corporations and service sector operations, where looks counted for success, helped fuel this intensification. Later marriage age, forcing men to put more effort into wooing increasingly independent women, may have played a role as well. Television surely loomed large. The medium exaggerated appearances of weight, and this bore on male stars and newscasters as well as women; to look good on camera, men as well as women had to be slim. Even before this, a generation of rock stars had featured impressively slender males, who had to keep up this youthful appearance even as their actual youth receded. Amid this concatenation of factors, the pressure to fight fat began to seem increasingly common across the gender divide.

Symbolic evidence for this shift came with the cartoonists' delight over the real or imagined weight problems of Bill Clinton. Rotund past presidents had not drawn great comment, though the actual build of presidents after World War I unquestionably shifted to a more fashionable slenderness. *Harper's Weekly* greeted the nation's fattest president in 1908: "We don't care how much Mr. Taft weighs. He is a good man and will make as fine a President, in our judgment, as the country has ever had." (It is worth noting, however, that even Taft deliberately dropped sixty pounds prior to his campaign.) Cartoons, while scarcely avoiding his girth, poked gentle fun at most: "a large, amiable island surrounded by people who knew exactly what they wanted." Hoover, the stockiest interwar president, was described as "[c]hunky, round face . . . , beaverish shoulders and neck," but his weight did not surface strongly in the increasingly bitter attacks on his presidency. Not so Clinton. Cartoons routinely exaggerated his size, while ridiculing his jogging habits. Bill pops a button when inaugurated; Bill, walking down Pennsylvania Avenue, gets winded and looks for a cab, stopping in a restaurant for a cannoli first; the initial state dinner includes four dessert selections, each labeled Bill's favorite. The contrast, not only with the treatment of past presidents but with the relatively gentle approach to recent, matronly first ladies such as Bess Truman and Barbara Bush, was interesting. By the 1990s, important men are supposed to demonstrate the same rigorous discipline as fashionable women as a proof of good character.[8]

By the 1990s, in this new atmosphere men began to report pressures similar to those encountered disproportionately by women during the midcentury decades. The director of an eating disorders program in St. Louis said: "I have men coming into my office telling me they're convinced they were passed over for promotion because the other guy was slimmer and they look more like a beach ball. Or their wife is unhappy with them because of their appearance. . . . With more men's fashion magazines on the market, more emphasis being put on the way men look. Now they're subjected to the same concerns about body image that have plagued women for years." Impressionistic reports of male affliction with bulimia and other problems, previously women's province, rose as well.[9] On a relevant front, by 1995 *Men's Health Magazine* was featuring at least one diet article per issue, just like its female counterparts; the emphasis rested both on health and on appearance, with men told among other things how they could recapture a thirty-two inch waist.

The process of intensifying the antipathy to fat during the twentieth century in the United States, and for using slenderness as a modern moral symbol, has been very powerful, even when specific versions target a particular group disproportionately. No racial group has been entirely exempt. African American outlets like *Ebony* treat the diet pressure distinctively, but they unquestionably echo it to a degree. Hawaiian culture, traditionally attracted to big bodies as symbols of power and sexuality, began to encounter an alternate image of beauty with the advent of tourism following World War II, along with the inevitable health warnings. The result was not a complete eclipse of the older preferences, but the concomitant projection of a new image, the slender hula maiden or surfer male, to rival the old. Amid these kinds of assimilating pressures, gender distinctions in the growing middle-class must not be exaggerated. Not part of the initial attack on fat or the impulses for moral compensation that lay behind it, the gender factor never fully predominated. Men enjoyed somewhat greater latitude for a time but no full indulgence, and then they were brought more completely under the most rigorous standards during the final quarter of the century. Men, too, needed visibly to demonstrate their capacity for self-discipline or be found wanting if they failed. It is time to return to the renewed connections between dieting and moral demonstration, as an economy of abundance increased the need for compensation or guilt regardless of gender.

Intensifications

This book has explored many of the aspects of the acceleration of the modern hostility to fat, but a brief review sets the stage for exploration of the most important specific facets. Above all, it is vital to remember that the process has been reasonably constant since the advent of the diet culture. The best-known surge after World War II deserves due commentary, though growing pressure during the 1920s must be noted as well, but once established, the standards of slimness seemed so logical, their role in providing an opportunity to prove self-restraint so serviceable, that they gained ground almost inexorably.

Several developments built on the existing weight control culture from the 1920s onward. Amplifying a theme already suggested by prewar gurus like Horace Fletcher, women's magazines began to tout miraculous success stories of heroic weight loss, complete with before and after pictures and using men as well as women as examples. The *Ladies' Home Journal*, for instance, featured Mrs. Jessica Bayliss, a Philadelphia Main Line matron, who in 1924 using "Mrs. Wallace's plan" dropped fifty pounds in a matter of weeks. This new genre was obviously designed to sell plans or products — Mrs. Wallace claimed immense success with a series of exercise records and diet tips, in a process that was "downright fun." But the miraculous cure pitch also appealed to the neoreligious aspect of dieting in revealing that no cause was hopeless, no sinner unredeemable. Diet cookbooks proliferated as well, deriving some the success of the first efforts by Susanna Coccroft. Even more than books, women's magazines filled with calorie-counting recipes, including some 600-calorie items for serious obesity. It was in the 1920s, also, that the use of home scales began to expand, providing a daily ritual for many adults in which the battle against fat could be assessed, guilt at failure intensified. It was also in this period that Charles Atlas began his muscular, fat-free displays for men, extending the bodybuilding discipline pioneering by Bernarr McFadden. Other sites showed how the antifat standards were settling in. By the 1930s the *New Yorker* magazine routinely used stout middle-aged women as figures of fun, their rotundity a visible sign of their general superficiality. Other comments continued the effort to tear down beliefs that fat people were happy: "it is a sad heart, black with melancholy."[10]

Drugs and creams to use against fat began to proliferate in the 1920s. Amphetamines were a popular item in the effort to reduce.

"Obesity specialists" began to sell quack medicines, usually at a cost of about ten dollars per treatment. Creams, according to one report, supported a $40 million annual business — some of them, interestingly, originating in France but obtaining the highest prices in the United States. American physicians looked more favorably on what they saw as a growing awareness of nutrition; as one noted, "the past year or two has witnessed an exceptional degree of interest on the part of the general public in problems connected with 'food values.'" Medical writing on the subject expanded, both in professional and popular outlets. It warned against quackery — one of the staples of American Medical Association columns. But it also pushed for food restraint, often explicitly furthering the theme that discipline, rather than additional exercise, formed the appropriate path to slimness ("Avoid physical overexertions"). If exercise had any place in a diet scheme, it was "subordinate" to the will power needed to reduce intake. Supplementing the medical approach were widely distributed insurance pamphlets by companies like Metropolitan Life warning of the dangers of overweight to life expectancy.[11]

The interwar period, in sum, extended the bases for a major diet products industry, increased medical involvement, and accelerated some standard promotional ploys like the dramatic weight-loss story. In the process, public interest increased steadily, furthering as well as reflecting these developments. It was public concern — in the view of physicians, sometimes unwarranted, given the small degree of overweight involved — that supported the product lines, led some people to risk dangerous drugs and untested products, and pushed growing numbers of patients into doctors' offices seeking relief from fat.

The explosion of diet paraphernalia in the United States after World War II eclipsed all prior experience, though the framework remained essentially unchanged. Weight-loss stories became still more common, the amounts dropped still more impressive, representing a distinctively American fascination with dramatic redemption: Mrs. Wallace's mere 50 pounds were easily surpassed by tales of 100- or even 200-pound reductions, bringing joy and happiness in their wake. More massive products became available, like a 1957 "leg ring roller" that weighed 400 pounds, which for only $995 would provide electrical massage to any part of the calf or thigh at forty-eight strokes per minute: "Five years of exhaustive laboratory experiments and use in salons throughout the world prove that you can guarantee results!" Fashion magazines for women proliferated, each with its diet message; this included magazines like *Seventeen*, directed to teenagers. Food products began to advertise on the basis of slenderizing qualities. Pepsi-Cola early staked its claim as a drink of slimness, even before sugar substitutes. Pet Milk and other companies urged the low-calorie virtues of their products. Even sugar companies briefly got into the act. Domino Sugar ran a delightful campaign in 1958 showing how three teaspoons of sugar were much lower in calories than half a grapefruit (54 to 75), releasing more "quick energy" besides. New diet gurus surfaced. The exercise leader Jack Lalanne began his work soon after World War II, a fitness advocate reacting to his father's death from a heart attack; revealingly, Lalanne compared himself to evangelist Billy Graham, the only difference being that his crusade was intended for the "here and now." Again, religious motifs surfaced quite explicitly as the momentum of the attack on fat carried forward.[12]

Several innovations marked the postwar phase particularly. Diet books multiplied and soon won a near stranglehold in the best-seller list. By 1959, ninety-two diet books were in print, and by 1983, this number had quadrupled. One study has suggested a twelve-fold increase in diet books and articles between the 1940s and the 1980s; by the latter decade, popular women's magazines like *McCalls* could average two diet articles per issue (along, of course, with recipes for pasta and cakes). Explicit diet foods won an ever-increasing share of supermarket space, thanks to new products like noncaloric sugar substitutes. Between 1950 and 1955, diet soft drink sales soared three-thousand-fold. Food substitute products like Metrecal were introduced in the 1950s as well, often with hundred-million-dollar annual sales within a decade. Forty percent of all Americans were using low-calorie products in 1961. Finally, joining the commercial parade, national weight-reducing chains emerged, building on the local massage and reducing salons of the interwar years. Weight Watchers, with $160,000 in annual business in 1964, was earning $8 million in 1970, $39 million in 1979. Not only Weight Watchers, but Overeaters Anonymous, Jenny Craig, and other syndicated operations enrolled literally millions of members each year.[13]

Along with new commercial fanfare, the basic measures of public concern persisted. Doctors continued to report steady pressure from their patients to guide heroic feats of weight reduction, with or without much effort. "Some patients expect dietary miracles. . . . There are individuals who do not want to sacrifice any gustatory delights, and present all kind of excuses." Successful dieters themselves spread the word, in personal interactions as well as the widely heralded magazine features. Talking about dieting, its stresses, or its contemplation became standard conversational fare. "How often we hear it said, 'I think I better go on a diet,' evidently hinting at some monstrous reform being under consideration." Worrying privately and publicly about weight, avidly considering helpful books, products and commercial courses became increasingly standard parts of American middle-class life. As one doctor put it in 1952, "Reducing, or the deliberate effort to lower body weight, may well be called an all-American preoccupation."[14]

There was no little irony in the postwar manifestations of diet concerns. A hostility to fat intended to compensate for consumer passion itself took on increasingly consumerist overtones. Ardent opponents had their diet groups to join, while more casual participants could hope to buy their indulgence by purchasing the more expensive foods that had sugar substitutes or some other weight-fighting attribute. By 1990 the overall American diet industry was an estimated $33 billion operation. Nevertheless, the moral content of the war against weight persisted along with the ups and downs of diet fads. Dieting, however aided, remained a visible measure of discipline in an increasingly indulgent society. A doctor noted that, along with all the valid health reasons for weight control, "a condemning moralistic undertone is seldom missing. A variation of an old saying is justified, that in our society 'Slenderness is next to Godliness.'" References to laziness and character defects continued to abound.[15]

For escalation was not just a matter of more products and sales pitches. It also involved the scare tactics of diet salespeople, whose messages have correctly been compared to apocalyptic religious tracts: "You know what you are. It bothers you. It depresses you. And it should frighten you." "You've been warned, time and time again, what that oppressive extra burden could mean to your health — high blood pressure, heart attack, diabetes ... early death." Escalation also occurred in postwar estimates of the problem of overeating, with figures like half the adult population routinely bandied about. As the *Ladies Home Journal* Diet Club proclaimed in 1969 (though modestly citing only 30 million overweight Americans), "Overweight is America's No. 1 public health problem." Hyperbole was a piece of the whole approach to dieting, partly because attendant health problems were severe, partly because it helped to sell diet-related products and publications, but partly because guilt was an important component — not simply an emotional by-product — of the whole endeavor. This same guilt could produce a growing number of deviations, including people who slimmed excessively or who rebelled against the pressure, but it described an important moral component in the daily lives of many Americans during the last two-thirds of the twentieth century.[16]

Sex, Health, and Work

Along with the steady crescendo of diet materials, dire warnings, and public concern about fat, several specific themes, already available in the culture, gained new prominence. Sexuality was one. Injunctions to keep excessive weight off during pregnancy and to recover normal weight thereafter increased steadily, as we have seen. Pregnant women should not compromise their sexuality by too much fat. Ballyhooed instances of movie stars recovering their figures (or their reluctance to risk losing their slimness through pregnancy) highlighted the pressures. Interestingly, during the 1950s when cultural approval of motherhood went up, women's fashions also relaxed weight constraints, as fuller-figured, and particularly fuller-busted, women regained attention in the era of

Marilyn Monroe and Jane Russell. This was a brief interlude, however, as exceptionally slender models took over fashion's center stage during part of the 1960s. Normally, without question (even in the 1950s), recommendations for dieting directed at middle-class girls routinely stressed the sexual attractiveness component. A 1962 list of diet motivations for teen-age girls thus began with "boys," then mentioned improved appearance plus the choice of better clothes and feeling better physically, before ending again with "boys." The magazine articles reporting on miracle weight losses by women invariably noted their desire once again to appear attractive to their husbands, as if a slender, youthful appearance now did for a wife in marriage what her moral qualities had been supposed to achieve in the Victorian era. The goal of self-restraint remained, but now focused on weight control. But men's diet stories referred to sexual attractiveness as well, if a bit more graphically than women's fare. Doctors, continuing their invocation of aesthetics in recommending weight loss, could now refer to fat making people look "older and less attractive from the standpoint of our national ideal of 'good looks.'" [17]

Even more obviously, health factors began to gain greater prominence in the diet argument; correspondingly, doctors played a greater role in diet advice than they had around 1900. Cholesterol started to receive attention in the 1930s as a villain in diseases of the heart and arteries, though the widespread campaign, adding to the theme of restraint in eating, awaited the 1950s. Doctors and patients alike became more knowledgeable about the kinds of degenerative problems excessive weight could generate. [18] Fat itself came close to a disease category, though it was never fully merged lest the character of fat people be exonerated. New groups like Overeaters Anonymous implied an addictive quality to excessive eating like alcoholism, with the same group support mechanisms needed to combat it. "Being fat is a sickness," proclaimed a popular diet manual in 1966, and the fatter you are, the sicker you are. Fat, continued the same pamphlet, is like a "60 pound tumor," with the same deleterious effects on the body. [19]

Growing focus on the health implications of excessive weight, along with the generally intensifying aesthetic standards, produced a recurrent redefinition of the widely publicized weight tables and calorie charts. Acceptable levels of one decade were denounced as lax in the next. Science here conjoined with subjective culture: actuarial figures were progressively refined, suggesting that lower weights were healthier, while the desire to discipline the body and to attack indulgence pushed in the same direction. Thus in the 1930s doctors began telling Americans that the previously cited figure of 3000 calories a day was too high; 2400 calories, perhaps even 2035, would be preferable for people with sedentary jobs. "It would probably be advisable for practitioners to bear these lower figures in mind, and when patients are obviously over nourished, much smaller quantities of food are desirable." Popularized manuals sometimes attempted to shift the definition of obesity from the standard 20 percent over norm to 11 percent (with a mere 5 percent qualifying as "overweight").[20] In general, in a trend that began around 1910, doctors and insurance actuaries began to push preferability of underweight to overweight, in terms of health and longevity. This was the conclusion of a widely publicized new table produced by Metropolitan Life in 1942 (Table 1). And the actual recommended weights went steadily downward. A medium-frame man of five feet eight inches in 1942, according to the Met Life tables, should weigh 145 to 156 pounds; his counterpart in the same company's 1959 tables (Table 2) was down to 138 to 152. In the same span, a medium frame woman of five feet four inches went from 124 to 132 to 113 to 126 pounds. Overall in this seventeen-year interval, the Metropolitan Life tables dropped by about 8 percent. Only in the 1980s was there any reversal of this steady push to increase the rigor of ideal weight definitions. But while a 1983 Metropolitan table moved back to the 1940s levels, other weight tables continued to emphasize greater rigor; a 1994 Centers for Disease Control and Prevention chart held the medium-framed five-foot-eight-inch man to 149 pounds.[21] For those alert to medical reports, the rigor of the weight charts was compounded from the 1930s onward by recurrent actuarial comment that health, or at least longevity, was best served by being under the recommended poundage; short of emaciation, skinny people lived longest.

What was happening, clearly, was a conflation of science with

TABLE 1.

"Ideal" Weights (in Pounds) for Men and Women,
Metropolitan Life Insurance Co., 1942, 1943

Height (in Feet/Inches, with Shoes)	Weight (in Pounds, as Ordinarily Dressed)		
	Small Frame	Medium Frame	Large Frame
Men, ages 25 and over			
5'2"	116–125	124–133	131–144
5'3"	119–128	127–136	133–144
5'4"	122–132	130–140	137–148
5'5"	126–136	134–144	141–154
5'6"	129–139	137–147	145–157
5'7"	133–143	141–151	149–162
5'8"	136–147	145–156	153–166
5'9"	140–151	149–160	157–170
5'10"	144–155	153–164	161–175
5'11"	148–159	157–168	165–180
6'0"	152–164	161–173	169–185
6'1"	157–169	166–178	174–190
6'2"	163–175	171–184	179–196
6'3"	168–180	176–189	184–202
Women, ages 25 and over			
5'0"	105–113	112–120	119–129
5'1"	107–115	114–122	121–131
5'2"	110–118	117–125	124–135
5'3"	113–121	120–128	127–138
5'4"	116–125	124–132	131–142
5'5"	119–128	127–135	133–145
5'6"	123–132	130–140	138–150
5'7"	126–136	134–144	142–152
5'8"	129–139	137–147	145–158
5'9"	133–143	141–151	149–162
5'10"	136–147	145–155	152–166
5'11"	139–150	148–158	155–168
6'0"	141–153	151–163	160–179

SOURCE: Emma Seifrit Weigly, "Average? Ideal, Desirable? A Brief Overview of Weight Tables in the United States." *Journal of the American Dietetic Association* (1984): 419–20; data prepared by the company from actuarial surveys and material on blood pressure.

TABLE 2.

Desirable Weights (in Pounds) for Men and Women,
Metropolitan Life Insurance Co., 1959

Height (in Feet/Inches, with Shoes)	Weight (in Pounds, in Indoor Clothing)		
	Small Frame	Medium Frame	Large Frame
Men			
5'2"	112–120	118–129	126–141
5'3"	115–123	121–133	129–144
5'4"	118–126	124–136	132–148
5'5"	121–129	127–139	135–152
5'6"	124–133	130–143	138–156
5'7"	128–137	134–147	142–161
5'8"	132–141	138–152	147–166
5'9"	136–145	142–156	151–170
5'10"	140–150	146–160	155–174
5'11"	144–154	150–165	159–179
6'0"	148–158	154–170	164–184
6'1"	152–162	158–175	168–189
6'2"	156–167	162–180	173–194
6'3"	160–171	167–185	178–199
6'4"	164–175	172–190	182–204
Women			
4'10"	92–98	96–107	104–119
4'11"	94–101	98–110	106–122
5'0"	96–104	101–113	109–125
5'1"	99–107	104–116	112–128
5'2"	102–110	107–119	115–131
5'3"	105–113	110–122	118–134
5'4"	108–116	113–126	121–138
5'5"	111–119	116–130	125–142
5'6"	114–123	120–135	129–146
5'7"	118–127	124–139	133–150
5'8"	122–131	128–143	137–154
5'9"	126–135	132–147	141–158
5'10"	130–140	136–151	145–163
5'11"	134–144	140–155	149–168
6'0"	138–148	144–159	153–173

SOURCE: Weigly, "Average? Ideal, Desirable?" 419–20.

cultural norms. Pushed by wider American beliefs, including the pleas of their own patients, doctors readily focused on weight as a key issue, and, of course, the epidemiological and actuarial studies did demonstrate a relationship between slenderness and good health, particularly in the cardiovascular categories. Both discovery and belief seemed to indicate that even more rigor would generate better health (and improved character besides); Americans should not be allowed to content themselves with the same restraint that their parents' generation had been satisfied with. "Flesh," in this mixed scientific and cultural context, began to take on unfavorable connotations, an association with excess, in contrast to scientific writing around 1900 that had regularly used the noun in a neutral fashion. This was the same science establishment, it should be noted, that tried to keep Americans on their toes by progressively redefining what foods were healthy and which were not; in the most striking reversal, during the 1970s received wisdom that had emphasized meat- and protein-heavy diets, against starches-heavy ones, was totally debunked in favor of a new scientific preference for the healthy qualities of pasta and insistence on the deleterious effects of meat. In this mix of science, guesswork, and culturally constructed bias, it was hard to rest easy — which was one of the points of the whole enterprise.

Increased rigor, enforced by science and fashion alike, continued to find new outlets. By the 1990s, teenagers, both male and female, began to refuse to take school showers together after gym classes. While complex homophobia played a role, so did embarrassment at displaying less than perfectly slender bodies.

The linkage of health as well as appearance with slenderness, along with the larger impulse to use a slim body as a talisman of a good, well-disciplined character, supported another new theme in the campaign against fat — the association of weight control with work. The initial turn against excessive weight around 1900 had certainly equated slimness with good job performance, but no concrete conclusions were drawn. "In love or business, the man with a paunch loses his punch," continued to be an advice theme.[22] It was only in the heightened fervor of the post-World War II era that various employers began systematically to exclude overweight applicants on grounds that their girth would interfere physically or aesthetically with their job performance, a trend that notched up still further by the 1970s as businesses sought to combat health costs by excluding poor insurance risks. The trend first emerged in the public sector, with policemen and military officers sometimes fined or fired during the 1950s for failure to lose weight. Cases proliferated in the 1970s, with female service workers the principal target. A female California law officer was punished and finally terminated for being 10 pounds overweight, while more obese males in the same unit were ignored. A number of airlines set stringent weight rules for their female flight attendants on grounds of acceptable appearance, while male workers like pilots were held to no specific standards. The TWA service manual required flight attendants to implement a weight-control program when weight detracted from appearance. To be sure, pressures eased somewhat with time, thanks to lawsuits that punished discriminatory treatment. Corporate interest shifted in the 1980s and 1990s to weight-reduction programs for employees of both sexes as a means of controlling health costs. It remained difficult, however, to win a discrimination case when one was not hired or was fired or fined because of obesity; "penalize the flabby and reward the fit" remained the unspoken policy in many companies. The U-Haul rental company, for example, charged overweight employees an extra insurance premium in the 1980s, while ignoring mere smokers. At the same time, weight reduction or low-weight maintenance became a central feature of the burgeoning "wellness programs" available to management and clerical employees. Companies like Apple Computer offered cheap "weight-management" courses ($60 per course, waived for good attendance) as well as counseling and exercise facilities; other firms offered pamphlets and prizes. The basic message persisted, however, even with some of the overt compulsion reduced: fat people and work did not mix well.[23]

The linkage between appetite restraint and work was an important feature of the postwar men's dieting culture and, again, often translated into corporate reality. One book advised that fat "can count against him just the same when promotions are being considered. Then, it's the vigorous, ambitious, dynamic man who usually has the edge — not his solid, calm, comfortably easy-going colleague who carries just a little weight too much." A teenager who lost thirty pounds was told that such strength of character in a fifteen-year-old-boy means "you can look forward to success in any future undertaking." Diet morality, easily measured, counted strongly in the job market.[24]

Intensification of weight standards, particularly after World War II, thus meant not only a persistent tendency to identify beauty with a slender form. It linked sexuality to avoidance of fat. It produced a growing scientific basis for weight-control goals and a pronounced tendency to redefine these goals toward ever-increasing rigor. And it attached the same goals to job acceptability. These trends went beyond formal matters such as weight tables and the ultimately disputed instances of dismissal for weight. They meant that many Americans increasingly encountered reminders about the need for rigor, and possibly growing rigor, when they went for medical checkups. Like the daily or weekly bout with the bathroom scales, dealing with one's doctor about weight became one of the real constraints in middle-class life, a public reminder of the need to attend to health and virtue. Slimness counted also in employable appearance, even when companies issued no formal directive. American Airlines, for example, stopped forcing chubby stewardesses to lose one and a half pounds a week on pain of dismissal, but they still imposed two pounds a month or moved the employee to another, less public job. The body still counted. Because excessive fat was increasingly scorned with a growing arsenal of reasons, a trim body mattered in interviews, just as in political campaigning; here was a sign that an individual knew the rules and could keep his or her appetites in check.

Fat and Morality

Ultimately, the intensified concern about fat from the 1920s onward heightened the role of weight control, or worries about weight, as part of twentieth-century American morality. Here a basic ingredient of the initial culture of dieting persisted, even as it was overlaid by additional arguments about health or job efficiency. At its base, the need to fight fat remained a matter of demonstrating character and self-control in an age of excess. Here, surely, was the reason that fat was long singled out over other known health problems — for example, smoking (until the early 1990s) or cancer-causing tanning or driving over speed limits to this day. Here was why fat was not fully a sickness in the ordinary sense, save for rare bursts of medical enthusiasm, personal defects always added in. Alcoholics might be sick, according to new definitions; fat people should be able to control themselves. Even when doctors called fat women "sick," they meant morally or mentally defective, not uncontrollably ill. A decades-long history had produced firm convictions about appearance and physical fitness, to be sure, but undergirding both was a conviction that fat denoted bad character.

The surge of suburban living, the expansion of the affluent middle class, and the burst of new consumerism by the late 1940s triggered a new need to use dieting to demonstrate virtue. Americans worried loudly about their values, even as they indulged an unparalleled standard of living. From the 1950s through the Kennedy era, the middle class was inundated with magazine articles and politician's warnings about a nation going soft. It was vital to demonstrate bodily restraint. As with the initial diet messages over a half century before, the drumbeat of slenderness made the linkage with compensatory morality quite clear. A *Cosmopolitan* article of 1954 described a successful businessman who worked and consumed too hard, never relaxing, never spending time with this children. Just in time, he decided to change his life; he and his wife were "now readjusting their values and recharting their course so they can enjoy more time together." Just as important, the man had dieted and lost sixteen pounds. Weight loss was part of the moralizing process and a symbol of ethical balance. Diet experts constantly drew the linkage between restraint and morality: "fattened wallets," chided one expert, made fattened Americans, while Hilde Bruch blamed the obesity problem on "pampered and undisciplined appetites." Or, as another article put it: "Overweight? Blame our Soft, Lazy Way of Life."[25]

The rhetoric was very similar to that of 1900 because the underlying moral causes were the same. Greater abundance and intense but not clearly meaningful work in corporate management and service jobs created a real crisis in values. Theologians and academics spoke of a national malaise, of a failure to adjust to a world of abundance or the lack of a need to strive for anything. Proliferating fast-food outlets brought new consumer temptations directly into food habits. Dieting offered a chance for demonstrating self-control, for displaying difficult virtue. The moralizing or self-satisfying results might genuinely make dieters more comfortable with the problems that unnerved them: the rapid pace of work, the parade of acquisitions, the limited time for family interactions.[26]

Furthermore, the ongoing extension and solidification of diet standards by experts and general public alike gave a new twist to the moralistic argument. The ideal of slimness was so clear and so widely acknowledged that people who did not live up to it (save for instances of glandular difficulties, which were given less and less credence) must have something wrong with them emotionally. Medical and psychiatric inquiry conjoined, in a novel way that simply carried older moralism to a new plateau. Compulsive eating became "an expression of emotional maladjustment." Rational people could lose weight or not gain it in the first place. By implication, overweight people were emotional cripples, eating to mask other problems. This argument created one source of the gullible public that responded to commercial miracle cures, hoping for magic reformations that would totally change their existence, along with body size. They could drop pounds and simultaneously prove mental maturity. Yet, the popular diet writers intoned, these same people could rarely lose much weight, which simply added to despair and renewed the overeating, "the most important means of relieving the felt dissatisfaction." Childhood problems, difficulties at work, sexual hang-ups — all could combine to produce the immature response of gluttony, with its visible penalty in obesity. Individual diet heroines like Helen Fraley, whose hundred-pound weight loss made repeated women's magazine headlines in the 1950s, not only reported their shame at their appearance before the miracle of reduction but also their awareness that their previous eating reflected emotional problems and immaturity that must be conquered through the symbol of attacking fat. The common wisdom was clear, as the moral degeneracy of fat translated into post-World War II psychobabble: "Circumstances leading to a high-weight mark usually stem from a fatal character flaw and other psychological manifestations."[27]

This theme had been abundantly prepared by the basic culture of dieting with its direct implications for character and its implicit service as moral compensation. Only the psychological sneering added a new ingredient. After World War II, the theme was repeated time and time again, with minor variants. Articles in the *Ladies' Home Journal* informed readers that many fat women suffered from problems in their love life, finding gratification in food. The *Journal's* top heroine dieter, Helen Fraley, wrote of her eating to compensate for stresses in the family, leading to further shame and dejection and still more eating until she decided to master her worries and get her body under control. *Seventeen* joined in for the younger set: "Only when you can face up to and come to terms with the reasons causing you to overeat will you be able to slim down and stay that way. . . . Or might it be fear and anxiety about sex that make you keep yourself unattractive?" Again the twin implication was that eating exposed a major character flaw and that, unlike a real illness, fat people could right themselves if they would only get a grip. Experts drummed in the same points, as many letters to the editor attested: "She says it's all in my head." "As long as the maladjustment persists there is a continuous increase in weight." "Psychiatrists have exposed that fat person for what he really is — miserable, self indulgent and lacking in self control." "The obese woman's very dimensions reflect her need for strength and massiveness in order to deny an image of self that is felt to be basically weak, inadequate, and helpless." Hilda Bruch, one of the more thoughtful postwar psychiatric experts, nevertheless saw a common psychological profile among the overweight, gifted people who "did not fulfill the promise of their early achievement" and who ate to "relieve the felt dissatisfaction." Quite correctly, overweight people saw the larger context as hostile and critical.

"Society feels we're lazy, that we have no will power; we just don't care." Only slender people, so popular and expert opinion agreed, really had well-adjusted personalities. "Girls get fat because they're emotionally disturbed."[28]

Assumptions about the basic inadequacy of the fat, which only rarely distinguished between massive and moderate overweight given the convenient carryall term "obesity," helped explain doctors' ambivalence or outright hostility to their fat patients, whose very problems would make them hard to treat. The assumptions underlay the nasty tone of the diet literature, not only toward women but toward men as well, with terms like "fatty" and "slob" tossed about as apparent motivators. In a middle-class culture largely devoted to relative care in conversation, with lots of emphasis on treating people "nicely" and maintaining a generally if superficially friendly attitude, the insults directed toward the fat truly stand out, marking the state as one of moral, not simply physical, degradation.

The same assumptions underlay the presentation of issues of overweight as matters of basic personal dignity and ethics: "Cake or conscience? which will win?" To be sure, one line of argument — designed to sell diet books or goods — pushed for ease, weight loss without effort. This is a common option in realms that employ religious-like intensity, where some sinners look for an indulgent path. Hence diets might tout their "painless" qualities — it should be no problem to lose a pound a week. (Even with this approach, to be sure, reality might subsequently force a confrontation with conscience: if slimness is so simple, what's wrong with me that I can't attain it?) But the more common argument stressed the need for great discipline and even pain. Exercise literature picked up this tone, talking of "workouts" and the need to "feel the burn" before any good was accomplished. So did more strictly diet materials. A man wrote of his successful effort to trim 150 pounds. First, he identified the problem as a moral one: "Most of them are fat because they overeat, because they are too weak-willed to say 'No' when the platter passes." "I was only half a man." But when determination finally arrived, the individual can (with sensible doctor's advice) win through. "Oh, there is a fierce joy in discovered strength, knowing you can resist something you want desperately. Like a man biting down on an aching tooth, I deliberately increase my efforts to harden my will." In an indulgent society, reluctant to talk of painful moral obligations lest they distract from consumer pleasures, the moral quality of dieting offered a stern contrast.[29]

This was the message behind some of the most common diet articles during the decades after 1920, which featured massive weight loss by individuals seemingly hopelessly obese. Even the most hard-hearted sinner could see the light and reform the will in order to prove character and win the bountiful joys of slimness. Of course, the striking success stories helped sell diet materials, but the moral lesson was vital as well: if such hopeless cases can achieve success, surely you, the garden-variety slob, can, too — or feel properly guilt ridden in your failure. The stories were always basically the same. A child grows fat because of inadequate willpower and indulgent parents, plus sometimes other pressures or character problems that force eating as compensation. Misery ensues: the fat person is too ashamed to function properly, ridicule abounds, joys of family and work are denied. And then, through a new determination and self-imposed hardship, success. "I was a hopeless fatty, now I'm a model." Work opportunities improve, popularity arrives, a spouse is found or regained; slimness brings heaven on earth: "Less than two years ago my husband and I regarded our marriage as far from ideal. . . . Now we are one of the happiest couples in town." "Poised and confident," Bettye Baker, an Arkansas secretary, "went out and got a new job at an increase in salary that [paid for her Dubarry Success] course many times over the first year." Once Helen Fraley emerged from what she called her "mountain of fat," she found it easy to get good jobs, when she was not busy being romanced by her newly ardent husband. Weight control and success both in work and family were fully joined, just as fat kept an individual mired in the hell of failure. Sometimes, of course, religion was more than an analogy, but was directly invoked. An African American pastor who lost 140 pounds attested: "I asked God to inspire me to lose the weight, and with the support of my family, I knew I could do it." Occasionally, of course, as with more traditional forms of sin, the same press that ballyhooed one of the successful conversions to slimness was forced to admit backsliding. Helen Fraley, the *Ladies' Home Journal* queen of dieting in the 1950s, regained a hundred pounds and had to begin the battle of self-respect and discipline all over again. It was not clear that she succeeded: sinners could be lost.[30]

The sinfulness of fat helped inspire the various new groups that sprang up in the 1950s and 1960s to support weight-loss efforts. Some organizations had commercial inspiration as well, charging fees and marketing a variety of products. But the congregational aspect, with deliberately religious overtones, played a leading role. Even diet camps for teenagers, as they began to spread after 1955, often warred against spiritual flaws as well as fat itself. Groups allowed members to confess their eating sins and, of course, to receive approval and absolution for the commitment and for actual weight loss. Organizations like Overeaters Anonymous, taking a page from the religious-like Alcoholics Anonymous, stressed the deep psychological problems underlying obesity. A fat person needed far more than a good diet; he or she needed a personal change, a spiritual rebirth, so that faith in a Higher Power would allow a control of eating that the individual, on his or her own, could simply not provide.[31]

The image of fat as essentially evil, the result of personal failure but the cause of additional failures in the outside world, reinforced the link between prosaic diet literature and the need for a moral counterweight in a society of consumer indulgence. Fat people had to wrestle with some inner devils and with the temptations of the outside world — the soda fountains and the food-laden party trays — in order to win. But they could triumph, aided by science and perhaps by God, but guided above all by their own willingness to persevere and suffer. The inspirational stories had to make it clear to fat people — even people only moderately overweight — that their bodies were badges of a certain moral failure, in addition to their unsightly and unhealthy qualities. The intensifying culture of dieting was a culture of shame and guilt in a society in which these emotions were in most other settings downplayed. Shame and guilt could motivate, which is what the success stories were all about; they could also simply fester, adding self-criticism to whatever other drawbacks inhered in modern fat.

Internalizing the Norms

Throughout a century of diet culture in the United States, it has been obvious that public concern and promotional ballyhoo were mutually reinforcing. New warnings about health and new efforts to make success at work contingent on at least reasonable slenderness undoubtedly spurred more people to worry about their weight. The vast expansion of the service sector and the middle class after World War II pushed more people into awareness of diet standards, helping to explain the great increase in weight coverage and in new books and products in the late 1940s and 1950s. Massive suburbanization placed more people under the scrutiny of middle-class diet values, just as their increasing consumer indulgence created wider needs for guilt and expiation through attacks on fat. But the various intensifications in modern culture of concern with weight, including their upsurges in each period of greater prosperity, followed from popular interest and popular need; they were not primarily the product of commercial or medical manipulations. Not only the basic culture of dieting but also its acceleration were widely internalized. Even groups that hung back because of different aesthetic standards, like African Americans, could not resist contact with the mainstream values, as outlets like *Ebony* carried materials on health standards and heroic diet successes while they gave distinctive support to people with larger builds.

The basic evidence for the widespread public acceptance of diet norms lies in the massive numbers of Americans who bought diet products, went on diets or talked about their need to do so, and crowded into doctors' office demanding help. We have seen their interest in achieving new control over their weight in the 1920s as well as the postwar decades when the rates of involvement are more precisely recorded. Magazines that carried diet articles, not only women's journals but also various popular health publications, achieved massive reader response. Two-thirds to three-quarters of the letters about beauty tips sent to the *Ladies' Home Journal* after World War II involved weight control and dieting: "With this year's tiny-waisted clothes I need to lose 2 inches around my waist." "I would like to lose ten pounds. Do you have any diet suggestions?" Inspirational pieces like the series on Helen Fraley prompted many readers to write in thanks, for the pieces helped them put their own agonies in some perspective and gave them hope that they, too, could win success through weight loss. Many middle-class Americans really did pore over calorie charts and daily weigh-ins on the bathroom scales, converting the concern with fat to a virtual obsession that expressed their desire to live up to public norms and their need to demonstrate virtue through discipline and guilt. "Calories are the No. 1 topic of conversation in bars, boudoirs and drawing rooms," a journalist noted in 1955. "Anybody who eats desserts is considered to be living dangerously." The growing popularity of the regular medical checkup provided yet another contact with slenderness standards, but also an opportunity to display achievements. Doctors might belabor fat, but they also rewarded even moderate success with assurances of their pride in some weight loss attained.[32]

Evidence of the acceptance of appearance standards comes in private comment as well as public display. One pregnant mother in the 1930s wrote in her diary of wearing a girdle into her seventh month to avoid looking fat, only reluctantly deciding that it was "more important for infant to have room than for me to have straight form" two months before the baby was born. Even after this concession, the diary filled with efforts at reassurance: the mother-to-be "still looked all right," and if she wore the right clothes, other people did not know she was pregnant. Only in the eighth month was the battle lost: "Fear my pregnancy pretty obvious now, side view at least." Many Americans, and not just the anorectic extremists, pushed their goals for slenderness beyond what was sensible, trying to fight what doctors often told them was their "natural" body build. To be sure, there was some variety. Certain overweight people came to terms with their shape and adjusted fairly well. Others, however, succumbed to the intense cultural pressure, becoming preoccupied with their weight and increasingly hostile to themselves, sometimes veering into mental illness as a result. As the diet culture intensified at least through the 1970s, it became harder to hold out; the latitude available, not just in public reactions but in one's own head, progressively diminished.[33]

For there is abundant evidence not simply that massive numbers of Americans bought into the antifat culture, but that they resonated to its increasing rigor. Belief in the problem of overweight increased rapidly. According to polls in 1951, 21 percent of all American men and 44 percent of American women judged that they were overweight. In 1973, the figures had increased to 39 percent and 55 percent, respectively. It was not just the change in percentages that was interesting but also its indication of a steady inflation of perception, for the 1973 percentages easily surpassed the actual figures of obesity. Efforts to take off the fat soared as well, which was not surprising: in 1950 7 percent of men and 14 percent of women professed to be on a diet, whereas in 1973, the numbers had risen to 34 percent and 49 percent. But the main point was the impact of the steady pressure of diet advice and the growing need to believe that discipline was required. Because the anxiety about fat went beyond the body to other tensions in a society of abundance, full correspondence between worry and physical reality was not required. It might even be uplifting to criticize one's shape more than was strictly necessary. Critics implicitly realized that dieting and diet worries were being pushed beyond reasonable limits — far beyond "the bounds of science and logic," as one observer noted in 1959 — because they served symbolic ethical needs.[34]

There was little question, as well, that the moral dimensions of the modern culture toward weight were deeply felt. References to conscience and guilt became commonplace as part of dealing with daily encounters with scales, mirrors, and peer review. A diet writer who noted that low-fat foods do not work for some people was bombarded with letters suggesting that she has missed the point, for the real issue was ethical: "Just because fat people can't control themselves. . . ." A 1994 study of morality drove the point home further. College students dealt with the capacity to restrain or lose weight as a moral category comparable to responses to sexual issues such as extramarital affairs or even to thefts. Another finding showed that Americans judged people who eat low-fat foods as more moral, in general terms, than others. The battle against fat had truly altered Americans' ethical compass, joining disciplined weight to much older ethical norms as a measurement of proper character. This, in turn, was why Americans elevated people in so many contexts by their body image, as a sign of an ability to resist temptation and unwanted appetite, a guarantor of moral reliability.[35]

6 Fat City: American Weight Gains in the Twentieth Century

No study of the modern American hostility to fat would be complete without exploring its great anomaly: during the very century in which diet standards have been ever more rigorously urged, average American weight has gone up, rather markedly. This is true even when weight gains are controlled for height, which has also increased. Foreign observers often note their surprise at how heavy many Americans are, but homegrown data are quite adequate to make the point. Indeed, a quite noticeable average weight gain during the 1980s and early 1990s made national news in 1995. It is just as important to note that even before this surge, American poundage expanded.

This is not a historical discovery, but it also has never been properly assessed. Hillel Schwartz's history of dieting notes weight gains, but only in passing. Schwartz clearly finds it amusing that amid all the diet fanfare Americans became fatter — and it is a real historical irony — but as an antidieter, he largely leaves his assessment with the implication that the joke's on us. Studies of American eating provide useful data, but they have not done much with the modern diet craze and so leave the obvious questions unexplored. This is not a richly researched area, and the tendency to separate work on eating from work on dieting compounds the problem. It is time to do better.

Clearly, the waves of diet advice and the pervasive cultural hostility to fat have not been fully effective. This does not mean that the culture we have been examining is insignificant. Many individual Americans have followed it and still more have tried, and where increasing fat has seeped through despite the culture, the result has been heightened worry and personal insecurity. But it does mean that the culture's impact is complex. It is not enough to characterize the culture as an obsession along the lines of some feminist analysis without noting that many, many Americans have ignored it in practice — and women, more overweight than men, have headed the pack.

A variety of factors have worked against the full success of the modern diet ethic. It is important to remember that the new standards began to kick in from the 1890s onward, a time when more people were becoming more sedentary and when both food and the money to afford rich food were becoming more abundant. Growing concern about dieting was not simply caused by the fact that it was now easier to put on weight — the new standards attempted to press for greater slenderness, not merely maintaining the status quo — but this was a factor. The inescapable datum that, for many Americans in the twentieth century, actual eating has outstripped actual dieting helps explain the growing rigor of the diet advice and the frequent desperation of many people who have found their bodies escaping their control. It is the combination of the diet culture with the actual weight gains that has made this whole area a matter of such public concern and, often, such private self-doubt.

Still, the tension requires further probing. Why have the diet worries been so frequently ineffective despite their intensity? This chapter proceeds in two stages. First, the problem is detailed with available data about weight gains. Then, several major explanations are offered, which in combination show why the pervasive cultural standards have not worked in as straightforward a fashion as might be expected and why the standards have in some respects been oddly counterproductive. This first analysis complete, we then turn in the next chapters — the book's final main section — to a wider analytical effort, where American history is combined with a comparative approach.

Tipping the Scales

Americans do not seem systematically to have gained weight during the later nineteenth century, despite the approval of plumpness in fashion and in health. Evidence is scattered, to be sure. The weight index of fifteen to twenty year olds at the Citadel Military Academy did not change systematically until the 1920s. It dipped a bit in the 1890s for most ages, regaining previous levels after 1900. But by the 1920s it rose about 10 percent. Thus the average nineteen year old weighed 144 pounds in the 1870s, 133 in the 1890s, 139 in the 1900s, but a strapping 156 in the 1920s and 160 in the 1930s. West Point Cadets were also quite thin in the nineteenth century: a student born in the 1870s at 5 feet 7 inches weighed an average of 127 pounds, less than women of that height do today. Evidence suggests that students ate large meals in the nineteenth century (more on this later) but must have worked them off with regular physical activity. To be sure, military cadets may have been self-selected for slenderness because of the need for good conditioning, but there is no reason to believe that the overall population was less stable, if perhaps a bit heftier.[1]

After 1920, weight gains seem to have been fairly steady in the American population as a whole. Straws in the wind: women's dress size twelve in 1939 was predicated on dimensions of 34–25–36; by 1971 it had been redefined to 35–26–37. In the 1960s, seats in the Los Angeles Colosseum had to be widened.[2] Estimates held that caloric intake increased on average by 6 percent between 1950 and 1978. And insurance weight charts told the same story more systematically (though inaccurate when based on self-report, they probably reflected efforts to minimize weight rather than any exaggeration). Between 1941 and 1963 (Table 3), the average weight of insured men increased eight pounds under age forty-five, five pounds for ages forty-five to sixty-four. Women's weight also increased under age thirty-five. Metropolitan Life tables (Table 4) showed an average weight increase of nine pounds between 1941 and 1967, with the largest increases in the eighteen to thirty-four age group. Short men (under five feet five inches) gained little, but men five feet six inches to five feet eight inches gained four

TABLE 3.

Trends in Average Weight (in Pounds), 1941–63

Sex, Age, and Height (in Feet/Inches)	1941 Metropolitan	1935–53 26 Companies	1963 Metropolitan	Change 1963 Over 1941	1960–62 U.S. N.H.S.	Excess U.S. Over Met. 1963
	Weight by Age (recorded weights adjusted to nude as indicated below)					
Males						
18–24	147	145	155	+8	159	4
25–34	153	155	162	+9	169	7
35–44	157	159	165	+8	170	5
45–54	158	160	164	+6	170	6
55–64	157	158	161	+4	165	4
Females						
18–24	119	119	121	+2	127	6
25–34	124	126	125	+1	133	8
35–44	136	133	132	−4	141	9
45–54	144	138	139	−5	145	6
55–64	145	141	135	−10	150	15
	Weight by Height*					
Males						
5′3″–5′5″	140	141	143	+3		
5′6″–5′8″	149	150	153	+4		
5′9″–5′11″	159	161	165	+6		
6′0″–6′2″	171	174	180	+9		
Females						
4′9″–4′11″	119	115	116	−3		
5′0″–5′2″	124	122	122	−2		
5′3″–5′5″	134	131	132	−2		
5′6″–5′8″	141	140	145	+4		

*Average weights by height for 1941 have been adjusted to age distribution of 1963.

pounds; those five feet nine inches to five feet eleven inches, seven, and those six feet to six feet two inches, eight. The mid-1960s showed a bit of weight loss among younger men, but they still averaged well above their counterparts in the early 1940s. Findings continue in this vein. A 1979 study found an average weight increase (height held constant) of five pounds, 1950 to 1971. Men gained a pound a year in their early twenties, .2 to .5 pounds a year through their forties, while experiencing a smaller increase in their fifties and a slight decrease thereafter. Women (height again held constant) gained three to four pounds. They were heavier after thirty than they had been in 1950, but actually lost weight compared to their levels during their teens and twenties. Between the early 1970s and the early 1980s, the average American gained two

TABLE 4.

Average Weights (in Pounds) for Men by Height and Age, Metropolitan Life Insurance Co. Ordinary Policyholders, 1941, 1963, and 1967

Policies Issued in 1941

Height Group (in Feet/Inches)	Age Group				
	18–64	18–24	25–34	35–44	45–64
5′3″–6′2″	160	155	161	165	166
5′3″–5′5″	143	135	143	148	150
5′6″–5′8″	154	147	154	159	162
5′9″–5′11″	163	157	165	171	173
6′0″–6′2″	175	169	177	184	187

Policies Issued in 1963

Weight Group (in Feet/Inches)	Age Group				
	18–64	18–24	25–34	35–44	45–64
5′3″–6′2″	167	161	169	172	170
5′3″–5′5″	145	139	144	148	153
5′6″–5′8″	156	149	158	160	163
5′9″–5′11″	169	163	169	175	174
6′0″–6′2″	182	175	184	189	188

Policies Issued in 1967

Height Group (in Feet/Inches)	Age Group				
	18–64	18–24	25–34	35–44	45–64
5′3″–6′2″	169	164	171	173	174
5′3″–5′5″	143	137	141	149	153
5′6″–5′8″	158	151	158	163	166
5′9″–5′11″	170	164	171	175	177
6′0″–6′2″	183	178	186	190	189

NOTE: Weight as ordinarily dressed indoors; height taken in shoes.
SOURCE: See note 3.

TABLE 5.

Overweight in America
(% of Each Group 20% or More Over Ideal Weights)

	1962	1974	1980	1991	Increase from 1980 to 1991
Both sexes	24.4	24.9	25.4	33.3	31.1
Men	22.9	23.6	24.0	31.6	31.7
Women	25.6	25.9	26.5	35.0	32.1
White men	23.1	23.8	24.2	32.0	32.2
White women	23.5	24.0	24.4	33.5	37.3
Black men	22.2	24.3	25.7	31.5	22.6
Black women	41.7	42.9	44.3	49.6	12.0
White, non-Hispanic men			24.1	32.1	33.2
White, non-Hispanic women			23.9	32.4	35.6
Black, non-Hispanic men			25.6	31.5	23.1
Black, non-Hispanic women			44.1	49.5	12.2
Mexican-American men			31.0	39.5	27.4
Mexican-American women			41.4	47.9	15.7

			Age Group			
	20–34	35–44	45–54	55–64	65–74	75 and over
Men	22.2	35.3	35.6	40.1	42.9	26.4
Women	25.1	36.9	41.6	48.5	39.8	30.9

All figures for women exclude pregnant women.
National weight surveys are presented for people 20–74 years old. Before 1980, Hispanic people were not treated as a separate category. Years indicate when surveys were concluded.
SOURCES: Centers for Disease Control and Prevention. National Center for Health Statistics.

pounds, when height and age were held constant. Levels of overweight with advancing age went up. By the 1980s, 24 percent of men and 27 percent of women were overweight, 8 percent and 12.5 percent severely, .6 percent and 2.5 percent "morbidly." Women went to extremes more than men, with more thin and more very heavy, which meant that female averages were less informative than those for males. Between 1960 and 1980, white women's weight increased 3 percent, that of white men 6 percent, of black women 7 percent and of black men 28 percent. A 1994 study found a quarter of all American children obese, up 54 percent from levels in the 1970s. More recently still, a 1995 study found 71 percent of all Americans over twenty-five overweight, compared to 58 percent in 1983 (using more demanding criteria than the previous 1980s survey) and 64 percent in 1990.

Putting these data together suggests a weight gain of about two pounds per decade from the 1940s to the 1980s (but a bit less for women), after a prior two-pound increase from 1920 to 1940. Then the late 1980s and early 1990s broke the scales with an unprecedented surge. The average American adult gained eight pounds between 1985 and 1995.[3]

While it is generally agreed that weight has soared, particularly during the past decade as many Americans admitted they were eating more despite acknowledged overweight and despite some attempts at concealment — a point to which we must return — it was the steady increase over a seventy-year span that is particularly impressive, coinciding as it did with rigorous hostility to fat bodies. To be sure, the weight gain seems to have begun a few decades after the modern culture of dieting first emerged, which confirms the independent causation of this culture. But it certainly indicates the ineffectiveness of this same culture in determining actual eating and exercise patterns, as more strenuous standards coincided with heftier bodies. The culture was not entirely irrelevant, to be sure. Women were more likely to be overweight than men (as they had been in the nineteenth century, almost surely, if twentieth-century standards had been applied), but they gained less, particularly during middle age and beyond. Here, surely, intense diet pressure paid off in part. Whites, more actively subscribing to the culture than African Americans, gained noticeably less. Younger adults gained more than their middle-aged counterparts in both genders, with only a few decades excepted. This division did not explicitly follow from the dieting standards but might suggest greater effort from people whose physical appearance was beginning to deteriorate in other respects. The same pattern may describe the weight-control success of shorter men, whose stature was a sufficient problem, given esteem for height, without adding unsightly pounds to the mix. The culture of dieting helps explain key variations, which means that its impact must not be slighted. It is also possible that the slight relaxation of the culture in the 1980s helps explain why weight exploded. Around 1990, various groups of spokespeople for the overweight urged pursuit of legal civil rights for the obese against job discrimination and social disdain alike, various cultural critics attacked the constraints of the dieting standards (particularly concerning women), and some doctors came out in favor of looser standards rather than recurrent fluctuations. Given a twentieth-century tendency to overeat, it may be that increasing the cultural rigor is essential to keep American propensities within bounds — an incomplete result of the culture, but a result nonetheless. All this said, it is also clear that the basic goal of the insistent preachments to keep weight down has not been met since 1920. The urgings have had an impact on certain groups and certain decades, but they have not triumphed over countervailing impulses. Given the culture's unquestionable power, this disparity must be explained.

Food and Subcultures

Two factors clearly contributed to shaping the difference between body standards and the seemingly inexorable average weight gain. The first involves the steady pressure to eat more, and more calorically, in a period when, thanks to sedentary jobs and automated transportation, the expenditure of physical energy declined for most Americans. The reduction in caloric output is obvious. The decades since 1920 have seen a steady trend away from agricultural and manufacturing jobs toward the service sector and, in all segments of the labor force, rural as well as urban, increased mechanization. The cessation of regular walking to and from the job has been a major development, particularly since the end of World War II and the big highway boom of the 1950s. As late as the 1930s, the vast majority of people in a city like Pittsburgh still walked to work.

Yet eating has, simultaneously, increased, according to admit-

An older ideal: Adah Isaacs Menken, a variety stage star regarded as the height of voluptuous beauty, in 1860. Courtesy Library of Congress.

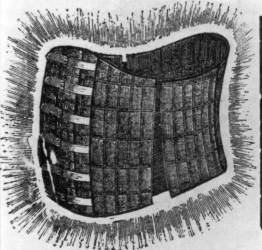

An early gimmick, 1892. The belts had over a hundred electrically charged magnets, plus medicated flannel, covered with silk. The electrical charge was supposed to disintegrate fat, as well as dispell intestinal gasses and tumors. From George Burwell, Obesity and Its Cure.

Life *magazine's Gibson Girl, shown here from an issue in 1900, both reflected and furthered the new fashion standards of slenderness for women.*

Advertisements from a single page of the Pittsburgh Press in 1905—a remedy for every body in a time of transition toward the more single-minded pursuit of dieting. Copyright © Pittsburgh Post-Gazette. Reprinted with permission.

The quick commercial appeal: this notice, in Woman Beautiful, *1910, drew 135,000 replies by 1914. Courtesy Library of Congress.*

An early version of the diet miracle photo. In contrast to later efforts, the "before" pose is mercifully absent. The use of a "society" woman suggests the top-down quality of diet standards. From Ladies' Home Journal, January 1924, 108.

WHY WE GET FAT
AND WHAT TO DO ABOUT IT

Too Bad That Our Customs are Such That Women of Means Cannot be Turned Loose on a Washtub Full of Soiled Clothes, for "Washing" Would Prove to be a Great Reducer

 By William S. Sadler, M.D.,
and Lena K. Sadler, M.D.

The disgusting fatness and laziness of rich women: "too bad" that they can't be made to do laundry, for it would get them active. From Ladies' Home Journal, August 1921, 91.

A relatively early, moderate version of the heroic weight loss story, where dropping nineteen pounds led to a better job thanks to a commercial beauty kit. From Ladies' Home Journal, *January 1942, 44.*

Bringing the standards, and the worries, to adolescent women. From Ladies' Home Journal, *April 1945, 140.*

From dowdy droop to thin-waisted model, thanks to the loss of 50 pounds. A typical Ladies' Home Journal *presentation from the 1950s (January 1955, 75).*

Carrying the message of slimness and muscularity to men: a faddist, "Prof." Paul Bragg, exposed by the American Medical Association. From Journal of American Medical Association, *January 1924, 288.*

I Cut My Weight by 150 Pounds !

By MAC R. TARNOFF

Six years ago I was a fat man. Not just a "fat man," but an oversized blimp who shot the scales to a quivering 337 pounds. Grotesque? Indeed I was. Today, after less than a year's diet, I weigh 187. I hope my story will help others in their fight against fat.

THE BEAUTY DEPARTMENT
EDITED BY DAWN CROWELL NORMAN

At 337 pounds (left) I couldn't get insurance. At 187 pounds (above) I have all the insurance I need. My reducing days are over, but to maintain my weight I shall have to watch what I eat for the rest of my life.

The heroic weight reduction, male department. A New Jersey man testified about his medically sponsored loss of 150 pounds. From Ladies' Home Journal, October 1958, 146.

Bialo

Cette jolie robe de dîner est
traitée en mousseline blanche
et dentelle de Chantilly noire
très apprêtée. Modèle de Bialo, 6, Place de la Madeleine

Le "Suffren", maillot de bain
d'une coupe parfaite exécuté
en un nouveau jersey fin et
très serré, bleu à rayures
blanches. Création Hermès 24,
rue du Faubourg Saint Honoré

Janine

Ses maillots de bains sont por-
tés par la femme soucieuse de
sa ligne. Aussi ses gaines
et ceintures-culottes pouvant
être portées sans bas. 30, place
de la Madeleine, Opé 86-9

Standards of the 1930s. Touting slimness, Vogue's swimsuit advertisement also sug-
gest the difference in rigor from postwar French standards. From Vogue, *June 1937,*
130.

The aesthetic of extreme slenderness, through careful eating. A transatlantic image, but with greater visual intensity in the French rendering. From Prima, June 1996, 127.

The fascination with reducing cream, against the dreaded cellulite. From Top Santé *magazine, May 1996, 41.*

Creams against the "culotte de cheval": the rigorous French standards for slender legs. From Top Santé, *May 1996, 6.*

tedly sketchy evidence. Even had older American preferences for rich desserts like cakes and pies persisted, weight gain would probably have resulted; but heightened consumption of meats, cheeses, and a veritable explosion of snack foods significantly upped that ante for all but the most faithful adherents of the new diet standards. Women's magazines, that staple source of pressure to lose weight, almost invariably intermix diet advice and health-conscious food suggestions with tempting, weight-adding recipes and advertisements. Not only traditional fare but also new products complicated the response to weight-control goals. The ice cream sundae was introduced in the 1890s along with the first weight-loss fads. The intensification of dieting in the 1920s was partially countered by innovations such as Eskimo Pies and a proliferation of commercial snack foods. Food promoters do their bit, deliberately trying to entice people to eat more ice cream or disingenuously claiming that their product, however sugary or fat-laden, really is not a major culprit. Devices to lower fat content sometimes combine a diet appeal with an invitation to substantial eating, rather like cost-cutting sales that distract from the high initial price. "No one food is fattening, it's the combination that counts. You can have your cake and diet too."[4]

In this context, the proliferation of low-calorie products made little difference when consumption of other items increased simultaneously, as was clearly occurring by the 1960s. People might pretend to meet diet goals by systematically converting to a sugar substitute (and typically paying a high price for the artificial product), while devoting little attention to their overall eating patterns. It was also true that the diet promoters had some self-interest in failure and recidivism, which would keep guilty Americans coming back for more paid advice, more special foods.[5]

And the temptation to gorge remained strong. Restaurants still called patrons with the distinctively American appeal: "all you can eat." (By contrast, French restaurants that offer "*à volonté*," or "at your will," have been much rarer — some are American chains like Pizza Hut — and the help-yourself buffet, which makes gorging really easy, is not usually a part of the deal. Only in the Belgian-founded Club Med is the opulent buffet widely available to the

French as part of their vacation.) In a culture already open to hearty appetites, the abundance of food, increased accessibility though ubiquitous fast-food outlets and snack bars, and enhanced commercial appeals to eat have all combined to play a major role in the U.S. disparity between accepted standards of slimness and actual patterns of weight. The result is not only the average gain but also a growing personal, sometimes agonizing, dismay about one's own body, which so clearly falls short of the aesthetic and health standards most Americans have accepted.

It is also true, as we have seen, that not all Americans subscribe to the same standards, and this is the second factor in explaining gaps between mainstream norms and national reality. The United States is a very segmented society when it comes to eating and diet goals. If a melting pot in some respects, in matters of body shape, the ingredients most definitely have not yet melted.

Three overlapping categories particularly defy the norms of slenderness: Americans in depressed rural areas are particularly overweight, with Mississippi and West Virginia offering the highest percentages of obesity, in that order. Also, African Americans and Hispanic Americans are much more likely to be overweight than are whites or Asians and, as we have seen in the case of African Americans, the rates of increase have been greater as well. Here are groups that participate so little in the consumerist culture or in the appearance demands of successful contemporary employment that some of the principal motivations of the white middle class simply do not operate. There is little indulgence to expiate by restraining appetite. In addition, traditional heavy eating and a positive valuation of big bodies add further motivation for putting on weight. Hispanic Americans stress the importance of substantial eating as a definition of family success, and we have seen that many African Americans maintain distinctive aesthetic standards when it comes to body size. Cultural tradition particularly explains the prevalence of overweight among women in these groups (as among older ethnic Hawaiians), which in turn helps to account for the greater national percentage of obesity among women than among men. Finally, increasing stress and deteriorating economic prospects, in places like Appalachia for rural whites and the inner city for African Americans, may have heightened the temptation to eat as a solace, helping to explain the recent intensification of obesity levels. Food has been available to subcultures that may particularly value it when other satisfactions, often including work itself, have proved harder to come by.[6]

Middle-class culture in the United States has been immensely powerful, particularly in the twentieth century, as it reaches the public through expert advice, school programs, and the media. There is no question that most groups are aware of the relevant standards, but many do not choose to implement them. The divisions in this respect operated even during the middle decades of the century, when by most accounts American culture homogenized to some extent. And less surprisingly, they have increased in recent decades, when social cohesion in the nation lessened in favor of separate group experiences and identities.

It is important to remember, however, that many middle-class individuals have deviated from clearly accepted weight standards as well. The average national weight gain occurred even when more and more Americans claimed participation in the middle class and by many measures, including suburban consumerism, lived up to their claim. The particular experience of certain minority groups explains part of the overall disparity, but by no means all. Even amid the distracting temptations of abundant food, packaged and advertised in newly enticing ways, there are other factors to explore, affecting minorities and mainstream experience alike.

Sparing the Child

Reports over the past decade have highlighted the extent to which many American children are overweight, setting up probable obesity difficulties in adulthood. The phenomenon is partly biological: fat cells can be shrunk but do not disappear, such that a chunky child always has greater potential for adult expansion than does his thinner counterpart. The phenomenon is partly recent and social: with television watching and middle-class chauffeuring, many children gained insufficient exercise, while abundant snacks, specifically advertised for this age group, encouraged extra eating as well. But the phenomenon is also historical: children formed an odd exception to the culture of dieting throughout much of this century. Their omission affected minority subcultures but also the mainstream middle class, whose valuation of childhood oddly conflicted with the body standards being imposed, in principle quite rigorously, on adults. Because children's eating habits were often relatively undisciplined, probably more undisciplined than in the nineteenth century, adolescents and adults often launched their diet careers with two strikes against them — an anomaly that helps explain why it was often only in early middle age that diet standards fully kicked in even for women, as young adults struggled more openly with weight patterns retained from childhood. The modern historical conflict between the valuation of children and the valuation of slenderness contributes to an understanding of the disparity between weight goals and weight results, even beyond the early years of life.

The context for this conflict lay in new attitudes toward children that had been developing for many decades, but had gained new urgency around 1900, right at the point when the dieting culture was emerging for adults. Historians have debated how much change can occur in standard parental attitudes toward children. An initial tendency to argue that premodern parents cared little for their children emotionally because of high infant death rates and the need to put young people to work at an early age has been modified. Signs of parental attachment, including considerable grief at a child's death, are not modern inventions in Western culture. Nevertheless, the intensity of parental attachment has probably increased since the eighteenth century. Falling birthrates helped focus emotional energy on each child who was born. As child labor declined, young people were increasingly viewed in terms of the love that would surround them; here was a reason to have children despite their cost and despite the birth-control devices that now permitted relatively free choice of whether to conceive or not. Nineteenth-century middle-class culture emphasized the loving and innocent qualities of children and the deep bonds they would form with their parents, particularly their mothers.

Ideas of original sin virtually disappeared in the mainstream American middle class, and of course, as innocents, children were exempt from any need to compensate for consumer indulgences in which adults might participate. Attachment to children, at least in principle, may have gone up still further at the end of the nineteenth century; certainly the middle-class willingness to shower children with gifts and other signs of economic commitment increased. Further, declining infant death rates helped focus attention on the possibility of eliminating this dread family scourge. If only one took proper care of young children, a family might — for the first time in human history — normally expect to avoid any deaths before adulthood.[7]

Along with growing affection for children, even their idealization in middle-class culture, and the instantiation in an intense desire to keep the young healthy as a sign of love and parental competence came some interesting complications. By the 1920s, middle-class birthrates had fallen so low that many families had only two children, a large minority but a single child. In this situation, a desire to keep offspring healthy could reach nearly desperate proportions. At the same time, previous assistance to parents within the home was declining: there were fewer older siblings to help, live-in servants were a thing of the past for most, and even grandparents were beginning to move out to establish separate residences. The responsibility for the child, and the tensions this could generate, fell more unambiguously on parents, particularly mothers, than ever before. It may have become more inviting to quiet an obstreperous toddler with candy or ice cream. Finally, the critique of motherhood, though doubtless qualified in actual beliefs, may have increased maternal anxiousness, making it tempting to work for short-term satisfactions among children lest dispute further challenge an already somewhat vulnerable adult authority.

The attachment to children and their feeding was social as well as familial. Waves of immigration around 1900 brought a new awareness of malnutrition that clearly offended middle-class ideals of the United States as a land of abundance, at least for helpless children. Immigrant parents came in for criticism in terms of inadequate care and knowledge, but a widespread concern for underweight children was nourished as well. "Are we in famine-stricken India?" a popular magazine article intoned. Data were then summoned about the shockingly high percentage of children who were underfed — a problem quite easily remedied, unlike some of the other difficulties attached to urban lower-class existence. Americanization was directly equated with ample food supply. An Italian mother was cited who did not understand that the "thinness" of her boy could be a matter of importance, but who finally exclaimed, "That boy! I fat him or I kill him!" Related targeting of tuberculosis among urban children drew attention to the need for solid weight. Amid these concerns, a problem of overfeeding might be hard to perceive.[8]

So much for context: how did it play out in the area of food and restraint? The logic, context aside, was clear. Two decades in which the importance of slenderness had been vigorously established for the middle class should have led to a growing awareness by the 1920s of the need to discipline children's appetites as part of inculcating good eating habits. This would be part of the intensification of the new culture of dieting, as automatic as, and perhaps in terms of long-term results even more significant than, heightened pressure on women or growing rigor in the adult weight tables.

Signs of this extension were indeed visible — even before 1920. As early as 1914, the government-issued pamphlet *Infant Care* — the most widely purchased publication ever federally sponsored, reissued recurrently — warned against overfeeding children. While noting that undernourishing was a greater problem and urging devices such as adding sugar to formulas to increase weight gain ("to furnish the necessary food stuff"), the brochure warned against flab. The goal was a "properly nourished" body, not a fat one. Too many mothers found a "fat, red-cheeked baby" a sign that "they are giving the best sort of care," and too many baby food companies promoted the fat baby image to sell their products. It was time for greater caution. This theme reechoed in subsequent medical literature. A 1937 article cautioned against "marked obesity," though this admittedly left the door open for some tolerance of milder forms. "This way obese children can be saved from much

ridicule and encouraged to take proper exercise with their fellows."
A 1954 pediatric text noted, revealingly, "It is interesting that parents worry so little about fat children and so much about thin ones," yet eating habits were so hard to change as children get older that it was best to correct overweight as soon as it began to show up. Not only adult slenderness, but also prevention of diabetes, called for parental and medical attention. A similar comment urged greater attention to problems of childhood obesity, which parents tended to overlook and even to resent having to acknowledge; it added, in another familiar link with the larger culture toward issues of weight, that children often ate too much because of lack of emotional security within the family. And in an equally fashionable swipe at mothers, it was stated, "To boast that a fifteen-months-old baby 'eats everything' is not a tribute to its precocity but to the ignorance or willful negligence of its mother." From the 1940s onward, doctors also noted that parents frequently brought children in for treatment because their fat made them look unfashionable or caused them to be teased — particularly in the case of girls. At all these levels, medical comment indicated clear contact with the evolution of the larger culture toward the body, the importance of a slender appearance, and even the extent to which fat revealed inner inadequacies (or parental failings).[9]

The urgency picked up in the medical literature from the late 1960s onward. By this point, the implications of the general culture were highlighted by specific findings about obesity problems among America's children. It was at this point that baby food advertisers slimmed down their infant logos. Pediatric texts were now noting that "obesity is a frequent finding" and urging parents to attend to the issue. Another new note was how recalcitrant children's fat was; "obesity is so difficult to treat it is best to avoid it." The warnings against traditionalism continued, as parents were urged that the days when the fattest baby was considered healthiest were long past. And the link with emotional problems persisted; the fat child, like his adult counterpart, had something wrong psychologically, and of course, parents could be called to account here, too. In other words, as with the general culture, signs of intensification of concern abounded.[10]

Yet the approach to fat children into the 1970s differed from the standard diet arguments in two respects: doctors and other family advisers sent mixed signals, in contrast to the virtually uniform attack on fat in adult prescriptive materials from at least 1900 onward. And many parents clearly embraced different standards themselves; more than individual failures to live up to approved norms were involved, for the norms themselves were contested. It was hard to shake off the admiration for a fat baby or even a stocky child.

Concern for underweight children vastly surpassed attention to childhood obesity problems until the late twentieth century. Both pediatric literature and (even more) popularized advice to parents reflected this imbalance. Doctors often preferred an overweight baby because this more clearly assured short-term health and easily brushed away undue attention to fat. Advice such as "try to watch it, but not serious," recorded in a mother's diary, seems to have been typical — even for a child twenty pounds overweight at age eight. A noticeable tummy was dismissed as "just little boy." In articles in family magazines, parents were regaled with advice about how to get recalcitrant children to eat: "Please, lovey, take one more spoonful for Mummy (or Daddy or Santa Claus)"; "I won't love you anymore if you don't eat." No device seemed too bizarre to coax the reluctant eater, who jeopardized his health but also called parental adequacy into question; one child ate only if his father "crawled around the room on all fours braying like a donkey." In a society of abundance, children's eating behavior may well have deteriorated as they learned they could manipulate parents without actually starving. A school report of a mildly under-weight child threw another set of parents in a frenzy. When their pediatrician brushed the problem aside as trivial, they shopped around for another doctor, who prescribed a high-calorie diet, which the parents forced on the child through spankings and other punishments. Recommendations of sweets were not uncommon, for it was vital to make sure children ate; hence between-meal snacks might seem to make particularly good sense.[11]

The childhood exception to rigorous diet advice followed both from a distinctive reality and from a clear cultural lag. Underweight children, particularly at birth, were at serious health risk; it was quite legitimate to worry about this more than about mild over-weight. Unlike adults, after all, children were supposed to grow, and abundant food played a vital role. Children also played power games with eating, refusing food in order to bedevil their parents; while sometimes this might best have been ignored, it was difficult to maintain equanimity when in some cases serious health problems could result. Growing knowledge of the spread of anorexia nervosa provided a modern twist to this kind of concern about assuring eating. So did reports of American children going hungry during the Depression or in recurrent comments about ongoing poverty in the 1950s and 1960s. Popularizers fanned the flames of worry about underweight even for the middle class. But it was also true that both parents and doctors maintained an anachronistic delight in seeing children eat heartily and, at least in the early years, present a well-nourished appearance. Improving appetites, rather than restraining them, took priority in this context. The disproportionate number of popular articles on underweight children both reflected and encouraged this parental focus. So did reports from increasingly ubiquitous school health officials from the 1920s onward. School notes frequently warned about under-weight, and diligent parents were eager to avoid this charge. Experts cautioned parents that even surface fat could mask that inner malnutrition: "He may appear round and fat but still be poorly nourished. The face of a child may look plump, owing to the particular cast of his features; but when he is stripped, noticeable depressions may appear between the ribs." As one doctor put it, "The safe policy is: Every child above his normal weight line." Lean children were troubling, but "sturdy" ones need "less special help." Popularizers frequently assured parents that moderate over-weight would pass with time; a stocky boy would slim down natu-rally, so there was no need to worry. Realization of how hard it was for adults to overcome childhood indiscretion lay only in the future, with the more systematic medical pronouncements of the 1970s. Until then, it seemed more important to avoid the lean and hungry look. "But a little padding on the frame doesn't hurt a child." True to the general sentiment, Dr. Spock, while genially urging that candy and cakes be postponed from a child's diet as long as possible, concentrated primarily on advising parents on keeping weight up and dealing with finicky eaters.[12]

While doctors and popularizers presented a divided image to the public, with promptings to encourage appetite on balance predominating, parents seem to have been even more single-minded in their desire to make sure their children ate. Of course, even before the 1970s help might be sought for the extremely obese child or for children who threatened to escape the constraints of fashion. Particularly when children neared their teens, and particularly where girls were involved, attempts to impose diets increased. But in most instances the concern was for good eating as a sign of health and cooperativeness. Doctors noted how often mothers insisted on force-feeding slender babies, despite medical advice to the contrary, "because they want to make their small children big and fat, like the wonderful 'bouncing baby' that is most admired on the block." More than appearance might be involved. Doctors also reported cases in which nervous mothers, eager to demonstrate how devoted they were, stuffed children with food to keep them contented and quiet. Again, providing frequent snacks played a common role in these efforts. A survey suggested that few mothers worried about children who ate too much: 29 percent of the relevant group expressed concern about the problem in general, and only 30 percent even opposed excessive consumption of candy. When overeating involved healthy foods, like milk or meat, concern dropped under 10 percent of those mothers whose children actually manifested these tendencies.[13]

At least on the medical side, including attendant popularizations, this ambivalent constellation did change by the 1970s. Even in popular journals like *Parents' Magazine*, the disproportionate focus on underweight children declined. Articles increasingly focused on the estimates of high levels of obesity among American children and on the importance of early medical attention. The sheer pace of this kind of advice picked up markedly in the 1980s, with emphasis on prevention. "Always remember that food should be given to satisfy hunger and to help your child grow properly" — and nothing more; the idea of food as a reward or as a symbol of parental affection was particularly attacked. The belief that emotional problems underlay overeating continued, amid some dispute as to how easy it was to preempt or solve the dilemmas of potentially or actually overweight children. Recurrent reminders of genetic factors further complicated any judgment about how remediable children's problems were.[14]

The removal of ambivalence in the relevant culture did not, to be sure, immediately echo in children's actual weight patterns. Problems of obesity if anything increased. Children began to get less exercise, thanks in part to television viewing. Parents, whatever their intentions, spent less time monitoring children's eating; as hurried working mothers became increasingly common, heavy meals replaced more careful cooking. Allowances, established earlier in middle-class families but now more generous, gave children independent spending money, with snack food a key consumer item within their grasp. Efforts to promote dieting could be counterproductive as children consciously or unconsciously found rebellion in overeating: "I dieted because my parents said I should. But I didn't really want to lose weight, and there were always fattening things around the house. So it was like telling me to do one thing and making it easy for me to do the opposite. Honestly, sometimes I think I eat out of spite."[15]

Children's eating patterns played an unquestionable role in the disparity between slender values and fat reality in the twentieth century. They translated the general abundance and promotion of food (and often some of the special issues of minority cultures) into physical form, helping to set up overweight adulthood. The vast majority — a 1968 estimate was 80 percent — of overweight children had weight problems as adults.[16] The dilemma was twofold. Balancing the need to feed children's growth adequately with the need often to restrain, was an inherently difficult task with regard to the many children who for whatever reason had a particular propensity to eat. But the cultural ambivalence, particularly visible in the United States, factored in as well. Because Americans valued plump-looking children and saw feeding children as an act of particular love and a special test of parental adequacy, because they continued to fight undernourishment battles long after the war had ended for the middle class they were incapable, in many instances, of translating the logic of the larger cultural hostility to fat into their approach to their own offspring. The culture toward childhood, sprung from a desire to show love and a desperate need to keep children alive and visibly healthy, warred with the culture of slenderness. Even when the norms applied to children were clarified with more uniform cautions against overfeeding, other factors continued to impede full translation of the norms into the actual experience of many children. This was more than a major reason for the weight-culture gap in adulthood. It also meant that many Americans entered adolescence or adulthood, when the aesthetic standards of slenderness could not be ignored, with a preexisting personal problem, setting up a need for lifelong bat- tle — a battle that enriched the coffers of commercial weight-loss operations and sustained the struggle imagery of American diet culture alike.

The Enemy Is Us

Plentiful and richly advertised food, combined with more seden- tary styles of life, minority subcultures, and patterns that encour- aged childhood eating even in the mainstream middle class to- gether account for most of the actual weight gains the American population experienced in the twentieth century. A fourth and final factor, less tangible, entered in as well, amid the very middle class toward which the attacks on overweight were aimed.

The American version of the war against fat could be explicitly or implicitly counterproductive, ironically encouraging some peo- ple to gain weight or subtly countenancing a certain amount of failure to live up to standards. On the explicit side, some of the diet injunctions were so stringent that they easily engendered a sense of hopelessness or rebellion: Thus the child eating to protest the injunctions of her diet-conscious mother. Thus the adult, a bit heavy after a stout childhood or because of genetic endowment, reluctant to take on the standards displayed daily by the slender models and television stars. Thus a resistance toward even more demanding weight charts or scrawny models; the ideals seemed impossible. Given the attractions of eating, it was certainly easy to pin hopes on some painless scheme — a few sugar-free foods or a pill or some "lazy person's" diet plan — and when this scheme did not work, give up the whole endeavor.

Diet culture worked on guilt; this was one of its main cultural functions, just beneath the surface of health and beauty tips. But consumerist outlook in the twentieth century was on the whole hostile to guilt, which was viewed as a damaging, anachronistic emotion.[17] From the 1920s onward, parenting manuals urged their readers to soft-pedal their inculcation of guilt in children lest it damage self-esteem. School discipline increasingly moved away from guilt, refusing to publicize bad marks and inflating grades in an effort to support fragile egos. Apologies for imputing guilt became common, for it was felt this should not be part of a healthy relationship. Too much guilt, after all, called consumer indulgence into question; guilty people might feel they had to punish themselves by denying this purchase, that treat. The attack on fat, and particularly the ideal of battling weight through worried self-discipline, deliberately countered this overall discomfort with guilt. Many people accepted, even unconsciously welcomed, the alternative, which helped them live more comfortably with other pleasures. But it was not surprising that some found the anachronism excessive: why deny in one area, when in most behaviors increasing hedonism was encouraged? Here, surely, was motivation for many, who were fully aware of the weight standards but ate more anyway.

Even where guilt was accepted, it could provoke eating because of the enhanced dismay at failure. "Dieting while growing fatter is an inverted spiritual exercise: every time your break your resolutions you eat even more, for consolation and in defiance. More fat motivates more desperate deeds, and the yo-yoing builds mountains out of it." The depression attached to obesity, because of stringent moralistic disapproval and self-loathing, could also prompt excess eating simply to lift the mood. The guilt culture, designed to restrain, could actually feed itself.[18]

There was a more subtle twist. Attacks on sin never eliminated it, even among believers. The same holds true for the American battle against fat, with its religious-like traits. Even when people did not lose weight, the cultural standards could be accepted, even internalized, precisely because they caused moral anxiety. Worry and a sense of guilt showed contact with a modern moral code, even when the practical results were absent. People accepted the weight-control culture partly because they really wanted to be slim, but partly because it caused a tension that could make other behaviors, like acquisitive consumerism or recreational sex, more ethically acceptable. The feeling of inadequacy was almost desirable in this context; it was a profession of concern about weight, a promise to diet soon, that counted, not necessarily victorious slenderness. Overeating in the process became a bit furtive, a quick relapse rather than a legitimate exercise of appetite, but as we will see, this meshed with some American traditions as well. On the basis of moral awareness and self-criticism, many middle-class Americans participated fully in the restraint of fat, even when they continued, apologetically, to put on weight. Here was the most subtle, but for many also the most important, result of a demanding twentieth-century culture.

And, of course, the strong links between dieting and moral compensation also weakened the hold of appetite restraint when, as in the 1980s, the level of affluence began to recede. With increasing job frustrations, unemployment, insecurity, and — for some beleaguered wage earners — heightened hours of work when jobs were available, the temptation to eat more as a quick solace might well have grown in any event. The American penchant for food in haste and quantity could easily be enhanced. But the obvious fact was that the need to discipline oneself as a payment for growing consumer indulgence declined as well. Even with full awareness of health consequences, restraint might diminish as the need for moral demonstration declined. Here, surely, is one of the keys to the odd clash between professed health concerns and actual weight gains during the past fifteen years.

Conclusion

The modern standards of slenderness had complex results. They made lots of people aware and self-conscious. The overweight knew that they were wanting in others' eyes, and this could be truly inhibiting. Some groups not only internalized the standards but lived up to them. Particularly impressive were many middle-aged women who bucked the overall trend of increasing weight gain; but individuals in every category of American society changed their habits and their shapes in response to the new norms.

Yet the countervailing forces were impressive as well. The unwillingness or inability to discipline children as much as adults sought to discipline themselves was a fascinating anomaly. Racial or ethnic subcultures that defied the mainstream standards expressed surprising strength of identity in their belief that weight embodied merriment, solidity, and sensuality, though at real cost to health and longevity, which dropped well below national averages. The same differentiation, of course, could quietly feed renewed social divisions in American society. Fat, overindulgent welfare recipients easily roused scorn. President Dwight Eisenhower in the 1950s responded with a dieter's lament when, confronted with data about the malnutrition of the poor, he argued that on doctor's orders he went hungry every night. Inequality might seem less dire when the middle class could note that it, too, suffered. Body shape and discipline, in other words, became a new class divide between the virtuous and the unworthy. For the middle class itself, the failure fully to live up to acknowledged standards is a comment on the inadequacy, to some extent even the perversity, of the modern American diet culture — but not on its irrelevance. Reasonably steady weight gain from the 1920s onward simultaneous with increasingly rigid, widely accepted norms of slenderness add up to a growing tension in personal life, registered daily on the bathroom scales or the furtive aversion to this same ritualistic device. In this respect, at least, Americans became more disappointed with themselves. They might draw some bitter comfort from their self-doubt, as it counterbalanced indulgences in consumer or sexual arenas that might otherwise be troubling. But they did not look the way they wished to look, and whether they admitted it or tried to conceal it, the fact cannot have been pleasant. It is time to turn to another approach to the modern imperative, to add comparison to the historical perspective, in order to understand more fully the culture Americans have subscribed to and the alternatives that may exist.

· III ·

The French Regime

7 The Evolution of Weight Control in France

French concerns about slenderness paralleled those in the United States in many respects. The two countries shared an artistic and Christian heritage. They industrialized at about the same times, though the American process was more impressive. Both, for example, passed the 50 percent urbanization mark around 1920, though for several decades thereafter the American rural population declined at a more rapid rate than that of France. France like the United States developed more sedentary work patterns plus a greater abundance of foods, including meats rich in fat. Both countries experienced a declining birthrate that could put pressure on women to demonstrate virtue in other respects, including a decidedly nonmaternal body shape.

More than parallelism and common background were involved. The two countries copied each other. Medical findings, where initially France (along with Germany and England) had a lead, were widely and quickly shared. French fashions and cooking styles influenced the United States, particularly by the later nineteenth century. In the twentieth century, cultural influence went the other direction: American diet procedures were widely imitated in France, though often with modifications and with a clear notation that these were foreign imports. Many of the best known (and slender) models in France — what the women's magazines by the later twentieth century ballyhooed as *"les supermodels"* in endless interviews, with endless personal details — were American, as were leading film and television stars.

The comparison between France and the United States must

thus be subtle and is all the more revealing for that reason. There would be little point in contrasting a diet-conscious country with one too poor to be worried about fat or so enmeshed in a culture of amplitude that norms diverged entirely; a brief comment on the massive differentiation would suffice. But the fact is that, because of parallels and mutual dissemination, France and the United States have been engaged for the past century in much the same process of weight consciousness.

Yet the process, for all its commonalties, shows important national strands. The French diet less but also eat less. They have gained less weight in the twentieth century, billing themselves in fact as the slimmest people in the Western world.[1] This is a fascinating outcome in itself, given the French joy in food, and it gains added significance in the comparative context. The French campaign against fat, it must be noted, has its own vagaries; this is not a simple story of European advantages over portly American bumpkins. The French are probably more prone to look for effort-free (and very dubious) antifat products than are Americans precisely because they have an even greater impulse to want to eat well and yet stay thin. They can say some remarkably silly things about calories in an effort to defend national food traditions. But there is no denying some real differences both in culture and in outcome, some of which at least redound to French credit. The French come closer to looking as they wish to look, at least in terms of waist size, than Americans do. We must first sketch how the French patterns emerged, remembering their many congruences with the American evolution without belaboring detail. Then we can turn to the fascinating issue of why both French culture and French realities took distinctive forms while participating in a common modern process.

The differences between France and the United States drive home the point, already established from the American experience alone, that modern weight-control interests were not simply an inevitable response to changing modern conditions. They were this in part; as Western societies became more sedentary and more prosperous, and as science advanced and concerns about the degenerative diseases of adults increased, some new attention to eating habits was probably unavoidable. We can expect to see similar developments in other heavy-eating societies as they move into mature industrialization, though the example of the West will add to the causation. This said, the nature and meaning of the dieting process, and its impact on individuals, vary depending on the precise nature and timing of standard developments, such as the achievement of mass prosperity or quality of traditional food tastes as people encounter new abundance. Above all, they vary in relationship to different cultural needs. Some of the values involved are explicit, like French pride in fine cuisine compared to a more instrumental American approach to food; others, including reactions to shifts in women's power or to consumerism, hover beneath the surface. France on the whole overlaid weight control with fewer symbolic purposes than did the United States, though the French expressed some of the same tensions with consumerist indulgence and, even more, with changes in the status of women. Again, we need to see how a closely related, partially imitative pattern developed in order to explore what the differences signified.

The Baseline: The Traditions Surrounding Fat

France in the late nineteenth century harbored many of the barriers that any society offers to new ideals of slenderness, plus some additional specifics. The French had a traditional confidence in corpulence as a sign of prosperity and good humor. "Fat people, good people" was an oft-cited provincial saying, while the conventional image of a well-fed peasant reveling in the rural version of the good life was quite real, if not easily attained in a poor economy. And here was another issue: many peasants ate extremely badly; in the Nivernais, for example, bread baking occurred only twice a year, meaning that food was not only scarce but unpleasant, save on a rare feast. What would people with this background do when prosperity improved their access to finer things? Surely the temptation to enjoy abundance to excess would be very strong. At the upper-class level, France led the world from the late eighteenth century onward in vaunting its fine foods and rich cuisine. At all levels, rich and poor, the French also maintained an unusually strong commitment to meat. Even as vegetarian options were proposed (often through foreign inspiration) around 1900, it was hard for any French commentator to subscribe; meat was the basis for strength as well as good eating, which meant that cutbacks in this area might be dearly bought. Nor did the French develop any particular concern for heart disease comparable to American anxieties about stress that first emerged under the heading of neurasthenia in the 1880s. On into the twentieth century, the French preferred to worry about the liver, and while anxieties about this could be translated into some diet restrictions, they focused less readily on sheer body weight. Indeed, the odd French dance between alcoholism and liver worries bears interesting resemblance to the American ambivalence between overeating and heart disease.[2]

The French also targeted two other problems in the late nineteenth century, quite correctly, that could distract them from attention to overweight or even make the condition seem positively desirable. First, the nation suffered from unusually high rates of tuberculosis, probably because of an excess of old, damp housing. Countering this problem, a well-fed body seemed both preventative and a symbol of the alternative to tubercular emaciation; and indeed early discussions of weight loss had to bow to its compatibility with defending against tuberculosis. Then there was the notorious population problem. The French birthrate lagged behind that of its competitors, notably Germany. This prompted national attention both to encouraging maternity, with lots of propaganda aimed at girls and women about their obligations to the fatherland, and to protecting those infants once born. Doctors and national commissions agonized over France's high infant death rate. A "science" called *puériculture* emerged in the 1860s to work on solutions including much more adequate milk supplies and nutritional advice for mothers. As in most traditional societies, many French mothers already saw in fat children a sign of health and parental success. The *puériculture* movement, with its massive propaganda apparatus and many clinics and nutrition centers, might easily have heightened this impulse, leading to a tendency not only to feed but to overfeed the young.[3]

On the other hand, France harbored some bases for a modern weight-control effort that the United States had lacked. There was a longer tradition of philosophical and scientific interest in promoting longevity, dating back to the great biologist Buffon and the eighteenth century Enlightenment. The French medical establishment was better developed and somewhat wider ranging. More French doctors than American had at least a smattering of classical training, which meant that they could cite Seneca and other authors on the virtues of moderation and the perils of over-weight. Galen's warnings that fat people rarely lived a long life cropped up recurrently. While Benjamin Rush, a Francophile, demonstrated a similar impulse at the end of the eighteenth century in the United States, his nineteenth-century colleagues were more inclined to play things by ear. France also maintained a somewhat more eclectic medical stance, with homeopaths holding their own, in contrast to their defeat in the United States. Homeopathy, in turn, and vaguely homeopathic beliefs in the general public, could draw attention to the need to adjust intake to maintain overall chemical balance in the body.

Finally and most specifically, France sponsored a massive medical research effort during the nineteenth century, which the United States began to catch up with only around 1900. Little research, it must be noted, went toward issues of weight. But the Belgian statistician Quételet began as early as the 1830s to establish ideal weight tables, which were recurrently repeated in French medical texts and refined further by Charles Bouchard in 1899 to 1900. This gave knowledgeable doctors a standard if rough and ready formula — height in centimeters - 100 = desired number of kilograms — on the basis of which obesity could be determined. French medical researchers after 1850 particularly excelled in pathology, and while this did not call forth immediate study of obesity, it certainly created a climate in which the impact of fat on organ deterioration could be readily determined. It was no accident that the unprecedented modern spate of research on obesity was triggered by Charles Bouchard's general treatise on pathology. And very scattered work directly addressed obesity through the later decades of the nineteenth century. Thus a dictionary article in

1871 noted the relationship between obesity and both migraines and diabetes. An 1864 treatise pointed to the link with heart problems and scrofula. A Paris thesis in 1875 studied the Banting diet that had created such a stir in England. Following the German lead, French scientists also studied fats and other nutritional subjects. This was sporadic work and often quite theoretical. Something of a debate arose in research circles during the 1890s about the role of water in obesity, with some experts arguing that if liquid intake were kept to a minimum the problem would be solved. The discussion was largely off the mark, but it indicated that the topic was clearly on the medical agenda and that, in fact, scientific interest was growing.[4]

Then there was fashion. French styles emphasized a good bit of flesh during most of the nineteenth century, for both men and women. Speaking for one group of men, the writer Théophile Gautier noted simply, "the man of genius should be fat," if only because he should be sedentary. As in the United States, this was seen as demonstrating both prosperity and good health. Romanticism in the 1830s produced some interest in frailness, particularly for young women, but the fad did not persist. Upper-class French women were held to the dictatorship of corsets, to pull the waist tight while simultaneously making fleshiness more obvious both above and below. Corsetry had reentered the French upper class during the First Empire after a revolutionary hiatus, and it seems to have been more widely accepted than in the United States, in part because the French upper class was itself better defined and more interested in expressing itself through fashion. Corseting drew a great deal of medical criticism for its real or imagined impact on female organs and diseases, and feminists joined the parade by 1900, blasting that device as an "instrument of torture" designed to force women to be idle. It most definitely distracted women from any need for slimness — indeed, the flesh must be available for distribution elsewhere — though, of course, it did provide a precedent for a slender silhouette for one part of the anatomy. Fashion experts adamantly defended corsetry into the 1890s, again suggesting both some preferences for selective flesh control along with a real appreciation of flesh itself. "Glory to the corset that spares us unpleasant sights. Glory to those clothes that remedy the ravages of the body." But, with Baroness Stoffe, "Strong women absolutely require the corset, which contains the opulence of their middle while supporting their bust."[5]

Phase I: 1890s–1914

In contrast to the United States, where fat fashion changed with a rush in the 1890s, signs of new French patterns emerged gradually from the 1860s onward. The Empress Eugénie was said to diet in order to be slim, even though empire fashions continued to drape the body heavily, making it fairly unclear what the actual form was like. The incomparable actress Sarah Bernhardt, naturally slim, managed to overcome prejudice against thinness on stage during the last two decades of the century and, in fact, struck a blow for the idea that slenderness might be beautiful and sexy.

Then in the 1890s fashion began to change more decisively, to emphasize a tubular shape that required thinner bodies. By 1899 Emile Zola, in his novel *La Fecondité*, blasted this new passion because of its obvious attack on France's great need for willing mothers. If women were supposed to be straight up and down, motherhood, already wanting, would become positively unfashionable, the novelist argued with some justification. Then in 1900 or soon thereafter (there is some quarrel about dates), leading French designers abandoned the corset. Paul Poiret was the daring innovator, soon followed by others. At about the same time, the French minister of interior also banned corset wearing by older female students in 1902. A combination of style shifts and health concerns began to undermine a key foundation garment, which meant that even to approximate the standards of the past toward an indrawn waist, not to mention to attain the new slenderness, women had to lose weight (or, if young, manage not to gain it).[6]

These were the same style changes that affected the United States at about the same time, though the corset debate lasted a bit longer across the Atlantic. The fashion impulse came from France, which was where such inspiration had come from throughout the century. Why did the French change after an almost uninterrupted century of assuming that fleshiness was good? Health considerations, including the trickle of obesity advice coming from the medical profession, might have played a role. Larger artistic interests were shifting. Early Impressionists, like Renoir, delighted in rendering female flesh, but now greater abstraction seemed to place a premium on slimness, even emaciation, as in some of the work of Matisse or the early Cubists, and style and art were tightly linked in France. This was not a definitive movement, as Matisse and his colleagues also illustrated fleshier women in many paintings; but whether in reflecting or causing fashion, available artistic renderings of slim women did increase. Was there a deeper undercurrent as well? The psychohistorian Rudolph Binion has recently ventured a theory about European intellectuals and artists in the last decades of the nineteenth century as they reacted to the rapidly declining birthrate they saw around them, even in their own families. The contrast with traditional fecundity, even that of their own parents, was striking, and prompted men and women alike to seek ways to express their disorientation, even guilt, at somehow failing a standard biological imperative. Perhaps slimming women down on canvas and in the great dress salons was a means of expressing some of this malaise, while potentially punishing women by imposing new restrictions in the process. Zola's perception was to this extent correct, save that he reversed the causal order: fashion did not so much discourage maternity as express its decline. Here as well would be a reason for some consumers to buy into the styles, to express their own willingness to deprive themselves to compensate for their own flight from traditional maternity. In other words, a factor that played into the American pattern a bit later may have entered the French scene from the start.[7]

Not surprisingly, French women's magazines quickly picked up on the new challenge. While not yet filled with diet advertisements — and while corsetry continued to draw its defenders among eager salesmen — the theme began to take on familiar proportions. The *Journal de la beauté*, in 1911, carried notices for pills and for slimming soaps — users were to just rub them on any parts that were "too voluminous." "Don't wait till obesity has invaded your tissues — *Marin* soap right away." More casual comments urged a reduction in fatty foods and sugar. Joining Zola's attack on the "Malthusian" qualities of French fashions, Emile Bayard lamented, "We're witnessing the eclipse of the stomach." Other observers raced for different explanations. They blamed feminism for making a boyish appearance fashionable: women not only wanted rights, they wanted to look like men. Or bicycle riding was at fault, by benefiting peddlers who were more in shape: "the thin, the light . . . are the big winners."[8]

In the new climate, a range of diet products began to hit the markets, some imported from the United States. It must be noted that, as across the Atlantic, considerable attention continued to be given to ways to fatten up excessively thin women — this was a transitional period in which older concerns persisted. But the variety of diet products, carefully promoted by brochures, was considerable. Triscuits, from New York, simultaneously attacked fat and diabetes. The French firm Heudebert touted its "essential bread" to replace the fattening real thing. Gymnasiums, machines, and exercise classes that included judo lured women — "to keep a young, slim and healthy body, to reduce *embonpoint*, to firm up the flesh" — this despite considerable traditional prejudice against physical activity for upper-class women. As a compromise, the Bergonnié machine, introduced in 1909, stimulated muscles electrically to displace fat. Sugar substitutes, like "Sweetina," made from gum, were urged, allowing an obese person to "see his bulge shrink." Advertisements played health as well as beauty games. "This affection [sic] is becoming more and more general" and, they warned, was a far more serious threat to health than most people realized. The culprit, said the makers of Gluten Bread (initially a diabetic product), was bread. Women over forty particularly needed to fight obesity, for it coincided "with their completely mysterious evolution." Finally, several spas converted for the diet craze: Brides, Salins-Moutiers, and at least four spots in the Jura mountains, including Vittel.[9]

As in the United States at the same time, the focus on women and their fashions was not the only facet of this new campaign, though it unquestionably drew the most attention contemporaneously and from historians since. It is in fact the range of innovations that indicated a really new body culture, not simply the style changes. Men were solicited; many of the product brochures were directed toward them. At a time when French security concerns emphasized military preparedness, it was not surprising that a growing appeal for physical culture and athleticism targeted men. Navy Lieutenant G. Hébert advertised the use of his exercise centers as a means of countering the effects of a sedentary life. During the 1890s and 1900s, Desbonnet chain of centers opened, with an even more explicit mandate against fat. Men must counter the "ravages of civilization" and the resultant "ridiculous obesity." "Obesity, source of so much suffering and also, why not say it? object of so much ridicule, is easily curable." To be sure, the center also helped build up skinny men; Desbonnet himself had been a frail child. But the increasing emphasis was on exercise as a cure for fat, given what was claimed to be the ineffectiveness of dieting. Examples showed a client who dropped from 112 kilograms to 82. "Don't forget that all obese people die *young* if they don't do physical culture. 'The stomach, this is the enemy.'" As in the United States, it is harder to trace this new pressure among French men for they had fewer gender-specific magazines. But there was no question of a new current and a vocabulary whose succinctness clearly indicated that it had won an audience.[10]

Finally, and even more than in the United States, medical research began to jump on the antiobesity bandwagon after 1900. Key studies of obesity, first dissertations, then large monographs, began in 1899 with the work of LeNoir. Between 1900 and 1914, twelve or fourteen major studies appeared, not to mention numerous articles in medical journals. Obesity was defined. The role of glands and heredity was explored, with heredity discussed in itself and in terms of family propensities. Regional and racial factors gained attention; for example, there was some belief that Jews had a particular propensity for getting fat. The deleterious effects of fat on health were clearly and repeatedly detailed: heart, blood pressure, kidneys, dyspepsia, sexual impotence. The treatises were quite clear on the main point: obesity cut the lifespan, with some arguing that it was rare for an obese person to live past fifty. The frequency of obesity in children was noted and deplored. The new wave of obesity research was directed quite explicitly against common errors, including the notion that getting fat with age was natural or that a pink face and fat cheeks indicated health. Common evasions were attacked; physicians shouldn't let a patient tell you he has big bones, for bones weigh very little. And a variety of treatments were discussed. Exercise was noted, though its effects seemed limited. Various water treatments and pills were discussed. Many doctors seized on the growing popularity among the general public of using thyroid extract pills and warned against their inutility and positive risk. Finally, various diets were laid out, for while doctors were fascinated by obesity causes other than simple overeating — glandular factors were far more interesting — they knew that ultimately eating habits had to be attacked. A few comments directly laid into the bad habits of *gourmands* and the idle, whose belief that they had to eat heavily was entirely artificial. One doctor, Albert Mathieu, specifically noted also the role of "intellectual and nervous overwork, so common in the wealthy classes of modern society." And all the treatises offered many pages of calorie-counting diet suggestions for all meals, with near-starvation variants for extreme cases, along with comments on clinical results among actual patients.[11]

French work was, of course, part of a European current, and the French periodically cited British and German colleagues. Even Chittenden, from Yale, drew comment, but Fletcherism never explicitly made it across the Atlantic, a gap comparativists may wish to chew over. (Though it is only fair to note that a more philosophical comment on long life did stress the importance of mastication. "With food that's well chewed, the stomach quickly says it's satisfied.") But this was a strong French thrust, deriving from earlier research interests. No one reported seeing more obese patients than before, though obesity might in fact have been increasing given growing affluence and a more sedentary middle class. On the surface, at least, the shift in medical interests flowed from research findings alone, gradually combined with a desire to reach out to a wider public through advice, at a time when many French doctors were hard up for actual patients but when Parisian specialists worked to maintain high standards for the field as a whole. There was even a somewhat distracting Cartesian game in this early material as doctors struggled to define whether obesity was one entity or several (a number of works pointedly referred to obesities) and whether simple overeating even qualified. Pages could be devoted to the balance between glandular and hereditary components versus simple excess at the table. Dr. M. Labbé was typical in laboriously concluding that much obesity resulted from a combination of factors, including overeating.[12]

The medical focus on obesity had one additional, double-edged feature common to the American counterpart that came a bit later. The term "obesity" was used and standard ideal weights were offered according to gender and height; Bouchard's charts and formulas were widely cited. But the clearest emphasis was on really excessive obesity. The pictures in the books were of monstrous obesity. Of course, this work was intended specifically for other doctors, but its tenor might either have scared the general public, worried that a common participation in obesity led inexorably to such grotesque extremes, or have encouraged a sense of irrelevance for the merely overweight who did not look nearly so bad. This was a tension that would persist in the medical approach for some time.

Along with medical commentary came a few more popularized efforts to discuss long life, part of a recurrent French tradition but given new credence by some of the medical findings, including Elie Metchnikoff's theories about the bacterial impurities in the body and how to fight them nutritionally. Vegetarianism drew some favorable comment in this context. But it was overeating that was particularly attacked. "Gourmandise is one of the great sores of humanity," argued Gaston Durville. The sage went on to claim that overeating caused tuberculosis, arthritis, and cancer — strongly suggesting that he was following his own drummer, not contemporary medicine. Attacking the French food philosopher Brillat-Savarin, he argued that gourmands, with their pink faces and prominent stomachs, might look healthy, but they died young. Almost all French kings, as Durville demonstrated in a tidy chart, died before they reached eighty, which seemingly clinched the argument for him.[13]

This first stage of the French campaign against fat resembled its American counterpart in many ways, beginning with virtually identical timing. It was multifaceted, involving men's body styles as well as female fashion, the eager commercialism of various diet products and exercise gurus, a few philosophical enthusiasts, and the medical community. Developments both in medicine and in style followed from a context of growing prosperity and consumerism and from changes in women's roles, expressed particularly through the visibly declining birthrate.

The balance, however, was a bit different in France. Independent medical research, though not yet systematically popularized, save as ordinary doctors, duly educated, communicated directly to their patients, played a greater role than in the United States. Few doctors, in fact, commented on how their interests followed from the pressure of their patients, in marked contrast to the American situation. It seems likely that, with unusually well-developed medical research facilities, the first phase of the French movement against fat depended on scientific findings in a context where sedentary lifestyles and the growing awareness of degenerative diseases played a major role.[14] This is not meant to exclude fashion or its fascinatingly separate origins. In fact, what is intriguing about the French pattern is the extent to which separate strands had yet to draw together. The promoters of new products came closest, in arguing both on health grounds and on those of appearance.

And there was one other intriguing twist: The French upper classes put up some definite resistance to the new promptings, particularly in the fashion arena. Their reactions went beyond simply not following the standards, however privately and with whatever embarrassment. Obviously, in neither the French nor the American case it is possible to talk about how many people, even in the middle and upper classes, tuned into the early statements of health and fashion. But we have seen that in the United States the subject became all the rage in an apparently quick conversion, at least at the rhetorical level. Not so, despite very similar timing, in France. Notwithstanding the consistency of the dress designers, actual French fashion remained rather varied, with concealing clothes still widely available. Artists, as we have seen, adopted no single standard. A handful of letters about dieting dotted the beauty magazines around 1900, but they vied with other pressing issues, particularly skin quality, and they simply did not suggest the level of interest in their American counterparts of the same years. Models pictured in beauty magazines continued to be fairly stout. In fact, one of the leading obesity doctors, Francis Heckel, writing in 1910, warned against fashion. In his judgment, women still assumed that they should be fleshy in their neck and chest, which he believed was the worst location of all since to obtain this the whole body had to be substantially overweight. Heckel also blasted continuing use of the corset, which misled women about their own bodies.[15] On another front, women's magazines, rather than simply trumpeting the new standards, more commonly argued that the main thing was for a woman to buy clothing that suited her body type. "There is no ugly woman," concluded an article that had praised a "big woman, with fine proportions in her lines." Another women's magazine article waxed ecstatic over the "thin young person, happy to show the gracefulness of her waist," but evenhandedly offered recommendations also "for a person less svelte." The problem was not fat, but taste. A woman shouldn't choose a dress that looks good on a "young and slender salesgirl," for "time is a terrible enemy of everything." And while it was easy to look "ridiculous" or "ugly" by trying to appear too thin, styles varied enough that "[i]t's easy to find what will accentuate our beauty." Here, clearly, the new standards were recognized but modified for the middle-aged in a way American commentary by 1910 did not allow (however many Americans followed such good advice in practice).[16]

An aristocratic beauty advisor, writing in 1903, put the matter clearly. Traditional standards still applied. "Obesity should never be confused with *embonpoint*: one is a fault, the other is a charm, rounding the angles, enveloping the dry line of the silhouette." Of course, women should not eat too much, for obesity caused suffering as well as looking bad. But thinness was ugly, too. The Countess de Tramar urged sensible diets, combined with massages, baths, electrical treatments, and thyroid pills if one's heart was strong. But she disdained the extremes of current fashion, which she took to be the thin simply taking their revenge after years of epigrams directed their way, "What had constituted beauty becomes a deformity," as the new clothes made all but the very slender look ugly. But the countess thought that this was a mere passing phase, even though with the new off-shoulder dresses it was impossible to use artifice to conceal a nice plumpness. Plump would rise again, however, "and women endowed with a pleasant *embonpoint* will triumph once more."[17]

Why this hesitation, apart from understandable good sense faced with dramatically new body standards? The firmness of the French fashion tradition played a role. Older women had believed so devoutly in the earlier standards of beauty, in contrast to Americans more open to faddish signals, that they did not surrender easily. Even a certain matriarchal element might come into play. Older French women expected power from their roles as mothers and mothers-in-law, and size, clothed in appropriate fashion, had long been part of this image. At the same time, while the health findings were accumulating rapidly in France, they were not yet widely publicized, and it was reasonable to assume that polite moderation would do the trick; no special gyrations were needed. The countess in no sense countenanced immoderate eating. And a final ingredient: while fat was unquestionably presented to the French as a major new issue between the 1890s and 1914, it was not for the most part a moral one. A doctor might hint at laziness, another might refer to the pressures of modern civilization, but there was no full link between fighting overweight and combating the evils of a consumer society. Overweight was a health problem or a fashion problem to be addressed in those terms. This context, different from the framework developing across the Atlantic, made it more possible for well-placed, fashionable people to dissent, while it slowed the overall pressure to fall into line. The first stage of the French campaign against overweight, in sum, developed impressive range but probably roused less widespread, crusading participation.[18]

Phase 2: 1920s–1930s

The interwar years were the decades in which French preoccupation with slimness became something like a popular obsession, with pressures from several directions. These were decades, indeed, in which French concern, despite what was in some ways a slow start, may have surpassed its American counterpart, with a surge more comparable to what was to happen in the United States in the 1950s. Correspondingly, relevant historical attention for the French case, while not embracing dieting as an overall subject, has focused on the 1920s, just as American work rivets on the post-World War II decades. Both approaches err in failing to note significant developments both before and after (this is particularly true, as we have seen, for the American work), but both correctly capture a major turning point, which was simply timed differently in France and the United States.[19]

The explosion and popularization of diet concerns from the 1920s onward built from the groundwork laid by earlier doctors and fashion leaders, some of whom continued to be active. Even more obviously, the cultural solidification of the new standards resulted from considerable fusion between health and fashion, with fashion tips routinely referring to health issues involved in obesity (if usually rather vaguely) as part of their appeal to the liberating qualities of modern slimness. Doctors, while not pushing dress styles, certainly commended aesthetic impulses as a motive for fighting obesity, if a wrongheaded one save when combined with a realization of what was at stake for health; they spent much less time chiding women for the shallowness of their fashion interests than did their American counterparts during the interwar years. Further, the doctors began systematically to move from laboratory to magazine stand as they penned an array of popular diet guides during the 1920s and 1930s.

Beyond the extension and popularization of prior trends, the 1920s surge obviously paralleled larger changes in women's lifestyles, the emergence, really, of a new generation after the pressures of World War I. Here lay the basis for the strong aesthetic impulses of this French diet surge, which carried some character implications — there were overlaps with the United States — but which focused more on beauty per se. While Frenchwomen did not get the vote, they did get new access to public leisure, nightlife, cosmetics — and slenderness. The links were explicit, as women's magazines trumpeted a slim body as part of the whole, desirable modern package for women.[20] As in the United States, however, different links, just as tight, were implicit: if women were to range more freely (and as the birthrate declined even further) they must be subject to compensatory discipline by maintaining a body image that would also make them look frail. As in the United States, a campaign loudly directed toward women was complicated with messages for men as well.

The new merger between health and beauty showed recurrently, helping to intensify the pressure overall. *Votre beauté* in 1934 excoriated fat people for their lack of willpower, but by the same token searched for an argument that would get them to realize what they were risking. The key was health: did the obese not see that they were cutting years from their lives? Fat would limit movement, hurt digestion, cause anxiety, emphysema, circulatory problems, heart difficulties, and impotence. Here and elsewhere, French references to fat causing fatigue were much more common than in the United States; it would be interesting to know why. The list of disease impacts began to remind of the putative consequences of premature sex in the Victorian period, and it had a similar basis in an attempt to use health as an ultimate warning for a newly proscribed social sin. Why were the obese so hard to treat? Because they were often "nervous, impulsive, unstable, weak-willed." Only 20 percent managed to keep weight off if they lost it at all. But *Votre beauté* was in this matter a crusading periodical, no mere fashion rag, and it embraced health as a logical extension of its commitment to appropriate standards.[21]

Doctors readily repaid the favor. Dr. Ruffier's book, pushing exercise, pulled no punches. "It's true that fat is the great destroyer of female beauty." So women, too often passive or at most interested in massage treatment, had to begin to get used to exercise along with dieting. Or Paul Mathieu, in a book that went through several editions, said the doctor must insist that the real problem of obesity was its impact on health, on the heart and kidneys. But aesthetics counted as well: Women wanted to wear the latest styles; Men were embarrassed when their pants were too tight, even more embarrassed when they had to get new measurements from a politely sneering tailor.[22]

Signs of the broadening and intensification of the campaign

against fat proliferated. Women's fashion was unquestionably one of its centers. Boyish styles in the 1920s particularly demanded slenderness, but even with longer skirts in the 1930s, the emphasis on slimness remained. To be sure, models in some store windows might remain stout, particularly for a poorer clientele, so as not to intimidate; and even in *Vogue*, a pinnacle outlet, body shapes in swimming suit articles were considerably chunkier than would be recommended by the 1950s. Nevertheless, the direction was clear. *L'Illustration* in 1933 claimed that science was making it easy for the modern woman to be beautiful. "And the obligations which the modern woman faces for the necessary care of her beauty have become very light." It really boiled down to avoiding heavy eating, for which a woman should be willing to make "every sacrifice." "In our days, the beauty of woman rests in the delicacy of her contours and the slenderness of her lines." Unlike her mother, the modern woman couldn't hide under voluminous clothing, and the growing popularity of sports clothes revealed even more. So the advice was to eat lightly and use slimming baths and other techniques if necessary. As early as 1924, *Vogue* somewhat ruefully listed the demands on "the unhappy woman who is resolved to maintain an ideal weight": girdles, thyroid pills to dehydrate, massages, and sessions at the gym. *Vogue* styles insisted on unprecedented slenderness (even if time would show there was more to be done); a bathing suit section noted that the modern woman was "careful of her lines." At a time when the French nation devoted itself to misguided hopes in the Maginot line, *"la ligne"* was coming to mean something quite different, and more demanding, for hosts of French women.[23]

Here again, the magazine *Votre beauté* was particularly strident. Obesity itself was beginning to become a fault, like skinniness used to be, along with the health hazards involved. Women should catch a tendency to overweight before it led to obesity, for a mere four kilograms extra distorted the face, hurt the skin, and sent a woman down the slippery slope of aesthetic disaster. Obesity was a real illness. The main response had to be in diet, cutting the calories. Of course, this was hard at first, but the goal was well worth it: "a light body creates complete euphoria." And the achievement was wide open. "Everyone can lose weight if he wishes. Its a question of reasoning and then of willpower." The magazine repeatedly offered diets, along with scorn for those who couldn't modify their habits in the interests of shaping up. "Not eat bread? many people feel incapable of this. So much the worse for them, they won't slim down." "If your weight doesn't drop, you and only yourself to blame, you and your lack of will power." But with a bit of attention, plus some exercise, it was easy to drop a kilogram each week. Predictably, in a time of growing concern, the magazine regularly received reader letters on dieting. One correspondent noted that she had stopped eating bread, but wondered if she could resume when she'd reached the right weight; yes, said the editors. Many wrote to thank the magazine for good advice, including the simple technique of weighing oneself twice a week. A regular column on slimming, "Maigrir," kept the suggestions flowing. The basic demand, with its aesthetic absolutes, recurred as well: "there are really too many people who impose completely remediable ugliness on us, and it's disgusting, when this ugliness is so easy to correct."

The fashion thrust had been foreshadowed in 1923 by Pierre Albert-Birot's "Cubo-futurist" history, *Femmes pliantes*, predicting that women soon would be so thin they could be bent and men could carry them under their arms. Artists like Matisse translated these themes of growing slenderness to canvas, in some of their images of women. Art merely exaggerated the styles being urged on women in every fashion outlet, even in the presumably more conservative 1930s.[24]

The second center of attack on fat came from the many popular diet books and comments on obesity put out by doctors, a veritable deluge. The centrality of doctors' cultural role in modern France, already important in shaping the diet campaign, took on novel dimensions, reaching further than in the United States at this time. Doctors themselves noted that in reaching out to the general reader they were trying something new in this area. Research on obesity went forward as well, but the new advice literature was really more important. Maurice Perrin and Paul Mathieu in 1923 reechoed the pre-World War I format in a fairly scholarly tome;

even here there was an effort to help readers identify particular diet products, like special biscuits, that could supplement the calorie charts. And the doctors stressed the deleterious effect of fat on the liver, playing up to a widespread French concern.[25] The more self-consciously popular manuals had fairly standard features. They warned about the health problems, particularly for the heart and arteries: "the obese person thus inevitably becomes sickly, always old before his age, having shortened his life almost by half." A number of manuals returned to the game of causal analysis, talking about endemic (overeating) versus exogenous (glands, heredity) obesity. "A detailed examination of the nutritional habits of the obese person, plus analysis of the urine . . . shows that in many cases . . . the food ration is higher than the age and body state require. But in what proportion does this eating vice play a leading role?" *Voilà*, three quarters: "In the great majority of cases, the obese person is a big eater." There may have been more than French-rationalistic game playing here. Doctors did have a research commitment to investigating causes, and it was important to identify people who had problems besides overeating. Besides, French high culture was devoted to good eating, so people may have needed some extra persuasion that this involved habits that required review, without moral criticism. Indeed a number of manuals made a bow in the direction of the great food philosopher, Brillat-Savarin. After the convoluted stipulations were completed, the doctor could go on to recommend "reasonable but severe" changes in eating patterns. Sedentary habits came in for comment as well: "the great scourge of civilized life with its pitiless obligations and imperious demands." Then the manuals discussed remedies, warning against dangerous quack medicines, particularly the thyroid extract pills; giving some credence to massage, electricity, and water cures; sometimes discussing American stratagems; but always focusing on diet itself. Calorie charts and recommended meals went on for many pages, with some doctors additionally riding some special hobbyhorse of their own. Joined to this drumbeat of popularized medicine was a steady rhythm of advice to parents about keeping their children from overeating.[26]

The doctors involved based their advice not only on research, but on growing experience with patients. Just as the women's magazines reflected frequent reader response, so the new medical push was wrapped up in an increase in actual consultations. Patients, as much now as formal research, gave doctors their evidence and allowed some realistic sense of what diet approaches worked most effectively. The same surge of demand helps explain why doctors thought it realistic to write for a wider public. And again, there was response, as several manuals went through a number of editions. The targets were men at least as much as women, perhaps because doctors still thought men were more important, perhaps because men were using medical recourse (as opposed to overt fashion advice) with new zeal. It was a man that Paul Deboux was addressing when he said, "You let yourself go to the delights of siestas after meals . . . of a little glass of liquor, followed by another, and then a third . . ." Another argument pointed in the same direction: you are praised for your ability to eat well. But then you can't fit in your clothes any longer. Your tailor tactfully tells you that you've become "more solid" *(plus fort)* than last time. You begin to find yourself short of breath. So you see a doctor, and rightly so: you need help in losing weight. And in the end, doctors, like the fashion magazines, sought to uplift: the problem was serious, but not hard to address. "No one remains obese who has the will power to slim down."[27]

The third center of attack on fat, related to the medical focus, was directed entirely toward men. The French army began cracking down on obesity, dismissing a few people each year because they were overweight. This military pressure was less salient in the United States and deserves attention as a quiet male standard setter, particularly in the absence of popular sports (like football) where weight would be an advantage. A mediocre 1922 novel by Henri Béraud detailed the pressures men were facing in ordinary life. The protagonist had always been fat, initially praised as a healthy baby by his gushy mother. He felt obligated to seem happy, for was this not what fat men were supposed to be? But his weight got him down. People laughed at him in restaurants, "There's someone who doesn't stint himself." An employer tells him he can't have a job unless he slims down, "We need active men, not fatsos *(poupards)*." Above all, women shunned him; they were looking for "the American type," slim but muscular. "It's the destiny of all fat men, the certainty of the cruelest disgrace: you've guessed it, the indifference of women." The hero tries gymnastics, diets, doctors; nothing durably works. "The day when I hit 100 kilograms, Ah! this day filled me with such a pathetic grief that, right there on the scale, I uttered a cry worthy of a tragedian." Finally, he resigns himself to his weight and does actually find a mate — a fate, feminists might properly note, not usually granted to fat women. Despite this fictional loophole, which could hardly be said to rescue fat men from the ridicule to which most of the book was devoted, the indications of male assimilation into the campaign against fat — through general public pressures, doctors, even women's magazine columns — were considerable. And fashion did its work here, too, not only through the embarrassing upper-class need to rely on tailors. "Modern clothing, there is the enemy! Long live the toga."[28]

The fourth center of the interwar intensifying concern about overweight involved the spread of standards to the lower classes, particularly in the case of women. It was in the 1930s that the Communist party, having failed to recruit many women in its youth movement, took a new tack, devoting considerable publication space to modern styles and appearances. Women were to be recruited by appealing to mainstream, bourgeois culture. Youth groups could help them learn about cosmetics and up-to-date fashions, as the party's journal, *Jeunes filles de France*, adopted the style of commercial women's magazines with articles like "Always Pretty." The tactic worked in bringing new recruits, whatever its dubious Marxist pedigree. The party's youth outlets (and also similar Catholic outlets) did not emphasize dieting per se but the "health and beauty" column did include exercises to flatten stomachs and firm up arms. Although hesitant about limiting eating because of health concerns, the Communist approach unquestionably helped disseminate fashion consciousness, including the new slenderness standards, and at the same time it reflected how widely these standards had already spread. The appeal of current beauty styles, after all, guided the new approach to young women in the first place. Inexpensive women's magazines, directed to rural and urban lower-class people who did their own sewing, were more actively pushing the new body standards. To be sure, 1930s beauty articles in outlets like *La femme chez elle* did not focus as strongly on slimming as their counterparts in bourgeois magazines. But the models sketched in the design sections, where patterns were offered, were extremely thin, indeed explicitly promising "to slenderize your silhouette." And the magazine regularly carried advertisements about slenderizing products. A vegetable cure boasted that it continued no thyroid. The Mexican tea of Dr. Jawas would avoid "superfluous fat and [lighten] the whole organism." Even if formal doctors were rarely used, the fancy beauty magazines, irrelevant, French lower-class women easily learned of the modern standards of beauty and gained guidance about how to appropriate them in their own lives.[29]

At all levels, of course, a host of new products proliferated. Girdles were one possibility, as a replacement for corsets; they were advertised as being "imperceptible," so supple that no activity was constrained, and also making one "slim and beautiful." As in the United States at this time, reducing belts offered great promise. The "Roussel belt," "Queen of elastic belts," would remove six centimeters in just eight days. Dr. Charniaux's belt was "medically studied" along with his reducing suits, while the "Sveltesse" belt offered massage that broke up fat tissues. Dr. Monteil's belt, "Goddess," slimmed thighs and stomach without diet or pills, "preventing and suppressing obesity"; the device was a rubber suit for the whole middle body. Electrical treatments were another possibility, in this case, directed more toward men. Exercise boosters took up the charge. "The modern silhouette of a woman, say the couturiers, is that of an athlete." Not so, exactly, for the "pipe woman" image of the 1920s was too frail. But women's athletics were the key to solid slenderness: "If a woman likes food too much to sustain the famous diets, if she distrusts iodide and thyroid products, she's condemned to sports," where in fact she can stay thin. Rowing and bicycle machines were particularly recommended. The magazine *Eve* filled with advertisements against overweight. Girdles, exercise routines, and slenderizing soaps were regular items. So were notices about diet gurus, to whom one had only to write for the mysteries of life to be revealed. "You must get thin ... to work without fatigue, to be healthy, or to be slim, elegant and in style" — readers were to write to Mme. Pasteur-Longard, no drugs involved. Various pharmacy products were touted. Tranol would allow one "to slim down rapidly, without altering your health; certain result." With Galton pills, based on sea plants, "each week the scales show the progress and your health is better." Mme. E offered the exciting possibility of slimming down any part of the body one wished, or making the whole body healthier. And so it went. In a two-decade period when the standards of slenderness were escalating and more of the French public was being reached through an interrelated variety of appeals, opportunities for gimmickry were almost unlimited. And the ads also played a role in driving home the central messages of slenderness, beauty, and health.[30]

In contrast to the first phase of the modern French concern about overweight, the interwar years tossed up no serious counterarguments to the diet pitch. People complained. Many ignored or failed to live up to the new standards. But the idea of continuing to argue that fleshier body types were good was now abandoned, a testimony to intensifying power of the modern standards. With no real overall orchestration, with mutual reinforcement between standard setters and an eager public, the notion of a need to keep weight down or take it off became inescapable. And the standards clearly attacked some rooted French beliefs in what eating was all about. Both the doctors and the fashion magazines, however gingerly, said that gourmandise could be overdone and that many people needed to rethink their habits rather severely. Doctors, to be sure, obfuscated just a bit in talking about "excusable" (that is, glandular or hereditary) or even "partially excusable" obesities, but they, and the fashion gurus even more, ultimately agreed on three overall conclusions. First, fat was bad, unhealthy, and ugly. Second, it was up to the individual to avoid or get rid of fat; there were no scapegoats. And third, it could be done with a decent amount of willpower (or, for readers of ads, some special gimmick). The matter was serious, but there was no great battle involved; grit your teeth and get started.[31]

The focus on diet in the interwar period, after a prolonged, somewhat disputed prewar prologue, highlighted the impact of fashion statements and of doctors' advice in a nation where physicians, often underpaid compared to their American counterparts, were particularly eager for new roles and where the research tradition provided a plausible base. Attention to women in the 1920s reflected some of the same desire to seek new constraints to counter new female freedoms (while calling the constraints liberating) as in the United States in the same period. But these were not decades of massive consumerist advance, and despite a few references to modern sedentary life, most French diet commentary did not imply moral compensation. Health and rigorous beauty standards were the key criteria.

Phase 3: 1945–Present

The sweeping nature of the interwar escalation of the campaign against fat inevitably made subsequent developments somewhat anticlimactic. Interrupted by the war (which reduced food supplies and made adequacy again the main goal, as well as imposing the kind of stress that drove some to overeating), the assertion of weight standards resumed almost immediately thereafter, without significantly breaking stride. A rhythm had been established that in many ways continues to the present day. Beauty, health and medicine, and commercialized gimmickry continued to combine to keep the goal of slenderness front and center. The general contours can be fairly easily illustrated, for they were by now familiar. The main change, and an important one, was the steadily increasing rigor of the definition of slenderness.

The themes and formats of the interwar years resumed very quickly. Doctors began issuing new diet books for public consumption in the early 1950s. Titles bore more directly on reducing than before; the interwar texts, still tinged with the research emphases, had referred to "obesities," but now the headings stressed how to get thin or how to treat obesity, though the contents remained about the same. References to the demands of patients increased as doctors claimed that the public at large increasingly saw overweight as an illness requiring treatment, as well as an aesthetic "disgrace" and an inexhaustible topic of conversation. Individual claims of having treated 15,000, even 30,000, overweight patients were common from the 1930s onward. Residual beliefs that plumpness was healthy were disappearing fast. Given a favorable atmosphere, the doctor's role consisted of motivation — including some good scare tactics if necessary — plus detailed diet advice. Several texts also suggested more rigorous definitions of the standard weight formulas, cutting the longstanding height-weight definition by 5 percent. Again, the formula of responsibility and feasibility was repeated. "You are the artisan of your own unhappiness" if you start a diet and fail to follow through. But willpower ("every decision taken is followed to the letter") really wasn't too hard, and the result would be splendid.[32]

Business as usual also characterized the women's magazines in the late 1940s and 1950s. *Marie-France* offered advertisements from 1946 to 1947 that were filled with much slimmer models than had been true of the interwar years. Advertisements, stressing the demands of fashion, offered pills (the "cure d'Antiges," taken twice a day, held the added advantage that no one would know you're taking them and were guaranteed to take off two to three kilograms a month) or health baths and massages (the *Institut de Jaegère* would reduce fatty body parts, such as the legs, while removing the breathlessness and palpitations that accompanied obesity). *Marie Claire*, resuming publication in 1954, offered a regular sequence of diet articles, along with slender models and fashions and advertisements for reducing girdles and other products. Josette Lyon, the beauty editor, insistently stressed adverse health effects of obesity, the burdens on the heart and the arteries and the potential for diabetes. There was no need to panic or to fall for quick cures. For most people, unless they were sick, dieting required "neither heroism or a fierce willpower." Various diets were offered, along with recommendations of sports and massage as supplements of limited value and some warnings against thyroid extracts. But while everything could be managed, there must be no question of who had to take the lead ("You alone are responsible for it"), for it was the individual who ate too much and failed to exercise. Nothing very new here, except the greater slimness of the models and some pressing reminders that fashions such as shorts and contemporary bathing suits required women to keep the weight off. With this came some more urgent comments on cellulite, that special accumulation of fat that could mar women (84 percent of all cellulite problems, it was claimed, were female) and that required particular vigilance, making it essential not to overeat in the first place and also to watch over the diets of children.[33]

Yet more substantial innovations, while hardly earthshaking, began to creep in. One involved increasing reference to developments in the United States. Somewhat ironically, since the United States was hardly a model of diet success, several American variants were recurrently grafted on to solid French trends. New pills were introduced, including *Préludine* (1956) and other amphetamines first widely used in American dieting. A number of American diet books were translated from the late 1940s onward, from Pennington in 1948 to Atkins in 1966, with his pure protein approach. Other American gurus were simply plagiarized, with titles like "Weight Loss Without Tears." Both beauty articles and doctors' manuals began to refer to the standard weight charts put out by American insurance companies; interestingly, French firms were much less active in this area, perhaps because doctors themselves had taken such an early initiative. Periodically, women's magazines carried long pieces about individual French women who had found diet salvation in the United States. *Marie Claire* offered a piece called "Diet without Suffering" directed toward older women. The protagonist had a long history of unsuccessful efforts. "The shame of weight haunted me for years. I belonged to the category of 'solid women' *(femmes fortes)*; it was horrible." She shunned fashions, never going to the beach, pretending she did not like to dance because of her need to hide her fat. Exercise, massage, steam, medicines, diets — nothing worked. Then came the visit to the United States, where she initially gained weight because, "in spite of its bad reputation" American cooking was quite good. The ultimate secret was low-calorie food. If she kept her calorie counter handy and avoided the calorie-laden foods, she could actually eat plenty and her weight began consistently to drop. Before and after pictures confirmed that this was one slender older woman who'd been quite a balloon before. None of this, of course, was really new in France; the article did not make it clear why calories became easier to identify because of American charts when there had been French charts for decades.[34] For the American influence clearly depended on the political and particularly the cultural ascendancy of the United States, not on any special wisdom. Letters from women and girls constantly referred to Hollywood stars (not all of them American, but tossed in the transatlantic pot). A teenager, desperate to lose weight, wanted to look like Audrey Hepburn. Doctors mentioned the great success Ingrid Bergman had achieved once she got to California in dropping five kilograms and keeping it off, despite having children by two different husbands.

From the 1960s onward, American influence meant one more thing, building on its apparent national leadership role in the diet field: the importation of additional American products and various novel organizations to France. Weight Watchers, rapidly expanding internationally in any event, was brought to France by a woman who had benefited from its programs in Kansas City. Well after its introduction in the United States, Coca-Cola introduced low-calorie versions to Europe in the 1980s (Coke Light), and gradually other diet concoctions based on Nutrasweet hit the French market.

The American influence remained limited, partly because some characteristic emphases were not congenial to French culture — more on that in the following chapter — but partly, of course, because it simply was not necessary, given the solid basis already established by the French themselves. Artificial calorie removal, for example, was less interesting in a society that liked good food and had learned that restraint in eating was desirable. The variable existed, however, as American stars and models increasingly dominated the screens and magazines, providing a disproportionate amount of the female imagery available to French viewers. (Even here, however, the advent of Brigitte Bardot in the 1950s, as a slim, scantily clad, newly informal, and very French standard, probably had a bigger impact than the American stars.)[35]

A second innovation, though continuing an earlier theme, involved changes in the women's clothing industry with the advent of ready-to-wear dresses beginning about 1949 (the term *"pret-à-porter"* dates from that year). Along with advertisements and movies touting the slender figure, ready-to-wear clothes increased the pressure on lower-class young women, including rural women, to shape up or be unable to fit into the fashionable sizes. Standardization automatically increased, more powerfully and publicly than with mere weight charts. Here was potent support for the tendency toward cross-class beauty standards that had begun in the interwar period.[36]

But the most persistent change involved intensification, making existing slenderness standards more rigorous. Signs of this emerged, as we have seen, very quickly after the war, but they tended to increase from the late 1950s onward as French affluence began to reach new heights. Doctors played a role in this process as another round of books and pamphlets emerged in the 1970s, again with claims of tens of thousands of patients treated. A few of the items were idiosyncratic (some with American influence), like *How to Lose Weight by Eating 400 Grams of Bread per Day.* Others, like *Reduce and Eat Well*, largely summarized earlier wisdom. But several substantial efforts, popular but distinctly more extensive than their 1950s analogs, provided new detail on the health dangers overweight posed, including, of course, the new information about cholesterol. The recommended diets for those who did carry excess weight were increasingly detailed as well, now that not only calories but other aspects of food chemistry must be conveyed. *Nouvelle cuisine* in the 1970s attacked rich French food staples such as adding au gratin to vegetables. Suggestions by French experts (as by those in America) that it was most healthy to fall somewhat below the recommended weight charts also emerged at this point.[37]

To be sure, doctors carried forward some staples. Laments about modern times persisted. "Industrial civilization builds a pathogenic society for man, because it is not to his measure." While some criticisms of excessive concern for beauty surfaced, French doctors continued to be sympathetic on the whole. "It's sad not to be able to look at oneself in the mirror." What a pleasure, in contrast, to glide into tight jeans. "I can fit into all the ready-to-wear clothes."

Of course, enhanced warnings about stress on the heart and arteries were central. But the big intensification, along with the cholesterol warnings, involved the weight charts and definitions of obesity, which had already tightened in the 1950s. Gilbert-Dreyfus defined overweight at 5 to 15 percent above the recommended levels, obesity at 15 to 30 percent — potentially a more rigorous definition than that current in the United States. Trémolières and others redid the weight charts themselves, while making the rule of thumb for height-weight calculations (height in centimeters minus 100) again more rigorous by as much as 5 percent compared to the 1950s, 10 percent compared to the 1920s. Trémolières's chart pulled 8 percent from the recommended weight for a man 1.7 meters tall, compared to its 1920s analogue, and 6 percent from that of a woman 1.5 meters tall. Recommended daily calories dropped proportionately. Here, quite precisely, the demands for health and beauty were going up, in much the same fashion as in the United States in the same period.[38]

Along with the new medical specifics, fashion and leisure habits applied new pressure. Here, in fact, the rigor surpassed the concurrent American evolution. By the 1960s, items like blue jeans and T-shirts became common in France, making concealment of extra pounds more difficult than before. Brigitte Bardot, coming to stardom in 1956, was not only fairly slender; she also provided a model of freer physical action and informal dress that depended on firm body tone. Certainly previous complements like girdles, however imperceptible, no longer supported true fashion. Store mannequins became thinner than ever before. Then there was the increasingly popular annual rush to the beach and increasingly scanty attire seen there, which by the 1970s included topless sunbathing. Women, and men, too, who wished to wear the new minimalist suits, needed near-perfect bodies to look good. As early as 1956, *Marie Claire* began to provide annual spring and early summer advice, including diets and exercises, to help women tone up for the yearly challenge. This annual cycle became standard in women's magazines, and it continued into the mid-1990s. Unprecedented exposure — far more than American women, even with their reduced bathing suits, were asked to provide — raised the ante on weight control. In 1957 Josette Lyon noted that many women now "feared" summer, manifesting a "bathing suit complex." Even slim women had to worry about their hips and thighs. Never fear; *Marie Claire* had a plan of action: diet galore, combined with the additional suggestions of eating only fruit one of two days a week; eat an egg before going to a party because then it will be easier to turn down rich foods; massages and heat would attack areas especially afflicted with cellulite. For a time in the late 1950s and early 1960s, diet advice proliferated in the women's magazines because of the new standards, before settling down by the 1980s to more of a maintenance level, with an article or two each year in each main outlet.[39]

Another sign of intensification resembled developments in the United States. Pregnant women were urged to gain very little weight in both formal obstetrical literature and more popular manuals during the 1960s. "If you wish to recover your young girl's figure, after the birth, you should gain no more than 1.5 kilos during the first three months." Extremely limited diets were recommended, with emphasis on vegetables and light cheese. "Don't think I'm trying to starve you." By the 1970s, to be sure, this pressure eased, as doctors found they were generating too many underweight babies, but many women still stuck to fairly rigorous regimes.[40]

In fashion, in pregnancy, even in medical advice, intensification showed, finally, in stronger vocabulary. Fat stomachs made "disgraceful" folds, unless women not only dieted but exercised on something like a rowing machine. Doctors noted how often women reported even modest overweight as "a simple disgrace." Fashion writers added that ordinary dressmakers felt the same and told their customers so. The female form is "extremely sensitive to excess food." "Beyond fifty years of age, a woman can no longer claim full beauty; nevertheless aesthetic care, physical culture and fashionable artifice allow her to efface, to a degree, the ravages of time." Lest there be any doubt, older artistic presentations were subjected to rigorous scrutiny. In Courbet's female figure in "La Source," for example, "the lower part of the body is invaded by fat." Aesthetic disgust, in other words, seemed to be reaching new levels.[41]

Particular attention was now directed to a woman's thighs, partly, of course because new fashions more commonly displayed them.

Women themselves, it was argued, were quite conscious of the problem. "They themselves know how thickenings in this regions are disgraceful." Cellulite, of course, was a major problem, to be attacked with general dieting but also specific massages, creams, and other products. Most revealingly, an explicit term became fashionable by the 1970s to generate automatic attention to problems of fat in this part of the female anatomy: *culotte de cheval.* The phrase, "riding breeches," was not new, but its routine application to the body was, and there was no escaping it in the women's magazines and the doctors' manuals. Here was a pointed indication that women, even if slender overall, faced some particular challenges that required more vigilance than ever. (One could say that, as use of this reference spread, French people for the first time in history united behind the goal of becoming *sans-culottes.*) Small wonder that by the 1970s reports of women's awareness of dieting, plus their search for additional support in new products, even surgery, escalated. Surgery, including laser treatments by the 1980s, was particularly directed at the dread *culotte de cheval.* "It pleases her to be able to parade around the swimming pools." By the 1980s, sales of reducing creams exploded, rising 18 percent a year during the early part of the decade. New weight groups, like the International Slimming Centers, opened, while older ones, including Weight Watchers, expanded a bit. Beauty institutes, a staple for decades, expanded, with new chains opening up. Even stolid daily newspapers, like *Figaro* and *Le Monde,* began carrying diet articles, as well as reports on the phenomenal increase of interest. The French diet game was not easy to win because the rules kept getting tougher.[42]

By the 1980s, 90 percent of all French people were reported to be worried about their weight, in what *La Vie* called "the dictatorship of the scales." Some doctors, turning a bit skeptical, claimed that a third of all the people who saw them about reducing were not really fat, but merely responding to "absurd" criteria. Parents worried about their children, particularly daughters, and tried to monitor their consumption of snacks and candy. "If she gets fat, she'll have a different life. We live in a world where such people are discriminated against for their ugliness" — sometimes not even allowed in certain nightclubs.[43]

Yet the older theme of reassurance did not disappear. The standards were demanding, but they could be met. Josette Lyon in 1959 reported that a fifth of all Frenchwomen had perfect measurements already; a full 54 percent were within target range in terms of weight size. This was a triumph for modern French dieting. For "only a minimum of willpower" was needed, and when they had to, "everyone [could succeed] in slimming down." There was no need for excess, just to cut back a bit; even cellulite could be defeated by moderate but persistent measures. With rare exceptions, no glandular or hereditary barriers would keep anyone from success. Slenderness was democratically available to all.[44]

Contemporary Patterns

Estimates vary concerning the number of French people actually on a diet by the mid-1990s, from about 12 percent to 40 percent. The figure is lower than its American counterpart. Correspondingly, French middle-class women's magazines curtailed their explicit attention to diet issues by the mid-1990s, settling in to one or two articles a year, often timed for the prevacation frenzy of body toning, spiced occasionally with personal tips from a star like Catherine Deneuve (who said she fasted completely about two days a month). At times, slimness seemed to have nestled into place among other beauty issues, including a new "obsession" with face-lifts as the French population (like the American) aged. Yet it was because slimness standards were so firmly internalized, and not because they had receded in special significance, that a sense of routine set in. The popularity of reducing creams continued — "the body is progressively remodeled" with Biothem, or Minceur Beauté, Gel Remodélant, Corps Evolution, or Contour Femerté Corps (slimness beauty, remodeling gel, body evolution, body firmness contour). It was joined in 1994 by new excitement over a chrome pill that, it was hoped, might just be the magic solution. Exercise clubs spread — there were thirty-seven new ones in the Paris area by the early 1990s. Though exercise had held a somewhat ambivalent place in the French culture of slenderness, rates of participation were clearly rising. In 1967, only 8 percent of all

French adults declared themselves "sportif"; the figure was 46 percent in 1981, with 26 percent actually participating regularly in exercise. By 1990, the regular exercise group was up to a full third, including 60 percent in the bureaucratic and professional segment of the middle class, and the correlation between exercise and slenderness was high. Basic standards continued to intensify somewhat as well. *Marie Claire* was always ready to raise the stakes, as in a mid-1995 article on how to be beautiful "entirely nude" — a new declaration of war against cellulite, wherever it might be lurking. The goals remained transcendent. As one dieter noted, "I'll really begin to live when I'm through."

France, then, had developed at least as extensive a culture against overweight as the United States had; the culture permeated as many facets of existence and entered into basic definitions of what success and the good life were all about. As *Elle* put it for women, in an article praising a combination of eating restraint, exercises, and creams, the ideal body involved "sexy breasts, flat stomach, firm breasts, legs of steel." And the reader could get these — by surgery if all else failed. Yet, with all the familiar hopes and standards, a French tone remained. Dieting, said the latest fad book, involved "eating less but eating well." And maybe, some thought — hoping to have their cake but not its calories — good eating was a key to success. "The pleasure of eating fine cuisine burns more calories than eating an insipid dish; likewise the discovery of an original dish with unfamiliar flavors increases the number of calories burned, doubtless because of the emotion inspired."[45]

The French spirit in the modern zeal for slenderness involved more than reconciling new standards with old tastes as a century of intensification and dissemination drew to a close, interesting though this distinctive national contribution is. It is time to reexamine this century, casting a more analytical eye over all the principal features of French diet culture that showed some staying power — including the dilemma of combining a traditional self-identity of superb taste with a new, and very proud, identity as the slimmest people in the Western world.[46]

8 The French Regime

American and French patterns of weight control share a combination of consistency and change. Both established certain themes early on, some of them quite similar, some rather different. At the same time, both shifted considerably over what is now a full century of modern weight control history. Both, among other things, worked toward greater rigor. Both incorporated new medical knowledge and new fashions, as well as a variety of changes in specific strategies.

French weight-control history, as we have seen, went through three fairly well-defined stages, from a definite but contested first phase, through the intensification period between the wars, to the establishment of a fairly definite rhythm along with greater rigor after World War II. Yet a number of persistent features accompanied these shifts. Some emerge from the French materials themselves, for example, the openness to nondietary solutions — or hopes — that runs from the first commercial products offered to the recent passion for reducing creams. Other consistencies require at least an informal comparative context, like the tendency to emphasize standards and words derived from aesthetics over moralistic impulses. Before turning to a final comparative explanation that embraces both France and the United States, we need to isolate some of the chief French features for their own sake, including the striking relationship between culture and reality.

As it emerged after 1900, and certainly by the interwar period, the French approach to obesity harbored a distinctive internal tension, even beyond the need to confront a tradition of fine cuisine. The French strains differed from characteristic American ambivalence between an explicit focus on weight and a considerable interest in using fat as a symbolic surrogate for moral degeneracy. The French, as we will see, largely avoided this pairing. But they did dance between strong insistence on personal responsibility for fat (plus the aesthetically disgraceful consequences of failure) and a desire to argue that keeping trim posed no great difficulties. One of the reasons doctors long debated the role of inherent problems caused by real bodily infirmities, as opposed to simple overeating, apart from a Gallic delight in labeling, was to clear the way for a simple statement of responsibility combined with an equally simple indication of how the responsibility could be exercised. Thus Michel Perin in 1954 still worried about separating the overeaters from those "less responsible" for their condition. But while the obese person was usually "most responsible," another colleague had stipulated in the 1930s that "no one remains obese who has the willpower to slim down."[1] While there was no logical contradiction involved between pinning down causation and reassuring about remediation, there was a practical one. If it was up to the individual to live up to the standards of weight control, but the task was not too arduous, why then make much fuss at all? To be sure, once they settled into the new culture by the 1950s, the French did discuss the matter less than Americans. Reminders, not monthly reinventions of the wheel, often sufficed. Still, there was a choice to be made in most presentations between emphasizing the responsibility-dire consequences aspect and assuming the matter could be handled in routine fashion. A number of other French features, as we will see, related to this distinctive blend.

A first set of themes involves groupings, notably gender, class, and childhood. French patterns here illumine the general modern process of weight control, adding to American data, but also point up some decisive differences. Then there is the major division between aesthetics and morality, from which several tactical distinctions flowed. And finally, body reality provides a crucible for the impact of French standards, as the French translated their slenderness goals more effectively than their transatlantic cousins.

Gender

The gender implications of the modern weight control culture are less simple than appearances suggest. The American patterns indicate this complexity. So do the French, with some different specific twists. In both cases, the new body standards were imposed far more vociferously on women than on men. Women's magazines carried a commentary missing from men's reading, while women's fashions earlier and more vigorously demanded compliance — or visible failure. But men were involved early on, and their commitment may not have been as different from women's as the sound and fury imply. Doctors, while noting women's fashion concerns, worried if anything more about men than about women as the cardiovascular statistics said they should. And men, both in France and the United States, may have shared these worries early, though they left less explicit trace than the historian would like. The early appearance of a novel bemoaning the pressure on fat men suggests this kind of involvement in France. So do occasional asides, even in women's magazines, that suggest men were listening; *Marie Claire*, for example, in the 1950s occasionally featured offerings "for men only" about dressing slim and dieting. And so do many of the diet product advertisements, the muscle-building physical culture displays, and recurrent references to embarrassment in public or before one's tailor assume an attentive male audience. Explicit interest in weight loss, again both in France and the United States, increased among men by the 1970s, in part because of more visible involvement in service occupations where appearance counted. But this was less novel than observers thought; it capped a long if somewhat silent participation. Gender imbalance on both sides of the Atlantic was less great than has been assumed.[2]

But women did receive special attention, and this requires assessment. The French did not quite as clearly escalate the pressure on women as Americans did, particularly in the 1950s, though fashions did become more demanding, the topic more discussed in women's magazines. It was true that, despite medical attention to men, French women were more likely to consult doctors about diet problems and to see doctors about health issues generally, a disparity that has continued. A gendered implication of scorn and derision, however, has been much less apparent in France. Doctors, though they noted women's style concern and occasionally worried that this might distract from the real point, which was health, did not usually complain about women patients. In a country where a large minority of physicians could not earn a living around 1914, they may have been grateful for any patients at all, but the approach does contrast interestingly with the United States, again reflecting the greater habituation of French doctors to a tolerant guidance role. To be sure, the conservative Trémolières in the 1970s blasted women along with modern civilization: a weight-conscious woman, "rejecting what she is, has kept an adolescent concern for how she appears." But this was a strikingly unusual aside; most French doctors praised women for wanting to look beautiful and urged that fat women in no sense feel blamed. References to the fact that women are more often obese than men, though they occurred, were less frequent than in the United States and more matter-of-fact. Women's magazines themselves were less sneering about fat, even when they laid it on the line about personal responsibility; this was a particularly noticeable contrast in the 1950s.[3] At the same time, the new body standards were inserted in a French context in which worries about the sheer commitment to motherhood were much greater than in the United States. Zola in 1899, and occasional medical comments in the interwar decades, clearly suggested the contrast between tubelike fashions and the hope that women would become more, not less, willing to incur pregnancy.

Both France and the United States, finally, surrounded the new women's fashions with excited references to liberation and euphoria. Superficially, at least, slenderness was part of a new package of public freedom and leisure opportunities, particularly from the 1920s onward. Yet the fashions themselves were punitive, as both French and American feminists would point out by the 1980s. Surely, on the part of some proponents, women were being asked to compensate for new freedoms, including their lessened commitment to motherhood; France had at least as many reasons to work this trade-off as did the United States. Here is one factor, despite the more muted misogynist overtones, in the timing of greater fashion demands in the 1920s as the French birthrate reached new lows. Again, the combinations are complicated.[4]

Yet the French approach to women suggests a readier acceptance of aesthetic standards than occurred in the United States. Without trying to overdo national stereotypes, French commentators, whether in the beauty field or in medicine, found it easier to understand that women must try to live up to fashion demands. In this sense there was less obscurity in the French approach. On the other hand, French culture was in some ways traditionally less demanding of women: while women were held to be natural keepers of the home, they were not, in nineteenth- and early-twentieth century formulations, endowed with a superior natural morality.[5] To this extent, as they participated in new leisure activities and new sexual openness, they had less to compensate for; they were disappointing fewer traditional expectations. And, of course, their official power position changed less quickly than in the United States, with a two-decade difference in receiving the vote. Hence, along with very demanding weight standards, there were fewer critical undertones where women were concerned, amid a greater insistence on meeting aesthetic standards.

Race and Class

In the early 1990s, the French Statistical Institute, noting that the French had continued to lose weight or at least remain stable in relation to height during the 1980s, commented on the divisions among major social groups. Their data suggest a pattern of distribution similar in terms of social class to that of the United States, though in greater detail. Students were thinnest (which may differ from the United States, given greater American diet success a bit later on in life), but this was a comment on age more than class. Among adults, with both men and women essentially coinciding, the fattest groups were rural landowners and small business owners (but potentially including larger owners as well; no distinction was made). Agricultural workers were quite thin; urban workers, about average. Among women, housewives were a bit above average. The thinnest urban groups were professionals and upper bureaucrats, followed closely by employees. The modern culture of weight control thus proves to be predominantly urban (assuming that rural workers were thin mainly because of strenuous labor), with particular correlation with higher education and the service sector, where presentation to the public was particularly important. American data, as we have seen, confirm the tendency for a rural-urban split and support the education and service-sector relationship.

There were regional differences as well, relating not only to urbanism (though Paris averaged relatively low weights) but also food traditions. Alsace was thus relatively heavy, as it had been earlier in the century. But regional designations were not primary in relation to the social variables. Thus the South, rated as heavier than average earlier in the twentieth century, now reflected urbanization, the movement of urban people back to the countryside, and the fashion pressure of the beach and tourism; it fell among the low-weight areas in the 1980s.[6]

The statisticians, with fewer data beyond an additional questionnaire, went on to contend that France had developed two cultures of weight, one eager to live up to modern standards and quite conscious of health and fashion, the other, quite simply, uninterested.

To some extent, this division probably held true as a simplification of the gradations among social groups. But it risked being misleading, for example, in ignoring efforts on the part of many housewives to live up to standards even while succeeding incompletely. Compared to the United States, furthermore, the French commitment to modern weight-control standards seems relatively uniform. Despite often huge political differences — indeed, as we will see, in part because of the expression of tensions these allowed — the aesthetic commitments of major French social groups increasingly converged. Gaps among the leading classes in average weight (controlled for height, though not for age) ranged 7 percent or less. These were significant, but not overwhelming. For the history of weight-control standards in France, or at least of appearance standards, suggests an increasing cultural congruence, particularly in the cities. The early decades of French slenderness culture, to be sure, were more overtly class-ridden than in the United States, some early aristocratic stylistic quibbling aside. References to spas and expensive beauty institutes were much more common in France than across the Atlantic, in a pattern that continues to some degree. Certainly before the 1920s, up-to-date medical care and the latest beauty aids were prerogatives of the rich.

But this changed, partly because doctors and diet-fad salesmen reached out. The new standards democratized, if gradually. The push toward assimilating the lower classes during the 1920s and 1930s, through inculcation of dominant beauty and fitness standards (even on the part of the Communist party) and through the *puériculture* campaigns, clearly paid off in large part. While some groups and individuals showed less enthusiasm than others, there was no alternative culture maintained after 1914 in which fatter bodies were held to be positively desirable. To be sure, occasional reminders continued in the 1920s and 1930s that some men preferred plump women sexually (even when these women, attuned to the fashion standards, insisted on trying to slim down), and on an individual basis, these preferences doubtless persisted. It is also true that the communist youth magazine, *Jeunes filles de France*, warned against the rigid diets of the movie stars, which undermined health. There was, then, hesitation on the part of lower-class outlets in a depression decade when nutrition and health remained precarious. But there was no clear subculture offering a different definition of body ideals. Aesthetically, the society was surprisingly homogeneous, even conformist, as the widespread adoption of other habits, like the stereotypic vacation exodus, would soon confirm.

No one, for example, after the 1930s sought to court French rural or lower-class groups with stouter-than-average models where even a hint of fashion should be present. Some cultural lag unquestionably persisted even as affluence and ready-to-wear fashions lured the lower classes in the 1950s. Letters in popular women's magazines like *Modes et travaux* into the 1960s complained about some of the featured diets, arguing that they did not provide enough to eat and were appropriate really only for invalids: "Our ancestors didn't know this word [*dietetic*], and they ate better than we do." "I'm not a mannequin." But by the late 1960s, these complaints died off as the magazine, like some of its predecessors even in the 1930s, converted to articles on slim styles and health consciousness. By the 1980s, the magazine was indistinguishable in the nature and intensity of its diet advice from the slick bourgeois periodicals.[7] Indeed, by the 1990s, even throwaway tabloids carried their own articles about miracle slimming treatments. Impressionistic newsstand forays in 1995 suggested that the cheap press carried diet articles more frequently than the middle-class women's magazines, whose regular but calm cycles of interest have already been noted.[8] The dominant culture became pervasive, and an audience eager to catch up may have been the main result of lingering social and cultural gaps.

What happened in France, more clearly even than in the United States, was that lower classes and rural groups picked up the diet interest a few decades late. Their need for more strenuous physical labor; a traditional pride in fulfilling hearty appetites as a badge of success, particularly given frequent penury; and, doubtless, some lingering aesthetic difference held them back. But the difference, though its traces still linger in weight distinctions, was primarily one of timing, not a simmering cultural dispute. By the 1990s, to a greater extent than in the increasingly stratified United States, it became difficult to predict social class in France by girth.

Without question, French social-class divisions proved much more amenable to considerable homogeneity in aesthetic standards, at least by the second quarter of the twentieth century, than did key racial divisions in the United States. The French had their racist references, to be sure. The claim that Jews were particularly likely to get fat recurred through the first half of the century. By the 1980s, some observers held (without any more specific evidence) that certain immigrant groups defied French norms because they so enjoyed prosperity that they could not restrain themselves or because the tensions of immigrant life could be solaced by extra eating.[9] But, to date, even among French racial minorities an alternate vision has yet to be articulated. The contrast with African American and Hispanic American patterns is obvious.[10] It reflects a significant difference in overall cultural context, and it contributes to a substantial difference in actual weight patterns. Divisions in weight and in cultural emphasis must be noted as part of the modern French history of fat, with more modernized social sectors clearly leading the way, but they barely qualify the dominant cultural and physical trends.

Children

One of the keys to growing social uniformity in French dieting, and certainly a basis for the actual results of the modern culture of slenderness in France, involved the distinctive approach to children. The social implications were not complex: despite many differences in specific settings, the French seemed to agree, across class, that childhood eating required serious discipline. A group of devoted experts certainly stressed this theme, explicitly across class lines, as they tried to improve the child-rearing habits of workers and peasants. Here was a major divergence from American patterns, and from this a crucial explanation of why other aspects of French weight culture, and of success in restraint, diverged as well.

For a striking feature of the French movement to control overweight was its smooth mesh with dominant attitudes to children and children's eating. The contrast with the United States was both obvious and fundamental. American diet culture, despite its strength, had clashed with prevailing indulgence toward children from the 1920s at least into the 1970s in terms of overall recommendations and actual family eating patterns. Childhood was a time for pampering, including demonstrations of the nation's traditional abundance of food. Parents, particularly if guilty over other slights to their ideals of loving care, easily consoled their children with snacks and treats. The intensity of concern over inadequate feeding, however justified for the poor, reflected the childhood anomaly in American diet culture well into the 1970s.

Not so in France. Traditional childrearing, to a degree across class lines, insisted on childhood as a period of regulation. Long centuries of limited food supplies conditioned peasants, at least, to insist that their children neither waste food nor use it excessively. None of this was new, but it was given new attention as doctors turned their sights on obesity — and notes on childhood obesity occurred far earlier in French medical literature than in American, scattered references aside. Specific research on childhood obesity was underway by the 1930s, again in advance of developments in the United States. More important still, the idea of regulating children's eating gained both legitimation and wide publicity by its incorporation into the endless pamphlets and courses on child care that spread throughout France from the late nineteenth century through the 1930s as part of the *puériculture* campaign.[11]

Control of children's eating was not the main point of the *puériculturistes*, to be sure. Their target was infant feeding, with endless pleas for mothers to breastfeed, or if artificial feeding could not be avoided, to do so properly. Along with this came standard recommendations about inoculations and other health care issues. But it was the rare manual that did not also comment on the desirability of curbing any tendency to overeat. "It is wise to be moderate, avoiding food excess as well as insufficiency of food," noted an interwar manual that also gave calorie listings for major food types. Mothers must learn that customary notions that plump children were occasions for pride were wrong, really the reverse of the truth — this from a manual of 1896. More specifically, mothers too often tried to feed children adult materials too early, which could set up patterns of overeating later on. And it was vital to turn children away from sweets and random snacks, another maternal impulse that must be stamped out. It was in this same context that doctors worked to warn mothers that their legitimate concern about tubercular children should not lead them to overfeed; the problems were quite separate.[12]

Two standard concerns of the *puériculture* campaign helped develop the rhetoric of regulation, in addition to the overall interest in children's health past infancy. First, the zeal to attack the use of animal milk, save where there was no option, was enhanced when it could be noted that this was one of the sources of later overweight. Too many mothers, freed from the natural constraints of breast supply and perhaps a bit guilty besides, poured too much cow's milk down their children's gullets, creating later problems with fat. Second, and here particularly when breastfeeding had occurred, the issue of weaning came in for much discussion. This was a second point, still in infancy, when patterns of overeating could develop, for children often were encouraged to compensate for the denial of the breast by eating too much of other foods. Even meat, that semisacred staple of French good eating, might be overdone for children, leading later to gout and hardening of the arteries, "provoking obesity" (this from a pamphlet of 1914). Many manuals, directed to parents or for teachers to spread in the schools as ideas of *puériculture* were expanded through the curriculum, offered calorie counters and standard growth charts to help parents know when to let up on their feeding efforts. Several commentators noted, in case parents had missed the point, that children's own appetites were very bad guides; it was scientific calculation that should underlie food supply. Parents should weigh their children regularly — once a week was recommended — again, to be sure that their bodies were neither too little nor too large.[13]

Crucial in this voluminous literature — virtually a routine item — was the insistence on establishing regular meal times and sticking to them without food in the intervals. Most authorities found this desirable even in infancy, but it certainly counted after weaning had occurred. Children should have four meals: breakfast, lunch, *goûter* (snack time), and dinner. These meals must be scheduled; any departure from routine was very bad for children. "One can avoid overfeeding by strictly regulating mealtimes" was a standard theme, with the added injunction of no food between meals — "forbidding any food in the intervals except water (candy, pastry, bread, and so forth)." Some advice expanded from insistence on regular timing to other disciplinary comments: "The child should eat slowly and chew well. He should get used to eating alone, sitting down, at fixed times."[14]

A common pattern of advice developed, along with the insistence on regularity and control, that urged some reallocation of food among the four meals. This was particularly true from the interwar period onward as the diet ideas caught on and (with exceptions for the 1930s to some extent) the abundance of food increased. Breakfasts, it was argued, were often too skimpy; lunches were all right, though some school diets were scored on nutritional grounds; but the *goûter* was often too rich and too close to dinner. Here was where indulgent mothers erred, and the frequency of comment, while doubtless unable to reverse the tendency, surely helped limit the impulse. Some experts even wondered if the *goûter* should not be abolished so that children would be able to eat proper dinners.[15]

Another common target was the pacifier. Some popularizers saw themselves fighting a vicious popular habit, particularly when pacifiers were dipped in liquor. This device would "make your child a miserable being for his whole life, whose weaknesses will be directed by a brain weaker still." (It was not quite clear whether it was the booze or the pacifier most at fault here, but the combination was clearly lethal.) Some French parents were said to warn their children not only against pacifiers, but even against thumb sucking. "I'll cut your thumb off if you keep sucking it."[16]

Many experts counseled against having children eat with adults, at least until the age of five or beyond. Partly this was a matter of general discipline — it was hard to keep children in hand when the whole family was around — but partly it was a matter of restricting appetites. Children should not be tempted by the abundance of the family table or by some of the foods adults ate. Eating separately was desirable "in order to avoid arousing his desires."[17]

A few other themes dotted this extensive popularized literature. Some exercise enthusiasts chimed in with their recommendations as part of raising healthy, slender children (while noting that the subjects usually didn't like the practice). There was some concern by the 1930s about teenagers who ate too little because of the fashions. Augusta Moll-Weiss, a leading authority, commented on girls "obsessed with the shame of being big, fat." Dr. Rocaz joined in, "How many young girls' deaths have contemporary fashions caused!" But even here the balance had to be kept, for other children did overeat: "there are often *gourmands* whose appetites must be restrained and who must especially learn to eat slowly."[18]

On the whole, cautions in *puériculture* about overeating increased during the 1920s and 1930s from turn-of-the-century literature. This obviously followed from the heightened medical and popular attention being given to slenderness, while furthering the movement as well. As *puériculture* yielded to pediatrics after World War II, and certainly by the 1970s, the connections between children's eating and adult obesity were more explicitly noted, as in the United States at the same point. Doctors also were more routinely invoked: if a child seemed headed for obesity, the doctor would adjust his diet "to satisfy hunger while avoiding excessive *embonpoint*." "Our children have more chance of suffering from food excess . . . than from insufficiency"; any obesity was dangerous. "Very obese adults were often fat babies." And the state itself stepped in from 1970 onward by requiring regular weighing of children.

But the basic message was surprisingly persistent. Too much food was bad. Children must learn to discipline their appetites and eating habits, sitting for meals regularly, chewing carefully, expecting adult supervision. In dealing with food, parents should "never yield to the caprices of the child."[19] This was a very different conception of childhood eating from that prevalent in the United States during the same decades, stemming from a less indulgent picture of childhood generally. In addition to the contrast in the basic message, two American staples were simply missing. First, there was no great excitement about underfed children. Infants, yes — this was the target of much of the *puériculture* campaign. And, of course, the manuals urged against too much underweight. But there was no special excitement, and the underweight warnings were always balanced by the cautions, usually wordier and more detailed, against excess in the other direction. The symbolic resonance that children's underweight had in American culture was simply absent here.

And there was little concern about fussy eaters who must be enticed lest they somehow starve themselves. This was, of course, related to the absence of excitement about undernutrition past infancy, but it dovetailed also with the larger disciplinary ideas. Most manuals simply did not bother dealing with the issue. The few that did simply told mothers to let time solve the problem. If a child wouldn't eat one day, starvation would bring him to the table the next, and a day without food was no big deal. The same technique should be applied to particular foods: if a child refused an item, he should be given the same thing the next time: "this is the best way to teach a child to eat everything." "If he doesn't like it, it is because you haven't made him accept it. Be firm, don't yield." Even infants should not be coddled; parents must be careful not to respond to every cry with food. Granted there were some nervous babies, nervous but also "badly raised" *(mal élevés)* said the editorial aside, but they were really asking for extra attention, not food, and they should be kept in their place. Children should be taught to eat everything presented to them "in reasonable quantity"; personal whims and tastes need not be indulged. This maternal teaching "is a service she is rendering them for the rest of their lives."[20]

An advice literature, even with surprisingly consistent themes, is not, of course, family reality. Though aimed at the lower classes — unlike the doctors' diet books of the interwar years, with their references to tailors and couturiers — it is not clear how many families could take the trouble of having young children eat separately, carefully monitored.[21] It is certainly unlikely that all actual parents could be as blasé about fussy eaters as the manuals suggested. Personality variables aside (and some individual parents were clearly more indulgent, or more convinced that plumpness was healthy, than others), there is some evidence that by the 1970s and 1980s, maternal efforts to make sure that children ate enough, especially at breakfast, stepped up. The reason, according to one student of manners, was not nutrition but guilt on the part of French mothers, now working full-time and worried that they were not taking proper care of their offspring. Nevertheless, the clarity of the recommendations, both during the heyday of *puériculture* and later amid contemporary pediatrics, provided little extra encouragement to overfeed children, particularly by indulgence between meals. The contrast with the United States remained striking.[22]

Furthermore, aside from some very recent claims that childhood eating patterns have been changing a bit, the evidence for French distinctiveness in fact, and not just in recommendation, is strong.

The relative French aversion to snacking, compared to American proclivities, is well-known, established by comparative studies during the 1970s and 1980s and probable earlier. It is highly likely that the basis for this restraint rests in the patterns of child rearing, in other words, that the recommendations did coincide with parental practice. Certainly records from French boarding schools suggest restraint. Whether this resulted only from cost considerations (clearly a leading factor in the nineteenth century) or from explicit commitment to eating discipline cannot be determined and, in a sense, does not matter too much. The prestigious French military academy, Saint Cyr, for example, provided 300 grams of meat per day to its upper-class student clientele during the late nineteenth and early twentieth centuries (not counting bone), less than two-thirds of what was available at its American counterpart, West Point. Fat and protein content in other schools where data are available were even more constrained at all grade levels: primary schools offered 100 grams of meat in the main meal; *lycées* (the elite secondary schools), 100 to 200. Quantities changed little from 1850 to 1940. Desserts were only added to the principal school meals in the late nineteenth century, somewhat grudgingly and in restricted amounts. The French simply did not see childhood as a time for great latitude in the range and amounts of foods offered, and this regulatory approach has applied for many decades.[23]

French attitudes to children clearly made the transition to new restraints on eating relatively simple, in principle and often in fact. Assumptions about discipline joined with the desire to make children aesthetically pleasing, in contrast to the American temptation to grant childish innocence an exemption from adult standards. The *puériculture* campaign provided additional specifics and justifications, ultimately relating to concerns about adult overweight, to a wide range of French people. The idea of disciplined eating and the warnings against using food treats as a facile source of childhood comfort could have lifelong implications, just as the popularizers argued. Here was a vital means of translating the new culture into livable reality.

Aesthetics and Morality

Greater discipline in childhood eating relieved, and continues to relieve, the French from some of the compensatory diet rigor that forms such a consistent theme in the modern American experience. There are fewer overweight French teenagers and young adults confronting a decision to conform to rigorous standards for the first time in adulthood. But the differences in the French approach to rigor result also from the basis for weight control itself as it emerged from aesthetic considerations supported by health factors, with morality at most an occasional supplement. The French have been insisting on thinness for decades, but they have not used it so directly as a measurement of character and moral worth as Americans have come to do. The idea that fat people are bad people surfaces only occasionally, in contrast to the frequent accusation that they are ugly. This means that French insistence on conformity, though no less great, is less charged emotionally and less judgmental than the American norms that have developed over the same decades. We can establish this crucial aspect of French style by assessing doctors' characteristic comments since the early twentieth century and then return to the more basic distinction and its tactical implications.

French doctors from the early popularizations of weight consciousness onward professed great concern for reassuring their patients and fat people in general. Trémolières, for example, though patronizing to women in some passages of his 1970s manual, insisted that obese patients not be blamed. Rather, they deserved sympathy — many were victims of the "hard blows of life" — plus encouragement to take responsibility for their own bodies. Gilbert-Dreyfus made the same point that "an obese person should leave your consulting rooms confident and solaced."[24]

This reassuring attitude was compatible with high standards of health. By the 1970s, French weight charts were fully as demanding as American. Thus Trémolières wanted a woman the equivalent of five feet two inches (1.58 meters) in height to weigh 113 pounds, which rested exactly at the midpoint of the Metropolitan Life recommendations in 1959; a five foot ten inch man (1.78 meters) should weight 153 pounds, again right at midpoint. Clearly the expectations and data for health were the same in both countries.[25] And French doctors could, as we have seen, comment on the lazy habits and sheer indulgence of some of the obese, implying some of the same moral strictures that pervaded medical comment in the United States between the 1920s and the 1960s. Rarely they could also psychologize, as in Herschberg's blast against some obese women: "Her own (sexual) frigidity propels her toward oral compensation."[26] But there was no consistent attempt in the French medical literature to probe the mental problems or defects underlying obesity or to urge attention to character flaws. Jacques Moron's 1974 manual told an unusual number of stories about women who grew fat after suffering some misfortune like divorce, but it drew no general conclusions about psychological neediness. Research was conducted, of course, from the 1930s onward, but little of it found its way into the popular manuals. Gilbert-Dreyfus, for example, specifically argued that, while psychology occasionally required attention, it was not involved in most cases of overeating and must not pervade the doctors' approach to their obese patients. Nor was there any major attempt to claim that the obese were in some way at fault or demonstrating bad character. The hortatory tone recurrent in American health manuals was largely absent.[27]

Instead, while pressing for success, French doctors urged the importance of getting patients to like and to trust the practitioners. And they advised against trying to press too hard. Gilbert-Dreyfus said categorically: "I disapprove of famine diets." Herschberg similarly urged sympathy: "[the obese person] already suffers enough from being deprived of his specific desires and tastes." No one should be forced to be endure too much privation. "Slimming does not mean dying of hunger, it means eating differently." Herschberg even argued for allowing some bread in reducing diets, despite the caloric content, because of its symbolic importance. "Being deprived of it is felt deeply as a major frustration, an exemplary punishment." Since no fault was involved, a punitive approach was clearly unwarranted and unproductive. A similar effort to accommodate led some earlier medical advisers to go easy on exercise recommendations because patients, as busy people, would not find it congenial and because too much effort was involved. Francis Heckel in 1920 thus advised against insisting on exercise, along with insisting that successful diets must be moderate and need not involve hunger.[28]

For obese people were not guilty of anything and needed no chastisement. They had a weight problem and needed to change habits in order to address it, but they must not be made to feel culpable. While Gilbert-Dreyfus criticized some colleagues for an "antifat rancor," he was at pains to note that most French doctors shared his indulgent attitude. The tone of French medical presentation thus differed from much of the comparable American literature. This is not to argue that doctors in practice diverged so greatly; there was variety in both countries, and no definite measurement can be ventured. But the cultural context for French physicians was different. The doctors were urged to motivate amid a conciliatory atmosphere, noting the need for willpower but avoiding the implications of sweeping character tests. Their public spokesmen wanted their patients to come back and were quite aware that a critical attitude could drive them straight to the quacks (who were reproved just as firmly in France as in the United States). The medical community may, given French dining traditions, have sympathized with eating problems that flowed from too much enjoyment of good food, even though they had to urge restraint. The effort to enlist the French tradition by citing its most famous representative, Brillat-Savarin, rather than attacking it frontally, suggests this kind of sympathy, as opposed to some of the leading American diet gurus, from Fletcher onward, who sought to curtail the pleasure of eating. Above all, the French doctors who went public simply did not think of the obesity issue in ethical terms. Sharing the same health goals as American doctors, increasingly using the same data, they emphasized different values, sketching a "no-fault" approach in an area that in the United States was fraught with moral overtones.[29]

The same absence of moralizing pervaded the other major sites of French commentary on issues of overweight. Fashion articles from the 1920s onward certainly stressed high standards and obligation. Women "must" get thin; they alone were "responsible" for making sure their bodies looked good. But at the same time, the path to success was clear; there were no complex character issues. No one had to be ugly. Only a "minimum" of willpower was required, and no self-torture was involved. For it was beauty, not moral improvement, that was involved. Fat was disgusting; this is where the demanding standards came in. "Are you fat? This disgrace is visible to the naked eye. If others don't see it, you've noted it yourself by looking in the mirror." But since the issue was aesthetic, there was no barrier to anyone's improvement. The contrast with the American moralistic approach was subtle but definite; if character came into play, everyone would be open to judgment but would require exceptional strength to improve. For the French women's magazines, the diets and aids available to beauty, thanks to modern "science," should make it simple to succeed; a 1933 article entitled "Easy Beauty" summed up the whole approach. Given simplicity, of course, failure was all the more inexcusable, but no one need feel deterred by the magnitude of the task.[30]

Words suggested the French emphasis. French children, like Americans, tossed around some nasty slang terms for fat peers; boys, particularly, might be called "Babar," "Jumbo," "Ten Tons," or "Fat Potato." But this slang literally never appeared in either health or beauty articles dealing with overweight. There was no reason to insult for there was no moral failing involved. Rather, effective neologisms focused on ugly body parts, notably the "*culotte de cheval*" (a term without any common American equivalent as an epithet), for this was where the problem lay. On the positive side, the French titles for the new body culture downplayed the notion of struggle. Words equivalent to reducing or dieting were rarely headlined, while the more purely aesthetic focus of "*maigrir*" ("getting thin") was favored. A neutral reference to physical culture substituted for the growing American concept of "working out." Even the idea of *régime* (diet) could seem too demanding since the point was to elicit willpower without implying compensation for faults; not only was the word rarely used in headings, but some French commentators suggested replacing it with "rationing" or some other more flexible concept.[31]

Popular presentations, in their preference for beauty over character issues and in their emphasis on manageability, resolutely downplayed psychological ingredients just as most doctors did. During the 1950s and early 1960s, when American influence was at its height and enthusiasm for psychological explorations ascending within the United States, there was some interchange. A 1962 manual granted that sometimes an emotional crisis was involved in overweight and once in a while a tyrannical mother might come into play, but these concessions were grudgingly offered. The authors insisted that there was no set pattern, that the main thing was to emphasize sensible dieting and let individuals take it from there. Psychology must not be overdone. "It's obviously important to avoid excesses in this kind of concept, which is applicable only to certain cases of obesity." A 1953 account owed more to psychology. Women were sometimes "desperate eaters" because of problems in marriage, psychological emptiness, or a "frustration complex." The author made frequent and approving reference to American work in this area. But even in this unusual instance, the discussion quickly returned to the validity of willpower as a means of shaking off frustration, regaining mental health, and dieting; indeed, a successful diet might reverse the other problems on its own. Another popularized treatment discussed Hilde Bruch's studies of domineering mothers, explicitly claiming that they were inapplicable to France where the problem was "over-independence, to the point of indiscipline." Of course, excessive weight might involve psychological issues, but for the most part, this was not a fruitful line of inquiry. "I have no reason to think that you [an overweight audience] are psychologically less normal than the psychiatrists who write this stuff." You are not necessarily particularly passive, dependent, or troubled, save that you have a weight problem, which for the sake of beauty and health you must address. And most commentary simply did not raise this line of argument at all, even as American popular literature reveled in the undercurrents. Schooled already to think of fat as an issue to be resolved, not wrapped up in moral failings or wider social dilemmas, the French largely ignored the psychological turn. As long as people knew the difference between beauty and ugliness, realized the health factors involved, and were introduced to the remedies available, the cultural framework was complete.[32]

French disdain for character flaws and their resolute focus on aesthetic over ethical issues helps explain other characteristic qualities in their modern approach to fat. One of the reasons that exercise was less frequently recommended, particularly in the interwar decades, was because struggle against fat had no intrinsic merit since there was no guilt to expiate. French doctors often pointed out how much exercise was needed to burn off the kilos as an argument for their preference for restraint in eating, but an absence of moralizing clearly entered in.

The surprising persistence in the French interest in effortless formulas also followed from this particular version of the modern culture. Because the goals were aesthetic, and given repeated assurances that no tremendous sacrifices should be necessary, French consumers were unusually receptive to commercial shortcuts. To be sure, Americans and French alike provided ready markets for all sorts of reducing gimmicks, from 1900 onward; there was a great deal of explicit overlap. But the most open American interest in belts, lotions, and other tricks of the trade seemed to peak in the interwar decades. After that, the national focus rested on a procession of highly touted diets, involving major changes in eating habits and, often, major reductions in eating enjoyment, often supplemented by physical workouts. The French unquestionably picked up on some diet gimmicks, importing by the 1950s some of the American variants, but their interest was less great. The most common diet advice stressed the variety of foods still available and the pleasure that sensible dining could still provide the palate. At the same time, however, the fascination with facile beauty treatments burned bright. The possibility of surgery was more widely and approvingly discussed. More revealingly still, the revival of interest in reducing creams in the 1970s and its persistence in France to the present day simply had no American equivalent.[33]

Pressed by demanding standards of beauty, but convinced that fat had nothing to do with character, the French quest for a magic formula made perfect cultural sense, particularly when a preference for fine cuisine was added in. There is no clear difference in realism here. American diet approaches involved at least as much hyperbole as did the French quest for beauty. Thus an

American breakfast cereal, recommended over an implicitly more delicious doughnut, will "begin to turn your life around" just as surely as any reducing cream or chrome pill in France. But the characteristic American magic is supposed to involve some definite sacrifice because of the moral issues embedded in fat. Relevant foods are supposed to taste worse (or be oddly surprising when they do not); good food must be bad for the eater. In France, by contrast, there is every reason to be open to a shortcut, given the fact that the dominant culture stresses that good eating can continue at the same time it ignores any need to improve one's character while achieving slenderness. Thus chrome could be advertised as "favoring weight loss with no change in eating or exercise" with none of the sense of moral sidestepping of the sort that would occur, for example, when an American health food is apologetically touted as also tasting good. When the aesthetic issues focused on particular pockets of fat, shaped by the omnipresent cellulite, the attraction of reducing creams was all the more enhanced.

Correspondingly, American diet crazes often seemed absurd to French observers, despite a certain cachet — just as the reducing cream fetish is likely to strike American observers as oddly superstitious. Fad diets were usually held to be too rigorous, requiring too much punishment and denial, and too inflexible. In the French view, after all, eating was supposed to remain a pleasure. American diets like the Scarsdale diet ignored this need (as well as claiming unrealistically quick results): sensible people would "get tired of it quickly." Gilbert-Dreyfus made the more general point in the 1970s that "[t]hirty million Americans follow more or less ridiculous diets launched amid great publicity." A nationalistic reaction to undue American influence surely colored these sentiments, but so did the difference in cultural context. Punitive diets made sense when personal faults must be overcome, but they missed the mark, and might even drive people away, when fighting fat was directed at enhancing beauty and could combine with continuing pleasure in the good tastes life had to offer. A popular culture that embraced American examples of beauty — the stars and supermodels — thus equally firmly rejected the American strain of moralism and self-sacrifice.[34]

The absence of guilt played a role in another intriguing tactical difference between French and American approaches to dealing with fat. The French have been notably less open to group sessions concerning weight, even as these became something of a staple in the American arsenal. Correspondingly, French advertisements for beauty products, from diets to creams, have often been at pains to emphasize their privacy: "no one will know you are taking this." Groups did, of course, form, usually as extensions or imitations of American activities. Weight Watchers, founded in the United States in 1963, spread to France in 1973. It caught on slowly and incompletely. By 1984, there were 800 centers with 30,000 clients, a modest result compared to the millions served across the Atlantic. Specific French analogs, often formed by hospitals, similarly struggled. The Club Diététique of the Saint-Michel Hospital in Paris, for example, encountered substantial resistance before folding in the 1970s. These results followed the general lines of the French-American cultural contrast. There was overlap, and overt American influence, so that differences should not be overemphasized; Weight Watchers did surge a bit in the early 1980s to reach its 1984 figures, even drawing in some men. But the differences remain striking.

French commentary has tended to dismiss group efforts for two reasons. First, the French are individualistic. This is an important claim, as it echoes speculations about national character in a number of historical settings including voluntary political associations, where the French have often been held to be less likely to join organizations than Anglo-Saxons are. The claim, though part of the French self-image, is not necessarily true, and it is not clear that it usefully explains much in the diet field. Americans in recent decades do seem to be more likely than the French to refer to others for approval; when jealous, for example, they characteristically check with friends to see if they are behaving properly, whereas comparably jealous French simply get angry. In this sense, more than in some abstract individualism, the weight groups may indeed be less suited to the French context. The second explanation stresses the unduly rigorous, "childish" rules that most group work involves. Weight Watchers, for example, tried to catechize its

French clients, having them repeat phrases like "far from the hands, far from the eyes, equals far from the mouth." While this injunction highlighted psychological problems less than some other American groups, there was an emphasis on self-improvement and rigor that repelled many potential French members: dieting was a hard job, requiring constant alertness and massive support. Other American organizations that emphasized spiritual deficiencies and the need for rebirth, like Overeaters Anonymous, had no echo in France at all. Beyond this, group work involved public declarations of effort and failure that simply did not mesh well with the larger French culture of slenderness. Where obese people were seen to be fighting moral failings, as in America, they might welcome the chance to parade their guilt and win congratulations for their struggle. When slimming down involved meeting beauty standards, the group reference was less relevant and might even be positively undesirable: who would wish to exhibit disgraceful ugliness more than necessary? [35]

The pillars of the growing French commitment to slenderness thus differed from those underpinning the American struggle against overweight. Both cultures generated tremendous pressure to conform and massive shame at failure. But while many goals and techniques were shared, the divergence between beauty and morality as priorities remained substantial. Americans referred to beauty frequently — this was a major aspect of the often hostile focus on women between 1920 and the 1960s. But they did not rest with a sense that fat was ugly, moving quickly to a moral or psychological judgment; ugliness, in itself, was not sufficient critique. Nor, more positively, was beauty in itself a sufficient goal. Americans, when caught in the diet culture, tended to think of the pleasures that would be authorized once slenderness was achieved: better jobs, better love lives. The French used such references less frequently, for beauty and health would be their own rewards. And they thought in terms of minimizing the sacrifice of pleasure during the process of achieving or maintaining slenderness, for there was no personal demon to exorcise.

Results: Obesity in France

Supporting the characteristic French sense that fighting fat did not require a pitched battle was the insistence that the actual dimensions of the problem were manageable. Individuals might be extremely obese, and certain modern tendencies were worrisome, but the issue at a national level was not out of hand. A more flexible approach, in turn, may have contributed to better results; this was certainly what many French doctors claimed in arguing that American rigor inevitably caused failures, which led to more eating, not less. A diet that was impossibly demanding lured people in with false promises, only to add to their problems when the bubble burst. Culture and reality in France intertwined.

For the French did not gain weight steadily during the twentieth century. Detailed studies of long-term patterns in France are not available and, partly as a result, comparability with the United States must be stated approximately at best. French insurance companies, less troubled with overweight as a health problem, did not publish the same kinds of records that their American counterparts did. With all this, however, it is clear that, when controlled for height, the French have not gained as much weight during the twentieth century as Americans have and that, at least in the past two decades, they have actually lost. Relatedly, rates of outright obesity in France in recent decades have been noticeably lower than those in the United States.

A slight weight increase may have occurred between the mid-nineteenth century and the early twentieth. A study of polytechnical students from the 1840s to the 1950s emphasizes an increase in height above all, while suggesting relatively stable weights. But an early twentieth-century estimate of average male weights by Lenoir at sixty to seventy kilograms for men ages twenty to thirty, though not radically different from A. Quetelet's estimates sixty years before, may have moved up modestly (Quetelet focused on about sixty-five kilograms for twenty-year olds, sixty-six for men at age thirty). Estimates for women were more stable (at fifty to fifty-five kilograms).[36]

The big news during the first two-thirds of the twentieth century, particularly after World War II, was a massive height increase among French men, reflecting substantial changes in health and nutrition. Weight probably increased slightly as well (assuming that Quetelet's nineteenth-century figures are roughly accurate). Thus a man standing 1.72 meters tall weighed about four kilograms more in 1970 than his mid-nineteenth century counterpart, while a woman at 1.58 meters had gained about three kilograms. (These estimates exaggerate the change slightly because of differences in ages involved since the French tended to increase in weight until their fifties, and Quetelet's estimates focused on thirty-year olds.) In rough outline, then, it can be suggested that French patterns of weight gain were similar to American in terms of rates through the 1960s, a function of better nutrition and more sedentary lives.[37]

During the 1970s, however, average French weight, controlled for height, declined absolutely, even as height continued modestly to increase (Table 6). The average French male in 1980 dropped by a fifth of a pound, while the average woman went down a full 2.2 pounds. These patterns seem to have persisted during the decade after 1980 as well. A study of female department stores clerks showed that the majority held their weight steady in the late 1980s, despite increasing age. By 1990, the average French person, though

TABLE 6.

Average Weight (in Kilograms) According to Height

Height (in Centimeters)	Men		Women	
	1970	1980	1970	1980
150	62.0	63.1	53.2	52.4
155			55.7	54.8
160	66.2	65.8	58.2	57.0
165	69.4	69.0	61.0	59.9
170	73.0	72.0	63.8	63.2
175	76.4	75.2	67.4	65.6
180	80.8	79.0	70.4	68.4
185	84.4	82.0		
All heights	72.2	72.1	60.6	59.6
Standard deviation	10.6	10.9	10.8	10.8

SOURCE: Compiled from the materials cited in note 38.

only a bit shorter than his or her American counterpart, weighed about seven kilograms (14.0 pounds) less. Figures on percentage of the population overweight varied, depending on criteria and data, but they uniformly pointed to much lower French rates. Thus one study cited 4.5 percent of French males as obese (defined as 40 percent or more above desired weights), compared to 10.3 percent of Americans, and 8.9 percent of French women, compared to 19.0 percent of Americans.[38]

Clearly, the French culture of weight control was having a demonstrable impact by the 1960s and 1970s, more among women than among men. It took some time for this culture to begin to neutralize other twentieth-century factors pushing toward weight gains, but it did ultimately kick in. The American battle against fat, it should be recalled, could also claim some effect, particularly in the middle and upper classes, in early to midadulthood, with women in these categories more clearly responding than men. But the U.S. achievements were far more limited than the French. Greater internal social diversity, a different involvement of childhood, and possibly the more moralistic and punitive tone of the culture itself combined to differentiate American from French response. The dramatic widening of the gap in the past decade, with American rates soaring while French restraint persisted, also owed something to singularly unsettled conditions in American society, including the growing income stratification beneath the upper class; and it is fair to note that more Americans stopped smoking in this period than did their French counterparts, which may have exacerbated weight gains as well. Nevertheless, the longer term patterns suggest that far more was involved.

Changes in French eating patterns supported the findings on loss of weight. The number of courses in restaurant meals fell back during the 1970s. Caloric consumption, particularly given less intake of bread and potatoes, seems to have fallen even earlier. Snacking, never a major French commitment, was increasingly confined to a small minority.[39]

Different realities, juxtaposed with demanding weight-control cultures, had one other interesting effect by the later twentieth century. Americans by the 1900s were more likely to conceal their weight situation than were the French, at least from outside inquir-ers, possibly from themselves. A comparative attitudinal poll sug-gested that, while the French worried about health far more than Americans, Americans claimed that personal responsibility, as op-posed to chance, was far greater in this area (though both countries produced large majorities who believed that illness can be avoided by a healthy lifestyle). More Americans than French claimed that their society had slimmed down on average — a difference that flew in the face of actual comparative trends. Americans were also far more likely to argue that they had changed health behaviors, decreased egg and meat consumption, and started exercising more. The pattern seemed clear and interestingly paralleled American patterns of concealment concerning reproved emotional outbursts. The need to adjust deeply held beliefs with contradictory behavior prompted prevarication or self-deception in the United States — an ironic testament to the power, though also the limitations, of mod-ern antifat culture. The French interestingly faced a somewhat similar gap concerning smoking, where far more people claimed to have quit than seem to have done so. But where slenderness was concerned, the majority of French people, having genuinely changed behaviors, moved closer to reconciling standards and re-ality.[40]

Mutual Reactions

Implicitly or explicitly, French culture and behavior diverged from American in several crucial areas during the twentieth century, even though some of the most dramatic results appeared only toward the century's end. The French tended to stay away from the American impulse toward crash programs because they interpreted differently both the problems underlying fat and the desirability of moderation and good eating. Their interest in remedies that in-volved less food restraint, however, remained higher. While child-hood eating was more regulated, ideas about guilt and moralistic responses to fat were far less common, whereas the aesthetic stan-dards imposed gained higher priority than in the United States.

Group remedies were less attractive, in part because the need to display moral commitment was minimal. With less involvement with guilt, and with greater control over children's weight, the French approach to slenderness, while rigorous and highly conformist, involved less of a sense of struggle.

For their part, Americans, as the more dominant mass culture, had less occasion to respond to French approaches. After all, French popularizers were motivated partly in a proud desire not to be as silly — as fad-ridden or moralistic — as the transatlantic upstarts, though this merely enhanced differences in national approach. But a window opened briefly in the early 1990s with widespread American news reports about French success in weight control. How could this be, given French passion for rich eating? Some American accounts merely reported the apparent findings, including some belief that red wine improved the management of cholesterol. Beyond the facts, American response seemed, predictably enough, to emphasize considerable denial. The French weren't really much healthier, they just had lower rates of heart disease — look at their greater cancer problems. And they ate more cheese, high in fats, while not getting enough carbohydrates and definitely failing to exercise enough. "Butter and cheese fill French veins, organ meats and goose fat load their tables." The fat facts, in other words, could be obfuscated by a larger reassurance that Americans had little to learn. The important thing was to claim virtue: less cholesterol, more physical activity, and, of course, less smoking and drinking. This claim staked, the objective data mattered less; American cultural concerns, if imperfectly met, had been reasserted.[41]

The tantalizing differences both in culture and behavior had one final impact, also most visible in recent years, as both Americans and French who were obese sought to counteract the dominant standards. American group reactions began far earlier. The National Association to Aid Fat Americans started in 1969, spearheaded by women and designed to rescue the overweight from their isolation and self-loathing. More widely publicized efforts emerged in the 1980s, fighting job discrimination and echoing group consciousness and rights agitation by women, gays, and other population segments. A French reverberation occurred only belatedly. The Association Allegro Fortissimo was founded in 1989, dedicated to opposing discrimination against weight. Members of the group expressed tremendous pain at being cut off from social activity, aware of their own monstrosity. In this sense, French standards were at least as alienating as American to those who did not measure up. But the tardiness and modesty of this French reaction, its clear dependence on American precedent, marked the endeavor as well, which flickered briefly and then returned to obscurity. With fewer obese people, with a culture that, however oppressive, did not directly seek to stipulate moral opprobrium, a liberation movement inevitably faced an uphill battle: it is harder to defend against charges of ugliness than against accusations of character flaws.[42]

In the broadest sense, of course, the evolution of French and American beliefs about weight harbored vital similarities through the twentieth century, and even the striking difference in behaviors should not overshadow this fact. Yet the distinctive approaches were fascinating, and not simply because each side of the Atlantic sought ways to sneer at the patterns of the other side. The distinctions revealed an unexpectedly wide range of differences between two kindred societies, as well as producing, at least for several recent decades, markedly divergent results. Before returning to the commonalties, with both societies trying vigorously to establish novel standards and tactics, a final comparative exercise is essential. Probing the underlying variance between France and the United States shows how a seemingly prosaic aspect of modern behavior, the daily anxieties about weight, touched on characteristics as far afield as politics and art.

9 Atlantic Crisscross: The Franco-American Contrasts

Explaining the differences between French and American approaches in a common cause — the battle against fat — requires some subtlety. Gross contrasts do not work. If the French were attuned more fully to the dictates of fashion, middle- and upper-class Americans certainly followed most of the same trends with considerable interest, diverging mainly after World War II in their more limited tolerance for partial nudity and the body exposure this entailed. While Americans did tend to eat faster than the French, with implications for the amounts consumed and the types of enjoyment and restraint available, French eating time tended to drop in the twentieth century, narrowing the time-at-table gap. The cherished French long lunch began to decline amid the pressures of doing business and commuting. To the surprise of many, fast-food outlets, introduced from the United States, did quite well in France from the 1970s onward; by the 1980s, over 10 percent of French restaurant eating occurred in these settings, whether homegrown or chain imports.[1]

Correspondingly, the fundamental imperatives requiring a new approach to restraint in eating easily crisscrossed the Atlantic. This is why the basic timing of two cultures was identical, with only modest differences in phasing. More sedentary work habits and less walking to work automatically created pressures on amounts consumed. Medical findings and health warnings, increasingly geared to the diseases of later age, pressed both the French and the Americans to watch their diet and their size. The impulse to standardization, which undergirded efforts to conform body sizes, resulted from a shared scientific and industrial pattern, and certainly a similar commercial zeal stood ready in both countries to capitalize on new weight concerns. Shared aesthetic standards, through fashion imports, films, international models, even beauty competitions, pressed for slimmer figures. While beauty contests were an American invention, they quickly drew in Europeans; France sent a contestant to the first Miss Universe competition (Galveston, Texas, 1928) with considerable fanfare and considerable chagrin at her failure to win. Finally, both diet cultures spread from the top down, with lower classes for a long time more preoccupied with simply assuring an adequate food supply, a concern that relaxed gradually and somewhat incompletely. Here was the framework in which both countries moved toward a new anxiety about fat and a new aesthetic for the body in many of the same ways.

The many shared impulses of two societies that were part of the same industrial civilization warn against any simple contrast of national characters. So do the important diversities within each society. The French are not uniformly devoted to moderation — witness their higher rates of cirrhosis of the liver due to excessive alcohol consumption and their surprising disdain for the environmental issues. They also have their own minority of overweight citizens, though it is as we have seen noticeably smaller than its American counterpart. Both societies harbor diversities, though for weight control and eating, they are greater in the United States than in France. Regional as well as class differences in weight control qualify any national generalizations.

Yet the divergences in behavior and cultural tone have been and remain real, and they pose a challenge for comparative analysis. Comparison itself is too rarely ventured in historical study, which means that what can be offered to explain the two cultures of slenderness is also an invitation to further work. We have already invoked some key variations in their approach to childhood. These pick up on the American indulgence for children, noted by foreign observers as early as the first part of the nineteenth century; but we need to explore further the distinctions in food discipline. Differences in medical patterns, though less great, also demand attention. Though the longstanding cultural significance of French doctors has been probed, diet history shows another facet in which French physicians gained influence more quickly then their American counterparts. A comparative historical analysis of health concerns would be welcome. Current polling consistently shows Americans claiming a greater interest in controlling health, but the record on dieting suggests acute awareness on the part of the French, at least about weight.

Two categories, however, created the framework that in turn prompted the more specific patterns that separated French and American bodies and beliefs. Both were rooted in the nineteenth century (if not before) and both extend into our own time. Comparative analysis must not be confined to these categories, but it need not be too diffuse. First, in approaching their own slenderness goals the two countries called on different traditions of dressing and eating, different despite overlap and mutual imitation of each others' traditions. These made achieving slimness more aesthetically pressing in France than in the United States, and also somewhat easier to obtain. Second, differences in the response to some of the issues of modern affluence allowed the French to invest their dieting concerns with less symbolic baggage than was true across the Atlantic, though some symbolism, particularly where women and women's power were concerned, was surely shared. It in exploring this second category that we are taken — with due caution — surprisingly deep into the cultures and even the politics of the two countries.

Clothes and Food

Fashion has been a greater imperative in modern French life than in the United States, at least for women. This is one reason that the French seemed to convert more suddenly to the standards of slenderness, with a wider initial range of commercial ploys, and one of the reasons that they have lived up to the standards more fully over the past several decades. When aesthetics called for slimmer bodies, many of the French felt compelled to respond.

American concern was substantial as well, but obviously somewhat less rigorous. There is admittedly some risk of tautology in this first line of argument: fashion determined more of French behavior in the weight-control area, therefore fashion must have been more culturally important. But it is possible to explore the factor a bit more fully.

The fashion industry became a French staple in the nineteenth century, influencing upper-class styles not only in France itself but throughout the Western world. The industry's success followed from France's historical lead in matters of high culture and from the aesthetic prominence of its aristocracy (even as it faced increasing political attacks). It corresponded to France's ongoing commitment to artisanal production and luxury exports even amid industrialization. The importance of clothing fashions in upper-class life within France itself solidified and intensified during the Second Empire period, from 1850 onward, when a parvenu imperial court tried to legitimize itself by stressing its aristocratic credentials. This was the same period, to be sure, when high fashion increasingly commanded attention in major American cities like New York. But with its styles largely imported, the hold in America was somewhat less fierce. Even words to describe high fashion, like "*chic*," came from the French (where it was itself a rather curious neologism of the nineteenth century, denoting the intensifying commitment to modishness within France).

One measurement of the difference in the commitment to fashion was the place women's styles commanded in intellectual and artistic life. In France, discussions of the latest dress styles and body shapes by 1900 — including the growing commitment to slenderness — formed part of a more general cultural commentary. Writers and poets like Mallarmé and Proust lingered lovingly over issues of fashion. Artists picked up fashion themes and furthered them in turn. Matisse's (admittedly inconsistent) interest in slenderness, plus the Cubists' mechanistic body portrayals, thus played a role in the French turn to slimness, and Surrealist art later contributed as well. The writer Colette penned fashion columns, and other writers like Cocteau maintained the tradition. This kind of interpenetration of fashion with wider intellectual standards occurred in the

United States only after World War II among certain circles in places like New York. In France, the mutual reinforcement of fashion designers and aesthetic commentary both reflected and furthered the impact that styles of dress and body shape could have. It is also possible that visual art plays a greater role in modern French culture generally; and the earlier and more dramatic birthrate reduction in France contributed, as we have seen, to a new rigor in women's styles.[2]

In addition to the greater economic and cultural role of fashion in the modern French tradition, certain distinctions in the valuation of women entered in as well. France, like the United States, experienced an increasing domestic emphasis for women during the nineteenth century. Women were supposed to guide and maintain the home. The importance of marriage increased for women. This trend was enhanced in France by the end of the century by tremendous concern about the nation's population lag, which furthered the emphasis on women as mothers (without reversing the increasingly low birthrate). But the French version of Victorian gender culture did not include the kind of moral apotheosis of women as occurred in Anglo-American middle-class idealism. Women were not held to be distinctively pure. This was one reason that French women had less success than their Anglo-American counterparts in appealing for the right to vote. They were different from men, but without the kind of ethical qualities that would allow them nevertheless to persuade a male constituency of their political utility. (Indeed, to the extent that many of them were actively Catholic, they positively frightened republican males.) In this context, with their economic functions on the whole declining (as in the United States) but without compensation from a new moral mission, the importance of looking good, of living up to the aesthetic demands of fashion, may have counted for more — first, in the upper class, but gradually, as fashion partially democratized, in other groups as well. Putting the contrast simply: American women valued themselves and their family roles for other attributes, viewing fashionability as a slightly more optional item.

Certainly comparative evidence outside the realm of diet per se continues to demonstrate the greater French preoccupation with beauty. French women are less likely than their American counter-parts to agree to disfiguring surgery, such as mastectomies, in the in-terest of health and are considerably more upset about aesthetic im-plications if such surgery occurs. American women who have experienced such operations are more eager to discuss their ordeal, while the French remain more silent, more eager to act as though nothing had happened, particularly in the younger age ranges. Rees-tablishing appearance had higher priority in France than in the United States, where keeping in touch with the doctor was im-portant but networking among female friends played a greater role.[3]

By the later twentieth century, French emphasis on appearance and fashion was heightened in other venues. The French began to place much greater emphasis on leisure. Vacation time, reaching five weeks or more per year for the middle class, greatly outstripped the more stable and modest allocations in the United States. Even in normal work weeks, hours continued to fall in France until 1984 when they stabilized; in the United States, weekly work hours began to rise after 1975. In this context, fashions that highlighted body display on the beach gave the French another reason to compel them to live up to slenderness standards. Americans were certainly attuned to the idea of shaping up for a summer at the beach or poolside, but with less vacation time, the goals may have mattered less.

There was also the greater celebration of nudity in France from the 1970s onward. The same basic sexual revolution hit both France and the United States in the 1960s, including new and widely disseminated forms of pornography. But while some sexual indicators began to tighten in the United States after 1970, includ-ing new restrictions on the availability of nude imagery, France continued to expand bodily displays, particularly female but male as well, in television and advertising. Actual sexual behavior may have differed little, but the open enjoyment of sights varied. This confirmed, though also may in part have resulted from, greater pride in achieving the ideal body shape.[4]

Fashion and slenderness thus reinforced each other in France more than in the United States, despite shared standards and models. The linkage had its origins in nineteenth-century traditions, including class structure, artisanal industry, intellectual life, and gender culture; France was prepared for greater responsiveness to fashion's dictates well before these dictates began to insist on slimness. For a variety of reasons, it mattered more to look good. These priorities have been maintained in the twentieth century, not only by the ongoing role of the great Parisian fashion houses but by new developments, such as a more ardent leisure culture.

Along with the priority of fashion, differences in eating habits, also predating the modern diet culture, have helped shape national responses to the hostility to fat. Somewhat surprisingly, French eating patterns in the nineteenth century were more easily adapted to the new norms of health and fashion than were American. This provides the greatest single reason for the differences in results, the fact that the French come closer to the recommended standards than Americans. Fundamentally, American food culture has tended to outweigh the intense diet emphasis — quite literally — whereas in France, with a different approach to food, the two areas have meshed more harmoniously, despite the decades in the first half of the twentieth century when weight gains outstripped diet pressures. The American clash between eating and slenderness is evident from actual weight trends in the twentieth century, but it gains added significance in the comparative historical contest. And food traditions also help account for the greater emphasis on struggle in the American culture: it is, in fact, more essential to combat the dominant food patterns in there than in France in order even to approximate slenderness.

France began to emphasize a pattern of fashionable upper-class cuisine in the seventeenth century with a growing use of butter in cooking and other changes.[5] This development was enhanced in the later eighteenth century, before the great revolution, by a proliferation of fashionable restaurants. Throughout the early modern centuries, stylish cookbooks gained a wide audience. French leadership in rich cooking rested on some of the same bases as did clothing styles: a wealthy upper class, including the aristocracy, bent on demonstrating cultural superiority and refinement of taste, served by an artisanal sector, in this case the chefs, in an economy where crafts skills retained validity longer than in other Western industrial societies. By the early nineteenth century, various French spokespeople were available to define the stylish approach to food; among them, Brillat-Savarin was an acknowledged leader, his work widely read and reproduced not only at the time but in subsequent decades and into the present. This was at the same point when the leading American commentary on food was work like Sylvester Graham's, in which food was used as a symbol of impurity and a terrain of combat.

The simple fact was that, without at all emphasizing rigorous slenderness, definers of French cuisine created a food culture in which good eating, even sublime eating, was not identified with great quantity. Though not true initially — fashionable seventeenth-century meals were huge — the idea of moderate restraint was beginning to take hold by 1800. By this point, moderation was typically included as an aspect of the discriminatory palate. This unquestionably facilitated the later acceptance of an ethic of restraint. Brillat-Savarin, writing in 1825, defined what would come to seem, with some exaggeration, a classic French approach to good dining. "The fate of nations hinges upon their choices of food. . . . The pleasures of the table are of all times and ages. They go hand in hand with all our other pleasures; outlast them and in the end console us for their loss. . . . The discovery of a new dish does more for the happiness of mankind than the discovery of a star." Or more prosaically: "Dessert without cheese is like a pretty woman with only one eye."[6]

Yet Brillat-Savarin, while extolling rich, high-quality food, made it clear that civilized dining required discipline. Eating must not be done hastily, but in association with good manners and elaborate conversation. Above all, it must combine with moderation. "Victims of indigestion are those who know not how to eat." True taste, or *"gourmandise,"* was "the enemy of excess," the opposite of "gluttony, greed and gross indulgence." The purpose of eating is aesthetic pleasure, not mere filling of the belly. "Let the dishes be few in number, but exquisitely choice." Good dining and cooking became part of a larger experience of beauty. And while Brillat-Savarin was no modern weight watcher, he explicitly wrote of the relationship between his idea of moderation and an appropriate physical form. He constantly struggled against a small paunch of his own — "a redoubtable foe" — and he urged those faced with real obesity that exercise and "discretion in eating" were indispensable habits. Women, particularly, had to keep their weight in check.[7]

This was not, it must be stressed, a modern diet culture. Brillat-Savarin approved of some plumpness, particularly in women. But the idea of combining quality eating and restraint was crucial. It was paralleled by increasing opprobrium attached to the word "*gourmand.*" Originally connoting quantity and quality, even as late as the mid-nineteenth century, the term by 1900 clearly referred to indiscriminate overeating, with both poor taste and excess called to account.[8]

Brillat-Savarin's approach set something of a model for French eating habits — hence the frequent reissue of his book. It was not modern. French standards of the early nineteenth century insisted on a great deal of meat (where Brillat-Savarin liked to economize was with bread or potatoes) and rich sauces. While high quality fruits and vegetables were praised, there was no explicit nutritional interest. Nor, parenthetically, was there much concern for hygiene; the French sage regarded undue concern for cleanliness as antithetical to his ideas of good eating. But there was a style here that stressed the enjoyment of high quality over quantity, in which moderation was not only consistent but actually required.

Obviously, French gourmet standards as defined in the nineteenth century were not a mass phenomenon. The main themes were echoed by many writers. Grimod de la Reynière for a time rivaled Brillat-Savarin as a philosopher of fine dining. His *Almanach des gourmands* was the first fine food periodical. Other authorities wrote of the principles of good eating later in the nineteenth century, while a number of gourmet clubs formed. Gourmet principles, in other words, were far more widely discussed and deeply rooted in France than in the United States, where there simply was no comparable genre until the mid-twentieth century. Always, in this French approach, praise of good food and esteem for a hearty appetite were balanced by warnings about abuses of quantity.[9]

French gourmet principles had concrete results. Banquets in the nineteenth century, though opulent by contemporary standards, were restrained compared to those in Victorian Britain and the United States. Five- to seven-course meals were common, but this menu tended to shrink after 1850 to a more standard soup, entree, fowl, salad, and dessert. A substantial amount of time was required for fine dining. Both features — a restrained number of courses and extensive duration for meals — contrasted with nineteenth-century American practice.[10]

Furthermore, some knowledge of gourmet principles penetrated well beneath the upper classes. Peasants could refer approvingly to their festival fare as attaining gourmet levels — the unwonted variety was described as *"grand gourmand"*. Normal peasant eating, however, was long a more restricted affair. Into the twentieth century, peasants in many parts of France enjoyed little but starch to consume and had to watch their food intake very carefully. Here was diet discipline, but of a different and more severe type. Children who attempted to eat between meals were seriously reprimanded, as in being branded a "liar and thief" by an enraged grandmother, concerned that the family's small allotment of sugar would be taken unfairly. Eating habits on other occasions, even during the special evenings where the peasant community sat down to share work and conversation, were regulated by social pressure; children tempted to overdo their intake from the loaded tables were criticized and learned to obey lest they be excluded the next time. Only at a few celebrations, such as weddings, was normal stringency really relaxed. France had no equivalents of rural Americana's pie-eating contests.[11]

Modern French eating habits were framed, in fact, by two traditions: the peasant concern for caution and regulation amid inadequate supply and the upper-class passion for quality along with an acknowledgment of moderation. Both traditions could blend with the distinctive twentieth-century appeal for slenderness, which had not been an explicit part of either tradition previously. Both traditions certainly helped support the disciplinary approach to childhood eating. From peasant caution came a continued interest in making sure that eating continued to be regulated, that family members not indulge in food outside of mealtimes, which as social occasions, would impose appropriate restraint when eating did occur. The gourmet impulse, even watered down to allow for less refined mass tastes, allowed growing numbers of French people to display their increasing prosperity by buying foods of higher quality, to participate in one of the true joys in life, without in general assuming that massive quantity was also part of good eating. It was not too difficult, in fact, to update the gourmet tradition to accommodate new strictures against fatty foods by such devices as the *"nouvelle cuisine"* of the 1970s, for the principles of beauty and high quality, amid limited portions, were directly translatable. Brillat-Savarin would not have liked *nouvelle cuisine*'s restrictions on red meat, but he would have recognized and easily approved its larger spirit, expressed in artistically arranged plates and a choice of the finest ingredients.[12]

Before the rise of modern weight consciousness, and long before specific responses such as *nouvelle cuisine*, the gourmet and peasant traditions of French eating showed in a number of distinctive habits. Meat portions were characteristically small, as in the later nineteenth century upper-class boarding schools. French butchers in the 1960s, asked to cut meat on a "per person" basis, aimed at 100 grams per portion (savvy American customers would learn routinely to lie about the number of persons involved to get what they regarded as a respectable amount of flesh). However, the French were willing to shell out a larger portion of their household budget to achieve foods of high quality — meats, but also garden produce. The frequency of elaborate meals in French films — a rarity in American movies, where such scenes depicted stiffness rather than pleasure — suggests the important place of the gourmet tradition. This interest in fine foods, and a willingness to pay to get them, has persisted in French dining culture, even as some of the common trappings of Western commercial foods sales — standardized packaging, fast-food outlets — have made headway in France.[13]

Some of the distinctive features of French food culture showed, not surprisingly, when French restaurants began to open in American cities like New York from the 1820s onward (with growing popularity in the 1870s and 1880s). French cuisine was associated with high quality ingredients and elaborate cooking skill — and with a fair amount of time for the act of dining. It was also linked to smaller portions than that to which American upper class was accustomed; the idea of restraint, developed early, showed through clearly in the comparative context. Here was another tradition that persisted. A French visitor in the 1950s, sitting down to his first American meal, noted that "it would serve three people at home."[14]

Other features of the culture have shown up more recently. When Eurodisney opened near Paris, something like American eating habits were largely assumed — yet the French refused to accommodate. In a Disney atmosphere, Americans snack frequently, allowing restaurants to operate throughout the day, expecting a fairly regular, and certainly massive, turnover. The French, in contrast, wanted their own style of dining even as they watched Donald Duck and Mickey Mouse parade by. They wanted good meals at set mealtimes; they wanted wine with their meals (a point that Disney, like MacDonald's before it, quickly had to concede); and they did not plan to treat themselves or their children to lots of munching between times.

American eating traditions, against which all but the most ardent dieters have struggled in the twentieth century, have been different. Neither the gourmet appreciation of costly quality amid restraint nor more severe peasant caution applied. Foreigners usually dismissed the quality of American cooking in the nineteenth century, commenting on its haste and inadequacy; even English observers like Harriett Martineau joined this parade. Constantine Volney, a French critic, found American pastry — a national specialty — "nothing but a greasy paste" thanks to hurried cooking. Brillat-Savarin, interestingly, was an exception during his American stay, for he liked exotic products like turkey. It does seem that in the newly settled society there was little time for careful cooking, though there were doubtless many exceptions. The same commentators, however, uniformly noted the abundance of fare, and they registered the haste with which most Americans liked to eat.[15]

Massive quantity seems to have been an American trait in the largest sense. Of course, there were settings — on the frontier or in urban slums — where it was hard to get enough. But plenty was the rule of the day from the time the Spaniards began to set up shop in Central and South America. (High rates of obesity in Canada suggest a similar disposition toward abundance to the north, while the Hispanic commitment to abundance, particularly in feeding children, contributes to one of the major subcultures within the United States.) The richness of American agricultural resources plus the new animals and crops brought over from Europe combined to generate an amount of food to which neither the Europeans nor the American Indians had been accustomed. Amid difficult conditions in other respects, when it was important to justify to oneself and any European visitors that the new society was a success, it was certainly tempting to exhibit large quantities of food as one of the benefits of the new land. We have seen that the same impulses emerged after 1900 in reactions to reports of immigrant malnutrition. In the United States, people became accustomed to viewing themselves as "people of plenty" in a number of respects, and food continued to be part of the American display. Huge meals were common in the nineteenth century, with many courses offered at banquets (twelve-course meals were not uncommon for the showy rich); sheer volume and ostentation, rather than quality that one could linger over, seemed to predominate. Perhaps most revealingly, the American breakfast set an international standard for amount and variety. New England breakfasts in the 1860s could include pigeon, fish, and oysters, as well as eggs and bacon, often all mixed up in a dish that gave some foreigners pause. To be sure, some medical people, like Benjamin Rush, urged a bit of moderation, but no clear American philosophy of food emerged to dispute the validity of quantity.[16]

Haste in eating suggested a people interested in disposing of quantity with minimal loss of time. Boarding houses were the quintessential American settings for haste, as boarders competed for the dishes set out by eating as quickly as possible so they could come back for more. This was as true among women in the boarding houses of textile centers as among men. Volney saw Americans consume fatty meals by "swallowing almost without chewing." Anthony Trollope noted that even in their homes, Americans "begrudge you a single moment that you sit there neither eating or drinking." Americans at table were devoted eaters, "who proceed through their work with a solid energy that is past all praise." Eating seemed to be regarded as an unfortunate necessity, a distraction from work, so that the only legitimate approach to banish sloth was through haste.[17]

Obviously, individual Americans might display a variety of personal approaches to eating; there is no need to homogenize them entirely. Different ethnic and regional traditions certainly varied the foods involved, and they could affect dining goals and styles as well. But some national impulses did seem to solidify early: quality was not a primary dining goal; quantity was much more accessible and seemingly more desirable; and speed permitted maximum intake with minimum loss of time.

These habits differed from key French traditions, and they set a more difficult context for the modern culture of dieting. They did not necessarily create heavier Americans (due to allowance made for greater average height) in the nineteenth century itself. American work (on larger farms, for example) may have called for more extensive physical exertion, making hearty appetites pay off. But the habits did portend problems when American physical activity declined and when tolerance for a bit of girth waned.

By this point — the 1890s — American eating habits had yielded another troublesome result that would continue to bedevil dieting in the twentieth century in ways the French food tradition largely avoided. Snacks have not, as we have seen, been a major part of French eating habits, whether because they threatened eating discipline and scarce food supplies or risked spoiling the focus on an artistic meal. In the United States, however, snacks between meals initially seem to have testified to the abundance of food of which Americans were so proud. Grocery stores in the nineteenth century kept cracker barrels, free treats that could be given to children, inexpensive pick-me-ups for adults. By the 1890s, this informal pattern began to be commercialized. Big companies like Nabisco began to package crackers and cookies, deliberately pushing their advantages as snacks. Hot chocolate was also widely touted as a food for any time of the day: "The Greatest Invention of the Age, Every Family Should Have It."

By the end of the nineteenth century, snacks were seen as offering a number of advantages besides sheer availability in a land of plenty. They could be carried anywhere, thus meeting Americans' apparent need to eat at irregular intervals. A small packaged cake was touted as a "convenient, palatable and healthful" food that could be packed by "bicyclists, tourists and students." Health and hygiene were other assets: snacks were now carefully wrapped, creating the impression at least of a high degree of sanitation; Nabisco products emphasized the "ceaseless care, absolute cleanliness and new machinery" of the company, plus their standard availability in stores across the nation. And, of course, they met the long-standing American interest in items that could be eaten quickly, without disrupting the pace of other activities. Some snacks were initially advertised as companions to regular desserts — this was characteristic of notices for cookies and wafers until after 1900—but quickly they began to take on a life of their own. By the 1920s, snack foods were being deliberately played up as items to be consumed at odd intervals, particularly by children: "Keep a supply of sunshine biscuits and give them to your children often." "Careful mothers know that is quite safe to give Jell-O to children, even after a substantial meal." By the 1920s and 1930s, Wrigley's gum was being added to the products many Americans had to have to keep their mouths busy during intervals between meals. Frequently fed children needed to keep chewing to feel content.[18]

Obviously, snack foods in the United States were prime candidates for commercial exploitation by the giant food processing companies, who applied the massive advertising and standardized production common to consumer goods of other sorts. But commercial success, while greatly enhancing the range and consumption of snacks, built solidly on preestablished American eating habits, including the desire to introduce children to the abundance of food as part of their enjoyment of a good life and a loving, caring family environment. Snacks also offered another quality that became increasingly important to American eaters during the twentieth century: convenience. As more demands were placed on women in the home and, by the 1950s and 1960s, as workers outside the home, ease of preparation became an increasing goal, meshing often with the even older interest in eating quickly. Women's magazine articles from the 1950s capture the theme clearly: "Slick Kitchen Short Cuts"; "Smart Cooks Cut Corners"; "Call Dinner in Twenty-Nine Minutes"; and "Dinner in a Jiffy."

Omnipresent snacks thus follow from several traditional American food commitments, with commercial pressures added in. The result structures American grocery stores far differently from their European analogs, with rows devoted to cookies and salted fried goods. And it contributes to a pattern of recurrent eating that the more disciplined French approach largely avoids. As one observer put it, "The slightest hint of hunger here instantly provokes a rush to snack. Americans eat all day long, and food is available everywhere. . . . In France . . . pleasure is not immediate; the meals install an economy of pleasure, which again means manipulating hunger, holding off eating in order to eat later with more pleasure and heightened discrimination." [19] With time, of course, the American penchant for snacking developed an additional advantage: snacks could be consumed not only quickly but often secretly, a furtive and very guilty defiance of recognized diet standards. People who were in principle devoted to losing weight, but angered by the deprivation or shamed by their failure, found it easier to sneak food than to indulge more openly in larger meals. Snacking, already being established before the antifat campaign began, thus took on new utility in a perverse interaction with the dominant official culture of slenderness.

The point is clear: Americans placed a number of values on food and eating that easily ran counter to restraint. The commitment to abundance was the most obvious issue, particularly as it spilled over into new habits such as snacking that featured high-calorie items that could easily replace or even exceed the large, nineteenth-century style meals that did begin to decline somewhat. Fast eating and increasing ease of preparation did not as a matter of course lead to weight gains, but they easily could. Neither emphasized moderation as a primary goal and neither featured the kind of eating pleasure that in the French gourmet tradition seemed most compatible with a willingness to hold down total intake for the sake of a savored experience. Finally, American food tradition meshed with an indulgence toward children, resulting in a much more child-driven eating pattern than was acceptable in France. Indeed, where parental discipline was concerned, the American food tradition promoted far more attention to cleaning one's plate, a moral and nutritional responsibility amid abundance, than to restraint. Injunctions to remember the starving children elsewhere made some sense in this context, at least to parents; urgings not to get fat were much rarer.

American eating traditions did, to be sure, include a concern for health. This lay at the root of Sylvester Graham's campaigns for food purity in the nineteenth century. It was picked up in the movement to professionalize the study and practice of dietetics in the early twentieth century, where food composition was carefully dissected and earnest scientists urged balanced meals on the American public. These concerns, along with the commercial pressures of the big food companies, did lead many Americans to a historic change in breakfast habits, toward consumption of cereals rather than the more traditional eggs and meat. This sober approach did nothing, however, to put more fun or intrinsic pleasure in American eating. Cookbooks in the 1920s and 1930s stressed ingredients, vitamin content, and the other trappings of nutritional science rather than taste, and many food advertisements picked up the same tone. The approach could be counterproductive, making foods that were touted as tasting good, like rich desserts, all the more tempting; if people sinned against science, they might well ignore any particular need for restraint, opting whole-hog for recurrent moments of indulgence. It was also true until after World War II that nutritionists seemed to emphasize balance in intake more than moderation.[20]

Unquestionably, however, the American patterns of eating contained some internal tensions that were developed further when juxtaposed to the steady pressure to lose weight. The interest in wholesomeness and the willingness by the twentieth century to judge food in terms of health and the findings of science could be used to introduce new habits more conducive to restraint and moderation. A comparative study (United States, France, Japan, and Britain) reveals Americans most likely to associate food with nutrition, least likely to pair it with good cooking. Yet, from a weight-control standpoint, there were obvious weaknesses in the tradition. The delight in abundance had to war against new diet motives. Commitment to plentiful food as a symbol of national success may have made Americans particularly vulnerable to stories of malnutrition or scarcity. Even though the nation faced far fewer actual shortages in the twentieth century than did war-torn France, the impact of news about underfed children early in the twentieth century and again in the 1950s and 1960s seems to have prompted even prosperous parents to intensify their efforts to make sure their offspring were surrounded by full larders. While middle-class Americans long stressed dinnertime as an occasion for family harmony, associating food with real or imagined values of family togetherness and love, the tendency to hurry and the lack of intrinsic emphasis on savoring quality could encourage high levels of consumption. With adults increasingly joining children in random snacks, chosen above all for convenience and quick relief, Americans translated some of their traditional food interests into other habits that complicated any program of weight control. Small wonder that contemporary Americans believe they are the least healthy eaters (and the French rate themselves highest).[21]

To be sure, Americans had other habits and cultural attributes that could help compensate for their embarrassed continuities in eating. We have seen that they were in some ways more health conscious than the French, more eager to claim personal responsibility for health, and certainly more interested in exercise (or in asserting such interest). Where these intentions carried over into fact, Americans could easily compete with their French counterparts in terms of fitness, even slimness. Overall, however, eating habits predominated over commitments to health and even exercise, partly because many Americans talked a better game than they played. Not only in comparison with the French but juxtaposed to their own lighter past, American advantages in the struggle for slenderness paled before their drawbacks. And the drawbacks centered on what Americans expected while sitting at the table and between sittings, relative to French preferences.

Both French and American traditions of food and eating required modification for an age of slenderness amid increasingly sedentary lives. Both, therefore, continued to promote some real personal and social tensions. French devotion to quality dining, even though modified in the day-to-day eating experience of most French families, could certainly collide with explicit restraints. Here was one reason for the ongoing French interest in deus-ex-machina remedies that would keep or take off weight without the need to deny too many pleasures at the table. We have seen that the French do often place more hopes in creams or pills than do Americans. The American tension, however, was on the whole more challenging, as it called for discipline in a food culture that had emphasized abundance and availability at meals and between them as well. In this tension lay one of the reasons American diet goals more often failed. In this tension, a sense of diet more as combat than a matter of simple restraint easily flourished. The French, with some difficulty and personal variation to be sure, could extend elements of their food traditions to meet the aesthetic demands of slenderness. Americans tended to have to do battle, to put on and take off pounds as they responded alternatively to the attractions of plenty and the calls to discipline.

Neither French nor American food traditions were uniform, of course. We have argued that France built a twentieth-century pattern of eating from a mixture of upper class gourmet goals and selective peasant constraints, transposed into an increasingly urban, prosperous society, particularly after World War II. It remained true that the refinements of expensive dining differed greatly from the ordinary meals of ordinary people. A history of shared and disputed food goals and habits in a France deeply divided by class tensions remains to be written. Nevertheless, the widespread acceptance of weight-control goals in France suggests some common components in the nation's aesthetic and dining culture, in which quality (however interpreted at different socioeconomic levels) eased an embrace of moderation. Only certain immigrant groups after World War II may have defied a national commitment to some degree of restraint, enjoying a demonstration of new prosperity by eating more or using food and attendant weight gains as solace against the tensions of a new environment. Such variety, clearly, was greater in the United States, with several subcultures (building perhaps on the national fascination with abundance) largely ignoring the new body standards. Others, who accepted these standards, actually opened to a rather French-like approach to food. Fascination with French restaurants in the nineteenth century provided the backdrop to ongoing interest in the French dining experience; *Gourmet* magazine, founded in 1941 and directed to the American upper classes, attempted to import the French philosophy of food and, with it, an increasing commitment to restraint amid high quality.[22] France, as we have seen, though open to American models of slenderness, accepted no such definitive pocket of foreign influence for its blend of food and moderation. A distinctive vocabulary for food, shared to some degree across class lines at least by the twentieth century, provided a constructive context for the French reaction to modern goals of weight control. Traditional American impulses toward food, along with more diverse subcultures where ideal body size and eating were concerned, created a more complicated arena in the United States. As one recent study put it, "Americans seem to have the worst of both worry worlds, the greatest worry and the greatest dissatisfaction."[23] In societies increasingly alike, with similar postindustrial urban economies, this difference may actually be expanding at the end of the twentieth century, as the purposes of food continue to generate divergent tensions and divergent evaluations.

The Symbolic Factor: Dieting as Discipline

Differences in eating habits and degrees of national homogeneity explain a great many of the distinctions between France and the United States, particularly in the actual weight trends of the twentieth century, but also in the imagery of moderation as an extension of restraint or a call to struggle. Another category of analysis must be invoked, less to explain the practical impact of diet advice than to probe its moral content. Americans load more values into their diet culture than do the French. Along with the fact that dieting is more difficult for Americans, given their food traditions, this helps explain why the subject is so inescapable in American popular culture and why such intense emotions, including self-loathing and disgust, are often felt. More than the French, who stick to vigorous but largely aesthetic and health criteria, Americans use discussions of dieting as explorations of character and as counterweights to some of the disturbing features of a highly commercialized consumer society. The French, enmeshed in just as much consumerism, at least in recent decades, treat the issue of dieting in a more straightforward fashion, with less hidden meaning. Traditions of food matter little in this second, less tangible facet of the modern culture of weight control. The crucial variable concerns the options available to express widely felt anxieties about meaning in modern life.

Since the increase of consumerism in the late nineteenth century, the French have worried just as much as Americans about corruptions of social and personal values; they may, in fact, have worried more, though the measurement is difficult. But they have had more explicit outlets to voice their concerns, which may ultimately have had the ironic result of making them more comfortable with the consumer society itself. Americans, quite anxious about distortions of purpose in a society where acquisitiveness gains ground and groups such as women alter their goals, have found it more difficult to voice frontal complaints. How can one openly attack the results of higher productivity or more democracy in a society long committed to these gains? Indirection is required, which means an unwitting reliance on symbolism — which has in turn included a deep, otherwise irrational devotion to the imagery of dieting.[24]

Because this aspect of causation is inherently abstract, reaching deeply into characteristics of both societies, it is best to begin with some specific comparisons. Kleptomania provides one rather precise comparative window. The rise of shopping and the creation of department stores with open displays of goods created the phenomenon of widespread shopper theft from the 1870s onward. The issue was quickly noted both in France and the United States. Expert observers on both sides of the Atlantic found the problem fascinating: here were thefts almost exclusively by women, mostly fairly affluent, who seemed to steal because of acquisitive compulsion rather than any real need. Burgeoning psychological experts had a field day assessing the thefts and publicizing their findings. Both French and American department stores responded as well, trying to play down the magnitude of the problem lest they turn away customers, while quietly beefing up security arrangements.

But other aspects of Franco-American commentary differed revealingly. American study of kleptomania was both less elaborate and more focused than French. Indeed, the French sponsored all the fundamental findings. American comment noted rather calmly that some ladies seemed to have a "mania for pretty things"; there was little general editorializing amid a number of anecdotal reports. Women's weakness was not played up, for the people involved were sick and atypical; nor, usually, were businessmen criticized for tempting their victims. The French tone was quite different: "These display case provocations are one of the causes of theft. . . . They are the preparation of an illusion. They fascinate the client, dazzle her with their disturbing exhibition." Modern stores, so the French experts tended to argue, could be called the "apéritifs of crime." They were "devilish," their temptations "better than Satan himself could devise."[25] For French commentators, kleptomania provided a forum, going on into the early twentieth century, to blast the immorality of modern consumerism and its outlets, as well as the sad frailty of women. For their American counterparts, implicitly convinced of the validity of modern commerce and acquisition, the same phenomenon was a finite problem, not an indictment.

During the crucial turn-of-the-century decades, when the cultural reactions to problems of weight were being formed, French critics had a host of opportunities to call the values of modern society into question. Emile Zola and other writers excoriated the lures of department stores. Zola's novel, *Au Bonheur des dames*, stressed the immoral seductiveness of modern shops, whose administrators were evil geniuses deliberately trying to trap hapless women. Middle-class newspapers picked up the same themes. An editorialist in *Figaro,* attacking the "great bazaars" in 1881, noted smugly, "I am one of those who prefers the individual ownership of a pot of flowers" to the growing cornucopia of trivial manufactured goods. Not only the mania for useless things but also the egalitarian tone and the invitation to women to enter new public areas stirred the ire of French traditionalists, who did not hesitate to speak their minds. Reactions of this sort persisted into the 1920s with journalistic attacks on an "age of pleasure," though the focus on consumerism per se became more diffuse.[26]

Rising anti-Semitism was another turn-of-the-century outlet for this kind of attack on modern values. Many anti-Semites blasted big business and the department stores, and while the values and security of small shopkeepers were most clearly in mind, the debate spilled over into general acquisitiveness and social disruption as well. Jewish merchants were among the Svengalis of modern artificiality. Socialism provided its own commentary on the frivolous expenditures of the middle class. A host of conservative writers, not necessarily anti-Semitic, provided even more explicit arguments as a major debate on luxury opened up in France (as in other European countries) in the 1890s. People like Emile Durkheim and Anatole Leroy-Beaulieu agonized over the moral crisis of modern society, in which "we are slaves to our needs." The envy of the masses was invoked, amid fears that they would "rise up against what they call the privileges of the rich." The ugliness of modern products came in for comment on the part of the critics of mass taste and bourgeois philistinism. Various reformers sought to revive artistic crafts and decorative tastes.[27]

Other targets emerged a bit later. Along with attacks on capitalism, on Jews, on debasement of art, and on female weakness and merchant greed, anti-Americanism played a significant role in venting anxieties about modern consumerism after World War I. It was in 1929 that the intellectual Georges Duhamel wrote his *Scènes de la vie future* after a trip to the United States, holding up American materialism as all that was terrifying in the world then taking shape. American mediocrity threatened to eclipse French civilization, imposing "needs and appetites" on humanity, which would demand more and more worthless junk. Not only American life in general but specific manifestations such as new kinds of stores, including chain stores of the dimestore type, drew the ire of French critics, who managed to restrict certain kinds of novel merchandising during the interwar years. The French parliament in 1936 forbade expansion of American-style outlets for a year on grounds that they "fooled" their customers and constituted a foreign intrusion into the virtues of traditional French commerce and taste.[28]

The levels of consumerism taking shape around 1900 caused concern throughout the Western world.[29] It was easy to worry about garishness, social climbing and envy, frivolity, misplaced goals. In France, as in much of Europe, it was also relatively easy to express these worries directly. A culture of increasing political extremes allowed attacks on consumerism from right and from left. Aristocratic and artistic traditions made it easy for intellectuals to blast modern styles in the name of older taste. Lingering social hierarchy facilitated assaults on the leveling, democratizing features of consumerism. Religion — in the case of France, a still-active middle-class Catholicism[30] — provided yet another basis for warnings about the foolish devotion to things.

Americans could be just as worried about consumerism — it is impossible to measure their levels of concern — but they lacked the outlets to say so.[31] Aside from a few blasts against corrupting French tastes (a theme of certain republican stalwarts around 1800) there was no foreign villain because the United States by 1900 was leading the consumer parade. A stunted socialist tradition limited attacks from the left. Trade union activity and strikes were vigorous, but on the whole, they sought a greater share in wealth to enable fuller consumer participation, not an alternative. Earlier Utopian alternatives faded with the collapse of the Knights of Labor well before the turn of the century. Anti-Semitism existed but was less open, and the lack of aristocratic conservatism and societal limits on intellectual snobbery restricted comment from the right. While many Americans privately believed in social class and privilege, American social rhetoric made it much harder to attack lower-class striving; the leveling effects of modern consumerism might be resented, but those resentments were very hard to articulate respectably. This is not to say that there were no open channels in which growing indulgence might be questioned. Populism, in its attacks on capitalists and city ways, provided a brief outlet, particularly for some farmers. Thorsten Veblen wrote his powerful *Theory of the Leisure Class* in 1899, but while it called consumer luxury to task, it focused on the idle rich, not on consumerism in general. If the rich behaved democratically, not too ostentatiously different in their consumerism, as many Americans have recurrently insisted, all would be well. American religion, a very healthy plant, gave many people spiritual supplements to consumerism, but as we have seen, mainstream religion converted to praise of consumer values by the 1870s. Only minority faiths provided real alternatives. Less politicized, less extremist, more openly approving of capitalism and trade, and less elitist, American culture provided far less opportunity than its French counterpart for people to express their nervousness about what modern consumerism represented.

Yet this nervousness existed. Limited in its explicit expression, it tended to seek symbolic outlet and, for many in the middle class, to turn inward to a kind of self-doubt that required a new vehicle for discipline and guilt. A passionate hostility to fat as the image of indulgence helped serve this purpose in a way most French bourgeois, whether critical of consumerism or not, simply did not require.

Different cultural patterns also limited the French need to use dieting as a means of attacking uppity women, though here there was more overlap with American imagery. Women had long held a more equal place in American private life than they did in France, and Victorian culture, stressing the special moral virtues of women, further enhanced female prestige in the United States. In contrast, as we have seen, the absence of comparable moral prestige helps explain why French feminism was more limited, and women-centered arguments counted far less in French than in American suffrage movements and welfare politics in the early twentieth century. American men could certainly criticize women's frailties and follies, but a sense of moral inferiority often limited the charge. It was hard to keep acknowledged angels in the house in their due place. The French, who kept their angels genderless and in heaven, had fewer hesitations in this regard. With women visibly gaining new power in the United States between 1900 and World War II, and with a culture that somewhat inhibited open attack, Americans were again more susceptible than the French to symbolic uses of new weight standards. French women, told less often that they harbored special ethical qualities, needed to feel less concern about their participation in new forms of consumer or sexual behavior, and on the whole they were less criticized by male observers. Their advances in public during the 1920s, for example, were more limited but less apologetic. Dieting in the United States, as we have seen, allowed many women themselves to compensate for a nagging sense that they were betraying the virtues of their sex. Here, clearly, was the primary reason for the greater venom of American commentary on fat women than that characteristic of French fashion discussions.[32]

French diet materials were not devoid of indirect meanings. In France, too, standards were particularly focused on women, who were disproportionately obligated to live up to fashion's dictates and whose new behaviors, including rapidly declining rates of giving birth, unquestionably caused concern. The ambiguities of the interwar culture, in which new fashions were discussed in terms of women's emancipation even as they imposed ever more rigorous limits on what fashionable women could eat, were clear enough in France as in the United States. "Modern civilization" was occasionally called to task in the French diet literature, as we have seen, from early laments about the nervous pressures of modern times to Trémolières's blasts against the unnaturalness of contemporary life in the 1970s. But these comments were unusual, and they lay in the background to the invocation of slenderness; they did not lead to an implicit, American-style insistence on thinness as a compensation for modern sins. Indeed, the emphasis on blamelessness clearly deflected French moralism. Consumer society framed the new French standards by coinciding with greater affluence and abundance, novel styles, and commercial gimmicks; this was clearly shared with the United States and supported the timing of the modern culture on both sides of the Atlantic. But the requirement of moral service as a reaction to consumer indulgence was largely absent. Any needs the French might have felt to express anxieties about modern life they could articulate more directly, even at cost to national political and social harmony.[33]

It is possible, of course, that American diet culture also picked up the age-old puritanism that is so often evoked in discussions of American character. Certainly American religion could generate extremes of self-discipline including fasting and mortifications of the body.[34] It is not totally far-fetched to see in the American approach to fitness a secular version of Calvinist salvation. The saved, in this regime, were those who carefully disciplined their eating and worked out, their fat-free muscles gleaming the superiority of the diet saints over the flabby damned. France, in this rendering, was content with a more Catholic appeal to the whole population, ready to join in sensible eating with no special heroics. Further, religion generally had declined far more in France than the United States, removing some sanctions for guilt. But the French Catholic tradition, particularly in its Jansenist phase, had harbored abundant sources of personal guilt and often encouraged phases of food deprivation and other self-punishments. The French interest in periodic sessions at a health spa, where normal eating was suspended in favor of extreme rigor, may indeed have evoked this religious heritage in modern guise — and here the French may have surpassed Americans in their willingness to alternate normal routine with recurrent self-denial. Their different religious heritage may still be involved in Americans' particular need for guilt, but the conclusion is not clear. A secularized religious input into both weight-control cultures is the more salient point. If a latter-day puritan ethic in the admittedly less secular United States can be added to the charge, it is not a free-floating ingredient. It operated in the context of a growth in consumer indulgence that Americans had trouble addressing directly, in contrast to French reactions that carried equal moral freight but could be separated from the slenderness baggage. One of the key reasons Americans worry so much about food, despite some conscious attempts to eat healthily, is they are seeking a very elusive higher virtue; the French are simply more complacent.

Conclusion

Two striking differences thus provided the distinctive contexts for modern weight-control efforts in France and the United States, reflecting fascinating and deep-seated divergences between two kindred societies. The first difference involved the ongoing impact of traditional patterns of eating and the satisfactions sought from food. The United States, a land of considerable private excess and impatience — including an impatience in waiting for food — needed a diet culture also prone to excess simply to compensate; and even then a gap between intent and result widened. The American fascination with salvation stories where grossly obese people achieved striking slenderness — the diet equivalent of sinners redeemed — was one measure of the moralistic approach in a land of plenty; it had no equivalent in popular French diet advice, where even temporary obesity would be visually unpleasant. The French, whatever their other faults, could operate within a more consistent band of moderation. The same differences in ethical overkill would show up from the 1970s onward in the tenor of later campaigns against smoking, with Americans again displaying a startling fervor.

The second difference followed from a common need for ethical ballast in an age where traditional limitations on material acquisition and traditional boundaries among social groups and between men and women were increasingly eroding. The French had a host of opportunities for public comment and political action. They did not need to imbue diets and restrictions on eating with strong moral overtones for they could express any larger discomforts they felt fairly openly. And, in any event, they saw more modern issues as social rather than individual. Not so many Americans. Here, as in other aspects of life, the limits on political vigor and acceptable social commentary in U.S. culture pushed tensions to the individual level. Here perhaps a puritan residue did persist, though updated through a middle-class rhetoric of achievement and fault. American culture liked to highlight personal responsibility over social failings, and the intensity of personal diet strictures was a daily reminder of this preference. It was up to each person to demonstrate some commitment to discipline and restraint, or to feel guilt in its absence, in order to justify the kind of acquisitive society that was opening up. Just as middle-class Americans tended to agree that there were few social barriers to achievement, merely individual problems of character and worth, so they created a hostility to fat designed to engender a new area of personal moral responsibility and self-doubt. Although they were less successful than the French in actually keeping weight off, Americans were a good bit tougher on themselves as they set goals and ruefully evaluated their shortcomings. Because of the moral service that their version of dieting performed, they needed to be. And this aspect of American dieting tended to persist. In France, after decades of adverse political and intellectual comment on the consumer society, a certain ethical acceptance set in by the 1960s and 1970s. Critics of consumerism remained, but the big disputes had been faced and seemingly resolved. Because the American debate was less open, more symbolic, it tended to fester. The need for some real moral discomfort persisted.

The two basic components that shaped particular directions for a common pressure to slenderize produced an obviously difficult combination in the United States. Committed to food abundance, Americans also sought moral solace in restraint. It was virtually impossible to achieve both goals, which is why so many Americans failed and why so many worried and obsessed as a result. French components, partly as a matter of luck — no one, after all, could in the past design the food traditions with modern diet needs in mind — blended more readily. Obsession, worry, and shame existed in France as well, but they were more limited in scope.

One final point, essential to any binary comparative analysis. Both France and the United States present some distinctive anomalies in the modern history of eating and dieting. The French philosophical passion for food finds no full match elsewhere in the Western world, while American moralism in personal habits seems durably distinctive. Neither society, in other words, is a clearly "typical" Western case. Yet, on balance, while urging fuller comparative study (in what turns to be a revealing as well as significant area of contemporary behavior), the United States stands out.

While British eating traditions have some important links with those in the United States (as in the abundant banquets served to the Victorian upper classes or high per capita sugar consumption), contemporary Britain's obesity rate is only slightly above that of France. Europeans generally cluster around fairly substantial spending on good quality foods, despite national variations in cooking patterns; they also seem to have been able to vent concerns about modern consumerism fairly directly, without requiring the diet field as an arena for moral combat. For better or for worse, Americans have developed some special tensions over food as they consume heartily and battle the results.

10 Conclusion: The Fat's in the Fire

Keeping to a diet is a serious component of modern culture and a major innovation in the panoply of personal concerns and commitments. The standards carry deep social roots as well as individual constraints, as weight control adds to but also reflects major features of modern life. The meanings of modern hostility to fat are particularly complex in the United States, but they run well beneath the surface in France as well. In both countries, anxieties about weight provide an essential balance to other modern trends; simply holding the line amid growing affluence, aging, and declining physical exertion requires a decisive new cultural statement. But dieting is fascinating beyond its role as a daily constraint because of what it may say about other moral uncertainties in modern life, because of its redefinition and standardization of physical beauty, and because of its symbolic testimony to good character and personal discipline. The religious analogy risks overuse for a secular age, but in this case it is real: a commitment to dieting (even without full success) can be a moral statement at a time when more conventional statements have less meaning.

In previous chapters, we have traced the formation of a pervasive new Western code, albeit with variant statements in the two nations we have examined. The code is still tentative, though it is invested not only with rational arguments but with the feelings of disgust for deviation that provide emotional underpinnings for fundamental social regulations. Many people have yet to live up to the code, and some of them may yet reject it — even in France. The tension between widely accepted standards and incomplete achievement is very real. It is conceivable that the code will be increasingly dismissed, replaced by a new tolerance and an admission that fat, too, can be beautiful. Recent American weight trends have been accompanied by pleas to drop the whole campaign. Even in France, reports of greater leniency in the feeding of children raise the prospect that other values (in this case, a desire to build new bonds with children, given the erosion of traditional parenting) could begin to undermine what seem otherwise to be widely accepted aesthetic standards. History, in this area, remains in process.

As a new code, whether primarily moral or more purely aesthetic, the modern culture of slenderness, perhaps by the 1920s and certainly since World War II, has definitely produced one of the inevitable by-products of intense standards: the creation of a new group of stigmatized, almost deviant people who for whatever reason fail to live up to the code. This is as true in France as in the United States, though the numbers are different. Shame, isolation, avoidance of public attention and even of mirrors — these developments, tragic for the people involved, mark the success of the new culture in creating a new dividing line in modern society. In this sense, the modern culture of slenderness, although not yet fully accepted, bids fair to join other standards that we internalize more automatically and that teach us that some people, in failing to measure up, are deficient as human beings.

The slenderness code, in what is still a formative period, also continues to carry social connotations, particularly in the United States. This culture began in the upper classes in France and America. Because the new standards derived from new fashions and from doctors particularly involved with treating various segments of the middle classes, they caught on most quickly with this group, which was also the group grappling with compensations for unwonted consumer indulgences and alterations in the roles of women. Active dissemination has occurred. It remains true that slenderness makes most sense for groups involved in the service economy, where self-presentation is a crucial ingredient of professional success. Lower-class participation in the culture occurs, but it lags, with pockets of active resistance. By the same token, fat can be an ingredient in social judgments, including work access; in societies facing new job competition in a period of economic dislocation, the fat can be locked out.

In this pattern, the slenderness standards constitute a dramatic extension of a process of bodily discipline that began in Western society in the seventeenth and eighteenth centuries. The process, first fully described by Norbert Elias in his theory of "civilized" restraints, initially applied primarily to outward manifestations of the body: gestures (including motions in eating), spitting, and toilet habits. It long helped the upper classes to refine and define themselves, while simultaneously pressing the lower classes to join in and criticizing them for lagging. One reason for the new attention to weight around 1900 may well have been a new need to define some other corporal goal that would again distinguish truly restrained people from cruder inferiors. Thus Elias's civilizing process began to apply not simply to movements but to basic shape and appearance.

Both in its larger historical context and as a response to the specific issues of advanced industrial societies, the antifat culture remains a substantial modern development, despite its drawbacks and incomplete adherence. It has changed the way most modern people judge beauty and character, and it has changed the way many people eat. In a broad sense, the widespread acceptance of this culture is part of a longer-term standardization of the human body as well as the acceptance of constraints over spontaneous bodily impulses. These processes began in the area of mechanistic body imagery and with novel manners at least as early as the eighteenth century. The insistence on fairly uniform slenderness, duly noted in fixed clothing sizes and weight charts, applies these processes to fat, forcing people to look at their bodies from the outside rather than, in more traditional fashion, attending to impulses from within. At the same time, though most thoroughly in France, the body changed from being an instrument of work to an agency of expression; expectations of beauty and of wellness shifted dramatically in this process. For all their important differences, French and American versions of the new code participated strongly in these basic shifts.[1]

This point needs particular emphasis because of several recently proclaimed studies contending that standards of beauty are essentially the same the world over and, by implication, timeless. We live in a period of great debate between those scientistic heirs of Enlightenment uniformities who believe that cultural differences aren't worth worrying about as they purport to show that people are people and those scholars (sometimes unduly defensive, sometimes jargon ridden and extremist) who conclude that culture counts. In the beauty field, recent research has concluded that people around the world pick the same kinds of faces and, to an extent, the same kinds of bodies as beautiful; the argument is that choices of this sort reflect evolutionary pressures to select sexually and reproductively desirable mates. Up to a point, perhaps. But beauty standards do change — even the recent studies suggest this, in showing how a very slender female form is rated among the top three types, far higher than it would have been in the nineteenth century (and moderate obesity is more roundly condemned). More important, the level of significance attached to beauty in assessments of others and of self definitely changes, for example, between cultures where mate selection is largely left to young people themselves as opposed those that assign choice to adult decision makers. This is where modern Western youth has upped the ante. The weight issue has been central to this process, with a combination of new and more slender body ideals and massive intensification of the criteria attached to body aesthetics and their symbolic implications. Culture does count, a great deal.[2]

The history of dieting thus reveals the power of beliefs under the spur of change. A shifting culture set new standards for body shape. This culture was caused by a variety of factors, including some social-psychological needs. Once formed, it recast what people thought they should look like, how they should judge themselves and others, how they should eat — though here the new culture could clash with other norms and habits. The culture of weight control gained momentum of its own, winning greater acceptance and assuming greater rigor with the passage of time and ardent preachments of assorted experts, pitchmen, and fashion gurus. The result over the course of a century was a significant change in people's worries, self-criticisms, and daily habits. From its beginnings onward, the heart of modern dieting rested in the realm of perceptions and values.

The cultural foundations for dieting are both surprising and anticipated. Modern Americans or French know when they diet or worry about weight that they are trying to obey styles and norms, so they are conscious of fitting a cultural image. But culture runs deeper. It explains why in little more than a century Westerners have become transfixed by slenderness — why "slender" is the most common descriptor in "love wanted" advertisements in the United States, for example. Only culture can explain why modern passions are so deeply engaged, reinforcing aesthetic preferences and motivating real disgust about fat, including the disgust Europeans claim about the shocking obesity they see when they visit the United States or the way the French stare at a seriously obese person in a public place. Modern Westerners use dieting not just as a personal decision about how to look and be healthy, though it is that, but to address some larger tensions in the relationship between individuals and an indulgent society.

In both France and the United States, the implementation of dieting has been associated with a rhetoric of emancipation. Twentieth-century consumers, especially those most successful in keeping up with changing fashions, like to tout their freedom from traditional constraints. Weight control can permit greater physical agility into middle age and beyond, and with it, a real freedom in this active sense. The rhetoric of emancipation was also true in a deeper, psychocultural sense; you could feel free to participate in modern hedonism if you paid your dues by restraint in eating. Here again, the analogy to religion is striking, for in religion, too, many people feel liberated by practices that any outsider would find confining. The hostility to fat counters freedom in crucial respects. It stands out as a new constraint, real and symbolic alike, a dramatic contrast in an age of growing material and sexual indulgence. In France, even more than the United States, we are dealing with a socially compelled, conformist regulation of striking proportions, all the greater in that many of its targets blithely assume their independence and self-determination.

Weight control is not the only aspect of modern culture harboring some misleading claims of freedom. Concerning emotions, contemporary standards, particularly in the United States, frequently trumpet a triumph over older repression while actually insisting on quite rigid if informal control over expressions such as anger or jealousy.[3] Indeed, the origins of the new approach to weight control overlap with modern emotional culture (and with other innovations, such as a more rigid rejection of homosexuality), forming something of an amalgam in which genuine openness (for example, to new acquisitiveness or to new sexual pleasure) was carefully if quietly and deceptively balanced by new constraints. As we have seen, the intensities devoted to the attack on fat were central to this counterbalancing strategy.

At this point, many in the small band of diet critics, particularly in the United States but also in France, jump in with a plea for greater latitude, even a lifting of the yoke.[4] They argue that dieting is so obviously cultural constructed, and for motives designed to make people feel bad about themselves or to undermine women's emancipation, that the tyranny must end. Certainly the diet culture can be pushed to extremes. When a person just recovering from major depression or an operation, nearly emaciated from the process, regularly receives praise for how good he looks — the assumption being that if you're slender, everything else must be all right — there is something amiss with our standards. The deviant downside of the diet standards, encouraging starvation tactics on the part of anorexics and bulimics, is familiar enough. So is our unwarranted hostility, even outright cruelty, to the obese. Surely we would be better off if we could jettison this anomaly of modern culture.

This conclusion merits attention, and it enhances the tentativeness we noted early on, but it is not my own. In the first place, the culture is so deeply rooted, for so many complex reasons, that mere talk about a brave, new, fatter world is not likely to have much impact. More important, all societies have constraints as part of setting agreed-upon standards and means of mutual identification. In a real sense, if we did not have weight control as a standard — particularly given our need to identify signs of good character amid the host of strangers we deal with as colleagues, customers, students, and neighbors — we would have to invent something else. But this is not to say that the attacks on overweight do not warrant review, even aside from the nastiness toward the obese. Medical experts themselves now debate in the United States whether we are best served by the most demanding weight tables or whether a bit more tolerance would better promote health, yielding among other things fewer fluctuations from the end of the individuals' diet to their regaining of weight. (A French sociologist has recently raised the same point.) In the United States particularly, the personal doubts and insecurities engendered by a demanding but often ineffective set of standards can also seem counterproductive, though we have seen that this self-criticism is a vital part of the culture as it now stands. It also seems probable that the sheer cultural fascination with obesity and the moral connotations attached encourage sloppy science. It is so easy for science publicists to find an audience with any weight proclamation that the need to refine research techniques and reduce disagreement is easily bypassed. Quarrels about the mortality results of moderate overweight (renewed in September 1995, when a Harvard report urged the benefits of underweight, to be matched by a Cornell study that asserted no harm from greater leniency, and unresolved as each side claimed superior science) leave the public bemused and possibly anxious. Reduced cultural intensity might improve technical reporting. The point is not, certainly, to hold the current culture of weight control immune from evaluation. It remains important to note that the mere fact that it constrains many modern Westerners or that it complicates dispassionate research is hardly a unique or intrinsically reprehensible social result.

Further, the culture directed against fat is not just a belief system; it also rests on real scientific evidence about what body contours are most conducive to health. While admiring subcultures that have managed to defy all the pressures of conformity in maintaining their confidence in corpulence, the fact is that the members of these same subcultures have shorter than average life expectancies. To be sure, longevity is itself a cultural goal, which I guess I share; it would be possible to argue that authorization to eat freely and enjoy diverse body types is a more important purpose. The main point here is to acknowledge that no enthusiasm for freeing modern society from the shackles of dieting should be allowed to ignore the mortality consequences or to imply that a social order can exist without constraints.

For one of the most interesting points about the modern culture of weight control is its subtle intertwining of science and constructed beliefs. There is no question that many doctors and researchers, for a century now, have become more excited about fat than the data warrant, with no awareness of their excesses. Sharing the general cultural preferences, they have assumed an importance for their goal that goes beyond the facts. True, weight reduction properly and permanently achieved helps health, but not necessarily all that much. We have yet to get as excited about other subtle killers like summer tanning or highway speeding. Speeding is an area where the dominant culture largely brushes aside scientific evidence; it's more important to drive fast than to maximize life. In the United States, current pressures push for higher speed limits despite incontestable evidence that more deaths will result; estimates suggest a 20 percent increase in mortality when speed limits jump from fifty-five to sixty-five miles per hour. Tanning, its mortality impact more subtle, offers significant scientific testimony but in a cultural context in which people vary in their response and refuse to join a moral crusade. In both cases, the contrast to obesity is fascinating, where culture helped create the scientific concern, sustains exaggerated scientific warnings, and elevates medical findings as moral guidelines. Culture further lends an aura of science to claims of the equivalence between fat and psychological disorder, with doctors easily racing past their own evidence.

Clearly, while the scientific warnings about fat are quite legitimate, they are culturally selected and, because of culture, overemphasized. Shared beliefs allow doctors and publicists to highlight correlations between excess weight and heightened mortality, sometimes with dubious precision and inflated statistics, correctly assuming that the public, well schooled in the evils of fat, will not dissent. The contrast with the long debate — now admittedly ended — over the validity of statistics on smoking and mortality is revealing; for here there was extended dispute between experts and a skeptical, sometimes addicted public. Where modern fat is concerned, we are not dealing with fully objective realities save insofar as deeply held beliefs and norms constitute realities of their own, and the public capacity to evaluate expertise is diminished as a result. It is also important to emphasize, given recent research on "obesity genes" in mammals and some anticipations of genetic cures, that the cause of increased twentieth-century fat, as well as the sources of the standards that lead to this genetic research, rest in what we believe about food, health, and bodies; genetics explains at most why some individual variations occur. Genetics may ultimately provide some remedies, but it does not account for why we collectively need them and even less for why we want them. Indeed, American enthusiasm for genetics reflect the moral pressure dieting and other restraints involve because it promises exculpation from blame. Genes, not character flaws, can be invoked, however ahistorical this explanation may be; hence, considerable public enthusiasm for this oversimple explanatory device.[5] But if greater palliatives develop, and we embrace them, as well—what new area of discipline will we need to invent?

We worry about weight because we hope to exercise greater control over our personal health and future, but also because of widespread aesthetic norms held by modern media, employers, friends, and potential sexual partners. We hold these norms, in turn, not only because we encounter them so frequently and give them exaggerated scientific status, which is certainly true, but because we have bought into their symbolic content: we need demonstrations of discipline and restraint in a society where greater license largely prevails. We can recognize the extraneous baggage we bring to this culture, but this does make the need any less real.

Understanding is, nevertheless, a key goal. We may continue to participate in the diet culture, priding ourselves on our restraint or lamenting our below-par, flabby bodies. I know I, a child of the culture, will do one or the other for the rest of my life for health reasons but also for culturally compelled self-respect. Hopefully, we can at least participate with an awareness of the historical enterprise we've engaged in. This may make us no less assiduous or self-critical, but it can provide a bit of perspective; it helps, in some ultimate sense, to be alert to the prisons we create for ourselves, even if we stay in jail. But the injunction of understanding may press further. Without jettisoning either the sound medical reasons for watching weight or even some of the larger moral qualities we seek to achieve through a commitment to dieting, we might be able to modify the culture to allow it to work more effectively. Here is where the combination of historical probing, explaining how American standards came to be as they are, and the comparison with France can be put to work.

Our own diet past raises several warning flags: we have sometimes attempted undue rigor, both in the general standards issued by public agencies and in the stratagems individuals employ. Too much diet heroism — reflecting a compulsive need to live up to demanding, youthful standards as well as a desire to prove moral worth in an age of indulgence — may not work, leading to disappointments and a kind of self-denigration that, while virtuous, may not be productive. Americans, as we have seen, because of their own complex, largely unrecognized cultural history, are particularly prone to grandiose campaigns that lead at best to temporary success, at worst to a sense of powerlessness and compensatory eating.

The weakness of the American approach to dieting has been particularly evident during the past decade. A strong culture that is contradicted by actual behavior makes for some agonizing social issues and self-judgments. With no official relaxation of standards, save for a bit of commentary on the rights of obese people and the possibility that different individuals may legitimately — naturally, and indeed genetically — have different weight potentials, Americans have become heavier. Their increased eating occurs amid full recognition, except in a few subcultures, that the slenderness standards remain valid. It occurs because the pressure to seek solace and satisfaction in abundant food — another cultural tradition — has become ascendant, particularly for the massive, aging baby boom cohort that adds pounds with years. It occurs also because the moral compass of American diet culture has been diverted. For the last two decades, middle-class Americans have seen their living standards stagnate and their hours of work rise. In this context, dieting makes less sense, work itself is penalty enough. There are no new consumer orgies that require moral compensation; the problem is that our consumer hopes are being disappointed. With less leisure available, the temptation becomes irresistibly great to enliven work with some of our ubiquitous

American snacks, providing comforting assurance that food, at least, is still available. Eating quickly, another tradition, provides a sense of release without loss of work time because haste supersedes restraint as the primary goal. Precisely because American diet culture rests on such complex underpinnings, apart from the apparent criteria of looks and health, it is vulnerable to larger disruptions in the national saga.

The French function better in this area, again for historical reasons. Their emphasis on aesthetic norms rather than a need to pay for life in consumer paradise has enabled them to approach weight-control standards in a less convoluted fashion. Their commitments have, as a result, varied less with economic oscillations; despite an aging population and some economic setbacks of their own, including high unemployment rates, the French report no recent significant increases in average weight.

There is danger, of course, in a book directed in part to an American audience, in touting foreign example too loudly. There are many things that the French don't do as well as Americans do; while I have always admired French culture, it certainly has both historic and contemporary blind spots. While more controlled in eating, the French have been less so in alcohol consumption and smoking, despite some recent rate reductions. But it is not true to see one excess in one nation neatly corresponding to another excess in another, as if there were a set amount of self-restraint available with only trivial choices of target differentiating various areas. French smoking does not primarily account for greater success in weight control, any more than Americans' greater withdrawal from smoking primarily explains the weight gains of the past fifteen years, though the factor does enter in. Correspondingly, French health, despite some of their distinctive problems, is better than American, and weight control has a great deal to do with this. To be sure, even in the weight-control area, the French approach prompts some remarkably silly statements and a troubling reliance on commercial remedies of dubious quality. Americans in this respect may be a bit more realistic, less likely to jump for the latest cream or machine and assume that all will be well. And at the level of standards, the French commitment to beauty —

the main motivation to diet — can smack of a rather shallow vanity.

Nevertheless, because of a historically determined approach to eating and an ability to deal with some of the moral dilemmas of modern society by open discussion and even political action, the French have developed a restraint toward food that is more effective and less obscurely punitive than its American counterpart. Their success, defined in terms of actual weight patterns but also a less agonized involvement with diets and self-criticism, suggests some possible modifications in the American approach. It would be fatuous simply to say that Americans should copy the French, even aside from our distressing national aversion to learning from others. The very cultural forces that have shaped the American approach and its deficiencies cannot be quickly or fully reversed. Merely because the French on the whole don't snack doesn't mean that Americans collectively can stop. Yet there are ways in which ingredients already operating in the United States could be furthered in light of the French model.

Certainly an extension of that American subculture, still largely upper class, that seeks a French-like appreciation for food in which quality replaces quantity and in which less rushing allows more considered eating — a sophisticated counterpart to Fletcherized chewing — might help a lot. We might benefit, as a philosopher has recently argued, from rekindling our appreciation of the place of good food and good meals in a civilized life — and have an easier time with our weight in the process.[6] Other French lessons are more prosaic. More rigorous discipline over snacks, starting with childhood, is advice often given by American diet experts. Its instantiation in French eating patterns adds support — with a reconsideration of eating goals, the game could be won. To be sure, American eating habits, like their cultural reliance on dieting as a moral statement, are deeply rooted. We have explored these roots in showing why the weight-control campaigns have operated as they have for the past century. Cultures do not change easily, and Americans may be rather comfortable with their strange mixture of rigorous self-assessment and lax enforcement. It would be historically misleading to suggest that current standards could be undone overnight, even if we could agree that they should be;

deep beliefs do not shift so readily. Still, knowledge that another pattern actually exists and works may be useful. It is also worth remembering that our own culture in this area is only a century old; as it was once shaped (just a few generations ago), it could be reshaped. Taking the opportunity to ponder how historical perspective and comparison conjoin to promote some rethinking of a cherished American commitment might generate some midcourse adjustments.

A few larger suggestions emerge as well. The American focus on dieting relates to a national preference for making political issues personal. Perhaps today, in a more politicized atmosphere, we can see more clearly how concerns about consumer excess or other aspects of modern indulgence deserve political debate, not merely personal grappling. The results, interestingly, would provide grist for conservatives, more openly concerned about national morality, but also for liberals, who worry that we displace too many social issues onto judgments of individual character and responsibility. The social class and race implications of American dieting merit attention as well, as they contrast with a more homogeneous French culture in this area. In a society that likes to discuss equal opportunity and resists class labels, the United States has used dieting as a marker among groups; middle-class people judge more obese inferiors wanting, while certain subcultures use girth to express defiance of the standards of a hostile mainstream. Clearly, more effective approaches to weight control require more explicit confrontation with deep divisions in our society, though this, at the current political moment, seems difficult to contemplate.

The modern culture of weight control is at once the product of some general changes in advanced industrial societies and a marker of distinct national characteristics. The changes are unlikely to go away: work becomes ever more sedentary and the abundance of food hardly diminishes, even as other economic uncertainties cloud the horizon. This book has covered the first, inevitably complex century of what will probably prove a durable set of constraints, in which modern people try to control their weights amid unprecedented opportunities to let themselves go. This formative period has also facilitated the combination of dieting with a host of other concerns: about beauty, about women's place, about morality. Here, different groups and, broadly speaking, different nations have produced distinctive amalgams, allowing basically similar standards to serve quite different needs beyond the imperative of physical slimness. At least during the past century, though in varying ways, weight worries have provided a challenge to personal discipline whose validity consists in countering some of the other impulses of modern society. While we can serve our weight control purposes better than in the recent past, the need for self-scrutiny and surrogate morality must not be taken lightly. Whether it tests our resolve or releases us for other pleasures, the insistence on one inescapable restraint usefully complicates the experience of modern life.

NOTES

NOTES TO THE PREFACE

1. Richard Klein, "Big Country: The Roots of American Obesity," *New Republic*, Sept. 19, 1994, 35. On success imagery see Scott Sandage, "Failure, Freedom and the American Dream" (paper presented to the Center for Cultural Analysis, Carnegie Mellon University, Sept. 20, 1996).

2. Mary G. Winkler and Letha B. Cole, eds., *The Good Body* (New Haven, 1994); Mike Featherstone, "The Body in Consumer Culture," in Featherstone, ed., *The Body: Social Process and Cultural Theory* (London, 1991); Susan Bordo, "Reading the Slender Body," in Mary Jacobs et al., *Body/Politics: Women and the Discourses of Science* (New York, 1990): Roberta Seid, *Never Too Thin: Why Women Are at War with their Bodies* (New York, 1989).

3. Elizabeth Hayenga, "Dieting through the Decades: A Comparative study of Weight Reduction in America as Depicted in Popular Literature and Books from 1940 to the Late 1980s" (Ph.D. diss., University of Minnesota, 1989) — a valuable resource but oddly wrong in terms of historical origins. Hillel Schwartz, *Never Satisfied: A Cultural History of Diets, Fantasies and Fat* (New York, 1985) — an excellent descriptive work, but analytically simplistic in relying on commercial ploys as explanation for American diet concerns. Revealingly, French dieting has been even less studied, a function of that nation's tendency to treat this phenomenon as a foreign intrusion. See Mary Louise Roberts, "Samson and Delilah Revisited: The Politics of Women's Fashion in 1920s France," *American Historical Review* 98 (1993): 679–81.

4. One sociological overview does comment, but without real historical perspective or accurate chronology; Claude Fischler, *L'Omnivore* (Paris, 1990).

5. Stewart Toy, "Guiltless Gorging in the Freud Fashion," *Business Week* (Dec. 30, 1991): 46; Laura Shapiro, "Eat, Drink and Be Wary," *Newsweek* (Mar. 2, 1992): 68; Daryn Eller, "How Frenchwomen Stay That Trim," *Mademoiselle* (Jan. 1992): 35.

6. Comparative social history is still too infrequently undertaken, even in widely researched areas such as gender. Slavery and emancipation and some aspects of working-class life form exceptions to this claim, but in a host of the

newer areas of social history, we remained unduly tied to one place. I would like to think that this effort, in a relatively new field, shows the possibility and profit of a wider venture.

7. Anne Murcott, ed., *The Sociology of Food and Eating* (Aldershott, England, 1983).

NOTES TO CHAPTER ONE

1. Hillel Schwartz, *Never Satisfied: A Cultural History of Diets, Fantasies, and Fat* (New York, 1983). For a medical history sketch, A. Bray, "Measurement of Body Composition: An Improving Art," *Journal of Obesity Research* 3 (1995): 291–93.

2. Lois Banner, *American Beauty* (New York, 1983).

3. Joan Jacobs Brumberg, *Fasting Girls: The Emergence of Anorexia as a Modern Disease* (Cambridge, MA, 1988); Walter Vandereycken and Ron van Deth, *From Fasting Saints to Anorectic Girls* (New York, 1994). While Brumberg makes a clear distinction between the sources of nineteenth-century anorexia nervosa and mainstream beliefs, Vandereycken and van Deth repeat the more casual tendency to identify a fashion change but assume that it originated almost magically. In their account, after a background of romantic fascination with frailty, the empress of Austria in 1866 rebelled against hoop shirts, setting in motion the growing commitment to natural slimness.

4. Rudolph Bell, *Holy Anorexia* (Chicago, 1985); Schwartz, *Never Satisfied*, 11.

5. Thomas Wright, *The Passions of the Mind* (London, 1630), 18–19.

6. William G. McLaughlin, "Evangelical Childrearing in the Age of Jackson: Francis Wayland's Views on When and How to Subdue the Willfulness of Children," *Journal of Social History* 9 (1975): 20–39; Anne Audier, *Le Temps écoute, comme on glane la memoire paysanne* (Saintonge, 1994), 46.

7. *Oxford English Dictionary*, 2d ed. (Oxford, 1989) s.v. "diet."

8. Banner, *American Beauty*, 62; Roberta Seid, *Never Too Thin: Why Women Are at War With Their Bodies* (New York, 1989), 23.

9. Brumberg, *Fasting Girls*.

10. John Kasson, chap. 6 in *Rudeness and Civility: Manners in Nineteenth-Century Urban America* (New York, 1990).

11. Stephen Nissenbaum, *Sex, Diet, and Debility in Jacksonian America: Sylvester Graham and Health Reform* (Westport, CT, 1980), 20, 141; Roy Porter, "Consumption: Diseases of the Consumer Society," in John Brewer and Roy Porter, eds., *Consumption and the World of Goods* (London, 1993).

12. Lois Banner, *In Full Flower: Aging Women, Power, and Sexuality* (New York, 1992), 250.

13. Banner, *American Beauty*, 100–125.

14. S. Weir Mitchell, *Wear and Tear; or Hints for the Overworked* (1887; reprint, New York, 1973); F. G. Gosling, *Before Freud: Neurasthenia and the American Medical Community* (Urbana, IL, 1987).

15. Henry Collins Brown, *Brownstone Fronts and Saratoga Trunks* (New York, 1935), 144; Helen MacKnight Doyle, *A Child Went Forth: The Autobiography of*

Helen MacKnight Doyle (New York, 1934), 63; Harriet Hubbard Ayer, *Harriet Hubbard Ayer's Book* (1899; reprint, New York, 1974), 252; Annie Wolfe, *The Truth About Beauty* (New York, 1892), 62–63.

16. Banner, *American Beauty*, 230–32; George Beard, "Physical Future of the American People," *Atlantic Monthly* 43 (June 1879): 725; Dexter William Fellows and Andrew A. Freeman, *This Way to the Big Show: The Life of Dexter Fellows* (New York, 1936), 93; Donald Barr Chidsey, *John the Great* (Garden City, NY, 1942), 147.

17. Martha Verbrugge, *Able-Bodied Womanhood: Personal Health and Social Change in Nineteenth Century Boston* (New York, 1988).

18. Waverly Root and Richard de Rochemont, *Eating in America: A History* (New York, 1976), 51, 138; *Godey's Lady's Book* (Feb. 1875): 183–84; (July 1878): 87–88; (Oct. 1876): 375–76; Elaine McIntosh, *American Food Habits in Historical Perspective* (Westport, CT, 1995).

19. Banner, *American Beauty*, 128–33.

20. "Sexual Imaginings: The Cultural Economy of British Pornography, 1800–1914." Lisa Sigel, (Ph.D. diss., Carnegie Mellon University, 1995); *And sic Instructive Story: The Simple Tale of Susan Aked or Innocence Awakened, Ignorance Dispelled* (London and New York, 1898), 12–13; *Sweet Seventeen: The True Story of a Daughter's Awful Whipping and its Delightful if Direful Consequence* (Paris, 1910), 10.

21. Banner, *American Beauty*, 149–153; Sara Schmucker, "If You Want Beauty, Think Beauty," *Woman Beautiful* 4 (Jan. 1910): 39; Grace Peckham Murray, *The Fountain of Youth: or, Personal Appearance and Personal Hygiene* (New York, 1904), 9.

22. Mary W. Blanchard, "Boundaries and the Victorian Body: Aesthetic Fashion in Gilded Age America," *American Historical Review* 100 (1995): 22–59; Jill Fields, "'Fighting the Corsetless Evil': Cultural Hegemony and the Corset Panic of 1921," (paper presented to the Organization of American Historians, Chicago, April 1, 1995), my thanks to Dr. Fields for lending her essay; on the evolution of American ready-to-wear, Doreen Yarwood, *Fashion in the Western World, 1500–1990* (New York, 1992), 107, 131, 149.

23. "Questions and Answers," *Ladies Home Journal* (Sept. 1891): 28 (hereafter cited as *LHJ*).

24. Joy Ruth Ashmore, "Side-Talks with Girls," *LHJ* (Dec. 1896): 345; Ashmore, "Side-Talks," *LHJ* (May 1897): 29; "Mrs. Roper's Answers to Questions," *LHJ* (Jan. 1898): 31; Emma Walker, "Pretty Girl Papers," *LHJ* (June 1904): 365; "Good Health for Girls," *LHJ* (Apr. 1904): 29; Emma Walker, "Pretty Girl Papers," *LHJ* (Jan. 1905): 33; Mrs. S. T. Rorer, "Dietetic Sins and Their Penalties," *LHJ* (Jan. 1906): 42.

25. "Mrs. Warren's column," *LHJ* (May 1900): 43; "Mrs. Roper's Domestic Lessons," *LHJ* (Jan. 1898): 20; "Mr. and Mrs. Waxman's Answers to Questions," *LHJ* (Oct. 1909): 39.

26. Harvey Green, *Fit for America: Health, Fitness, Sport, and American Society* (Baltimore, 1986); Kevin White, *The First Sexual Revolution: The Emergence of Male Heterosexuality in Modern America* (New York, 1993), 28–32; James C. Whorton, *Crusaders for Fitness: The History of American Health Reformers*

(Princeton, 1982); *Physical Culture* (Feb. 1919): 15; (Nov. 1918): 36; (Jan. 1922): 135; (July 1920): 21; (June 1918): 17, 80.

27. "Mrs. Warren's Column," *LHJ* (May 1900): 43; *LHJ* (May 1913): 80.

28. *Pittsburgh Press*, Feb. 14, 1908; Mar. 3, 1910; Mar. 5, 1910; Mar. 6, 1910.

29. Schwartz, *Never Satisfied*, 117–19, 165. Schwartz offers an excellent minihistory of scales; 750,000 home scales were reported sold by 1933. On the changing cultural role of life insurance in contemplating death, a shift which gave insurance reports unprecedented visibility and credibility by the 1890s, see Viviana Zelizer, *Morals and Markets: The Development of Life Insurance in the United States* (New York, 1979).

30. Harold Wentworth and Stuart Flexner, eds., *Dictionary of American Slang* (New York, 1975), s.v. "slob" 488; *Oxford English Dictionary*, s.v. "slob"; Schwartz, *Never Satisfied*, 93.

31. Edith Lowry, *The Woman of Forty* (Chicago, 1919), 33; Schwartz *Never Satisfied*, 140–93; Banner, *American Beauty*, 153–76; Amelia Summerville, *Why Be Fat?* (New York, 1916), 28–29; Simon N. Patten, *Over-Nutrition and Its Social Consequences* (Philadelphia, 1887); David G. Phillips, *Susan Lenox: Her Fall and Rise* (New York, 1900).

32. "On Growing Fat," *Atlantic Monthly* 99 (1907): 431.

33. Edith Wharton, *The Custom of the Country* (1913; reprint, New York, 1987), 20.

34. Francis Benedict, "Food Conservation by Reduction of Rations," *Nation* 101 (1918): 355–57.

35. Erving Goffman, *Stigma: Notes on the Management of Spoiled Identity* (Englewood Cliffs, NJ, 1963); see also, though not historical, the anthropological studies by Igor de Garine and Nancy Pollock, *Social Aspects of Obesity* (Melbourne, 1995), and Karen Way, "Never Too Rich . . . or Too Thin: The Role of Stigma in the Social Construction of Anorexia Nervosa," in Donna Maurer and Jeffery Sobal, eds., *Eating Agendas: Food and Nutrition as Social Problems* (New York, 1995), 91–116.

NOTES TO CHAPTER TWO

1. Carole Haber, *Beyond Sixty-Five: The Dilemma of Old Age in America's Past* (Cambridge, 1983); Peter N. Stearns, *American Cool: Constructing a Twentieth-Century Emotional Style* (New York, 1994), 224–27. On the other hand, a recent historical effort, though interesting, starts the relevant medicalization process far too late; Jeffery Sobal, "The Medicalization and Demedicalization of Obesity," in Donna Maurer and Sobal, eds., *Eating Agendas: Food and Nutrition as Social Problems* (New York, 1995), 67–90. On the basic health transition, Abdel R. Omran, "Epidemiological Transition in the United States: The Health Factor in Population Change," *Population Bulletin* 32 (1977): 2–42.

2. Thomas Krug Chambers, "On Corpulence," *Lancet* 2 (1850): 345; C. J. B. Williams, "Obesity," in John Forbes et al., eds., *Cyclopedia of Practical Medicine* (Philadelphia, 1845), III: 404; Charles Roberts, *Manual of Anthropology* (London, 1878), 32–33; Hillel Schwartz, *Never Satisfied: A Cultural History of Diets, Fantasies, and Fat* (New York, 1983), 393 n. 47.

3. Ernst Wagner, *A Manual of General Pathology*, trans. from 6th German ed. by John van Duin and E. C. Seguin (New York, 1876).

4. F. A. Packard, "The Prescribing of Diet in Private Practice," *University Medical Magazine* (Philadelphia) 10 (1897–98): 269–71; N. S. Davis, "Importance of Regulatory Dietetics in Harmony with the Physiological Laws Controlling Digestion, Nutrition, and Waste and Some of the Inconsistencies in Prevalent Dietetic Practices," *Journal of the American Medical Association* 31 (1898): 1393–95; S. E. Jones, "Some Remarks on Obesity," *Medical Brief* (St. Louis) 25 (1897): 1692–95; A. L. Benedict, "Practical Dietetics," *Medical Standards* (Chicago) 26 (1903); C. C. Douglas, "Starvation as a Therapeutic Agent," *Detroit Medical Journal* 2 (1902–3): 737–41; A. E. Taussige, "The Treatment of Obesity, or Corpulence of the Middle Aged," *California State Journal of Medicine* 1 (1902–3): 356–59; W. F. Morrison, "The Harmfulness of Overeating," *Providence Medical Journal* 5 (1904): 174–82. For the overall chronological pattern, see *Index Medicus* bibliography, 1885 onward.

5. J. E. Knighton, "A Discussion of Dietetics and Dietetic Fads," *Southern Medical Journal* 28 (1935): 1108; George Harrop, "A Milk and Banana Diet for the Treatment of Obesity," *Journal of the American Medical Association* 102 (1934): 2003.

6. L. H. Newburgh, "Foundations of Diet Therapy," *Journal of the American Medical Association* 105 (1935): 1034–37.

7. Alexander Bryce, "Personal Investigation into the Dietetic Theories of America," *British Medical Journal* 2 (1909): 1666; Schwartz, *Never Satisfied*, 119–140; Harvey A. Levenstein, *Revolution at the Table: The Transformation of the American Diet* (New York, 1988), 44–60.

8. G. J. Warnshuis, "Individualizing the Treatment of Obesity," *Medical Review of Reviews* 37 (1931): 676; Gavin Fulton, "Evaluation of Reducing Diets," *Kentucky Medical Journal* 34 (1936): 518, J. S. McLester, "Obesity, Its Penalties and Treatment," *Southern Medical Journal* 21 (1928): 196.

9. Ian Anderson, "The Dietetic Treatment of Obesity," *Practitioner* 162 (1949): 61; W. N. Mann, "Obesity and its Treatment," *Practitioner* 164 (1950): 436. It was also true, not surprisingly, that many of the overweight patients rather liked the idea of hereditary or endocrine causes, as it relieved them of accusations of "gluttony." Mann, "Obesity," 436. For an earlier, American attack on the endocrine distraction, arguing that obese people should be put on a low caloric diet and that they could lose weight ("any obese person will lose body *fat* on a low caloric diet"), see Hugo Rony, "Obesity and Leanness," *Illinois Medical Journal* 59 (1913): 310.

10. David Edsall, "Some General Principles of Dietetics, with Special Remarks on Proprietary Foods," *Journal of the American Medical Association* 54 (1910): 194; Beverly Robinson, "The Treatment of Obesity," *New York Medical Journal* 102 (1915): 329; McLester, "Obesity," 197.

11. Maclay Lyon, "What is a Rational Diet?" *New York Medical Journal* 92 (1910): 818–19; Woods Hutchinson, "Fat and its Follies," *Cosmopolitan* 48 (1910): 383.

12. The question of how much chewing Fletcher advocated is one of those fascinating unresolved historical debates. One source claims he insisted on a hundred chews; I have found references both to twenty and to thirty-two. Fletcher

himself went over seven hundred for certain foods like shallots. Other scholars may pick up this gauntlet for further research. Levenstein, *Revolution*, 86–98; John Harvey Kellogg, "Diet Fads," *Illinois Medical Journal* 51 (1927): 210–13, a fascinating effort by a faddist in his own right to distance himself from Fletcher and diet extremism more generally; Horace Fletcher, *The New Glutton or Epicure* (New York, 1906), 127–52. On Lindlahr, "The Catabolic Diet," New Looks Publications (Woodmere, NY, n.d.).

13. Levenstein, *Revolution*, 86–98; Russell Chittenden, "Physiological Economy in Nutrition," *Popular Science Monthly* 63 (1903): 123–31; Chittenden, *Nutrition of Man* (New York, 1907); Schwartz, *Never Satisfied*, 119.

14. Upton Sinclair, "Starving for Health's Sake," *Cosmopolitan* 48 (1910): 739.

15. "On Fasting," *Contemporary Review* 98 (1910): 381–84.

16. Bryce, "Personal Investigation," 1665; Levenstein, *Revolution*, 94–98; Kellogg, "Diet Fads."

17. William L. Gould, "On the Use of a Medicament to Reduce the Appetite in the Treatment of Obesity and Other Conditions," *New York State Journal of Medicine* 47 (1947): 981; Francis Humphris, "Electricity in the Treatment of Obesity," *British Medical Journal* 11 (1912): 493.

18. Lyon, "Rational Diet," 818–19; Edsall, "Some General Principles of Dietetics," 196; Bureau of Investigation, "Stardom's Hollywood Diet in which the Obese are again 'Kidded by Experts,'" *Journal of the American Medical Association* 102 (1934): 2041–42; Bureau of Investigation, "Professor Paul C. Bragg, A Food Faddist and Sexual Rejuvenator Debarred from the Mails," *Journal of the American Medical Association* 96 (1931): 288–89; Bureau of Investigation, "Another Brinkler Fraud Order," *Journal of the American Medical Association* 113 (1939): 1346–48; Bureau of Investigation, "Fayro, Another Quack Obesity Cure of the Bath Salt Type," *Journal of the American Medical Association* 92 (1929): 2121; Bureau of Investigation, "Obesity Cure Fraud, Nancy Hatch and Youthful Face and Figure Inc. , Barred from the Mails," *Journal of the American Medical Association* 112 (1939): 75.

19. Burton J. Hendrick, "Some Modern Ideas on Food," *McClure's* 34 (1910): 653–69.

20. John Wainwright, "Reduction Treatment," *Medical Record* 68 (1905): 934–35.

21. H. Stein, "Who Is Underfed?" *Medical Record* 65 (1904): 811–12. See also James S. McLester, "The Principles Involved in the Treatment of Obesity," *Journal of the American Medical Association* 82 (1924): 2103.

22. J. Di Rocco, "The Treatment of Obesity," *New York Journal of Medicine* 93 (1911): 376–78; Robinson, "Treatment," 329, 331.

23. Max Einhorn, "The Art of Increasing the Diminishing the Bodily Weight at Will," *Medical Record* 54 (1903): 91–92; McLester, "Principles," 2103.

24. A. W. Ferris, "Reduction of Obesity," *Medical Record* 89 (1916): 142–43; McLester, "Principles," 2105.

25. Schwartz, *Never Satisfied*, 157; John M. Keating, *How to Examine For Life Insurance*, 3d ed. (Philadelphia, 1898), 24; Lulu G. Graves, "Developments in Dietetics during the Year 1919," *Modern Hospital* 14 (1920): 203–6; Henry C. Sherman, *Food Products* (New York, 1914), 215–16; Levenstein, *Revolution*, 94. On

the doctors' involvement, Sobal, "Medicalization and the Demedicalization of Obesity," 79–90.

26. Alfred C. Crofton, "The Dietetics of Obesity," *Journal of the American Medical Association* 47 (1906): 820.

27. G. J. Barker Benfield, *The Horrors of the Half Known Life: Male Attitudes Towards Women and Sexuality in Nineteenth Century America* (New York, 1976); John D'Emilio and Estelle Freedman, *Intimate Matters: A History of Sexuality in America* (New York, 1988); Andrew Scull, *Museums of Madness: The Social Organization of Insanity in Nineteenth Century England* (New York, 1979).

28. Levenstein, *Revolution*, chaps. 6 and 7.

29. R. P. Neuman, "Masturbation, Madness, and the Modern Concepts of Childhood and Adolescence," *Journal of Social History* 8 (1975).

30. Robinson, "Treatment," 197; Lyon, "Rational Diet," 819; Crofton, *Dietetics*, 821; James Alto Ward, "Obesity and Its Management," *Southern Medical Journal* 38 (1938): 1282; Lulu G. Graves, "Coping with Overweight by Means of Diet Therapy," *Modern Hospital* 32 (1929): 62; Gavin Fulton, "Evaluation of Reducing Diets," *Kentucky Medical Journal* 34 (1936): 513.

31. McLester, "Principles," 196; Graves, "Coping," 63, 64.

NOTES TO CHAPTER THREE

1. Stephen Nissenbaum, *Sex, Diet, and Debility in Jacksonian America: Sylvester Graham and Health Reform* (Westport, CT, 1980), 20, 141. Lois Banner, *American Beauty* (New York, 1983), 153 ff.

2. Walter Vandereycken and Ron van Deth, *From Fasting Saints to Anorectic Girls* (New York, 1994).

3. Hillel Schwartz, *Never Satisfied: A Cultural History of Diets, Fantasies, and Fat* (New York, 1983); Kim Chernin, *The Obsession: Reflections on the Tyranny of Slender Men* (New York, 1981).

4. Roland Marchand, *Advertising the American Dream: Making Way for Modernity* (Berkeley, CA, 1985).

5. George Chauncey, Jr., "Christian Brotherhood or Sexual Perversion? Homosexual Identities and the Construction of Sexual Boundaries in World War I Era," in Peter N. Stearns, ed., *Expanding the Past: A Reader in Social History* (New York, 1988), 169–192; Peter N. Stearns, *American Cool: Constructing a Twentieth-Century Emotional Style* (New York, 1994).

6. Kevin White, *The First Sexual Revolution: The Emergence of Male Heterosexuality in Modern America* (New York, 1993).

7. Christine Ruane, "Clothes Shopping in Imperial Russia: The Development of a Consumer Culture," *Journal of Social History* 28 (1995): 765–82; Warren G. Breckman, "Disciplining Consumption: The Debate About Luxury in Wilhelmine Germany, 1890–1914," *Journal of Social History* 24 (1991): 485–506.

8. John T. Pressly, "Address to the Students," 1840, Pittsburgh Imprint, Carnegie Library, Pittsburgh, 24; G. W. Baxter, "The Wicked are Without Peace," *Pittsburgh Preacher* (Pittsburgh, 1832), I: 83; Paul Charles Hachten, "From Wretched Philosopher to Aesthetic Hedonist: Pittsburgh Presbyterian Attitudes

Towards Pleasure-Seeking, 1827–1885," (honors thesis, Carnegie Mellon University, 1991).

9. William McKinney, ed. , *The Presbyterian Valley* (Pittsburgh, 1958), 278–81; John T. Pressly, "Address," 1856, Pittsburgh Imprint, Carnegie Library, Pittsburgh; *Presbyterian Banner* (Pittsburgh), Oct. 18, 1871, and Feb. 28, 1872.

10. Hachten, chap. 4, "Wretched Philosopher"; *Presbyterian Banner*, June 7, 1876; Jan. 15, 1879; July 28, 1875.

11. Francis G. Couvares, *The Remaking of Pittsburgh: Class and Culture in an Industrializing City, 1877–1919* (Albany, NY, 1984); Roland Marchand, *Advertising the American Dream* (Berkeley, 1985); Vincent Vinikas, *Soft Soap, Hard Sell: American Hygiene in an Age of Advertisement* (Ames, IA, 1992). William Waits, *The Modern Christmas in America* (New York, 1993); Viviana Zelizer, *Pricing the Priceless Child* (Newport, 1986); Miriam Formanek-Brunell, "Sugar and Spice: The Politics of Doll Play in Nineteenth Century America," Elliot West and Paul Petrik, eds., *Small Worlds: Children and Adolescents in America, 1850–1950* (Lawrence, KS, 1992), 107–24; Elaine S. Abelson, *When Ladies Go A-Thieving: Middle Class Shoplifters in the Victorian Department Store* (New York, 1989); Patricia O'Brien, "The Kleptomania Diagnosis: Bourgeois Women and Theft in Late Nineteenth-Century France," in Stearns, *Expanding the Past*, 105–17.

12. R. W. Fox and T. J. Jackson Lears, eds. , *The Culture of Consumption* (New York, 1983). In their introduction, the editors attribute new consumerism to the new, more boring corporate structure of middle-class work, along with the sheer abundance of goods.

13. Thorstein Veblen, *Theory of the Leisure Class: An Economic Study of Institutions* (New York, 1912).

14. T. J. Jackson Lears, "From Salvation to Self Regulation: Advertising And the Therapeutic Roots of the Consumer Culture 1880–1930," in Fox and Lears, eds., *The Culture of Consumption*, 1–38.

15. Dominick Cavallo, *Muscles and Morals: Organized Playgrounds and Urban Reform, 1880–1920* (Philadelphia, 1981), 59; "Foods for Weight Reduction," *Journal of the American Medical Association* 107 (1936): 431.

16. John Brewer and Roy Porter, eds., *Consumption and the World of Goods* (London, 1993).

17. Mary G. Winkler and Letha Cole, eds., *The Good Body* (New Haven, 1994), 55; Susan Bordo, "Reading the Slender Body," in Mary Jacobsen et al., *Body/Politics, Women and the Discourses of Science* (New York, 1990), 88.

18. Simon N. Patten, *New Basis of Civilization* (1907, reprint, Cambridge, MA, 1969); T. J. Jackson Lears, *No Place of Grace: Anti-modernism and the Transformation of American Culture* (New York, 1981), 54; Simon N. Patten, "Overnutrition and Its Social Consequences," *Annals* 10 (1897): 44–46; Daniel M. Fox, *The Discovery of Abundance: Simon N. Patten and the Transformation of Social Theory* (New York, 1976), 77, 100.

19. Nissenbaum, *Sex, Diet, and Debility.*

20. John D'Emilio and Estelle Freedman, *Intimate Matters: A History of Sexuality in America* (New York, 1988); Steven Seidman, *Romantic Longings: Love in America, 1830–1980* (New Brunswick, 1992).

21. Rudolph Binion, "Fiction as Social Fantasy: Europe's Domestic Crisis of 1879–1914," *Journal of Social History* 27 (1994): 679–700.

22. Linda W. Rosenzweig, "The Anchor of My Life: Middle Class Mothers and College Educated Daughters, 1880–1920," *Journal of Social History* 25 (1991): 5–25; E. S. Martin, "Mothers and Daughters," *Good Housekeeping* 64 (May 1917): 27; Ruth Ashmore, "The Mother of My Girl," *LHJ* 11 (Sept. 1894): 16; "Antagonism between Mothers and Daughters," *Independent* 53 (Sept. 26, 1901): 2311; Gabrielle Jackson, *Mother and Daughter* (New York and London, 1905), 3, 63, 81, 85–86, 104, 114, 129; Jan Lewis, "The American Doctrine of Motherhood in the Nineteenth and Twentieth Centuries" (paper presented at the eighth Berkshire Conference on the History of Women, Douglass College, June 1990); Charlotte Perkins Gilman, *The Home, Its Work and Influence* (New York, 1903).

23. Lois Banner, *In Full Flower: Aging Women, Power, and Sexuality* (New York, 1992), 252.

24. I find no evidence for another possible correlate to the diet craze: concern about immigrants around 1900. This concern abundantly existed. It did generate some nutritional criticisms of immigrant diets, such as Italian starches or Polish sausage. But I have seen no comments before 1920 about particular immigrant overweight. Further, because diet concern also arose in the nonimmigrant societies of Western Europe at the same time, though admittedly with fewer moralistic overtones, I do not find the immigrant correlate necessary, however possible in theory.

NOTES TO CHAPTER FOUR

1. Hillel Schwartz, *Never Satisfied: A Cultural History of Diets, Fantasies, and Fat* (New York, 1983); Joan Jacobs Brumberg, *Fasting Girls: The Emergence of Anorexia as a Modern Disease* (Cambridge, MA, 1988).

2. Naomi Wolf, *The Beauty Myth: How Images of Beauty Are Used Against Women* (New York, 1991); Rosalyn Meadows and Lillie Weiss, *Women's Conflicts about Eating and Sexuality* (Binghamton, NY, 1993); Marcia Millman, *Such a Pretty Face: Being Fat in America* (New York, 1980). See also a recent book by Brett Silverstein and Deborah Patrick, which claims to break new ground by showing that women's constrictions have always promoted eating disorders — current standards have little to do with the case. The book, in fact, deals largely with recent patterns, and it may be quite useful thereupon; the historical references are misleading, totally scattered, and devoid of any comparison with eating disorders among men. The subject, in sum, continues to generate more gender heat than historical light. *The Cost of Competence: Why Inequality Causes Depression, Eating Disorders and Illness in Women* (New York, 1995).

3. *Pittsburgh Press*, Feb. 14, 1908; Schwartz, *Never Satisfied*, 93, 117–19; Sara Schmucker, "If You Want Beauty, Think Beauty," *Woman Beautiful* 4 (Jan. 1910): 39; Grace Peckham Murray, *The Fountain of Youth: or, Personal Appearance and Personal Hygiene* (New York, 1904), 9; Harvey Green, *Fit for America: Health, Fitness, Sport, and American Society* (Baltimore, 1986); Kevin White, *The First Sexual Revolution: The Emergence of Male Heterosexuality in Modern America* (New York, 1993), 28–32; *Physical Culture* (Feb. 1919): 15; (Nov. 1918): 36; (Jan. 1922): 135; Robert Ernst, *Weakness is a Crime: The Life of Bernarr MacFadden* (Syracuse, 1991); James C. Whorton, *Crusaders for Fitness: The History of Ameri-*

can Health Reformers (Princeton, 1982); Harold Wentworth and Stuart Flexner, eds., *Dictionary of American Slang*, s.v. "slob" (New York, 1975), 488; *Oxford English Dictionary*, s.v. "slob."

4. John M. Keating, *How to Examine for Life Insurance*, 3d ed. (Philadelphia, 1898), 247. J. Di Rocco, "The Treatment of Obesity," *New York Journal of Medicine* 93 (1911): 376–78.

5. Lulu G. Graves, "Coping with Overweight by Means of Diet Therapy," *Modern Hospital* 32 (1929): 62, citing earlier work; even here, references to women's difficult constitution (particularly, middle-aged women's) escalated in the 1920s: James S. McLester, "Obesity, Its Penalties and Treatment," *Southern Medical Journal* 21 (1928): 196; Gavin Fulton and Edward Humphrey, "The Management of Obesity," *Kentucky Medical Journal* 37 (1939): 110. On analogies with gender bias in neurasthenia, F. G. Gosling and J. M. Raye, "The Right to be Sick: American Physicians and Nervous Patients, 1885–1910," *Journal of Social History* 20 (1986): 251–68.

6. William R. Emerson, M. D., "The Over-Weight Child," *Women's Home Companion* (1920): 31.

7. Josephine H. Kenyon, M. D., "When a Child is Thin," *Good Housekeeping* (Apr. 1930): 108, and "Thin Child," *Good Housekeeping* (Oct. 1933): 98, 182. See also Charles Aldrich, M. D., *Cultivating the Child's Appetite* (New York, 1931), and L. Emmett Holt, M.D., "The Reluctant Eater," *Good Housekeeping* (Nov. 1956): 34–35 and, with Rustin McIntosh and H. L. Barnett, *Pediatrics* (New York, 1953).

8. Lulu G. Graves, "Should the Teens Diet?" *Parents Magazine* (Apr. 1940): 62, 72–77; Child Study Association of America, *Parents' Questions* (New York, 1947), 206; Clara M. Taylor, "Boys Eat Too Much — Or Do They?" *Parents' Magazine* (Aug. 1949): 45, 64–65; Elizabeth Scott Stearns, diaries, 1940s, in possession of Sarah Stearns Gipson, Indianapolis, IN.

9. Gladys D. Shultz, "Our Underfed Children," *LHJ* (Mar. 1951): 44–45, 129–30; Pauline Mack, "Do Children Need Sweets?" *Parents Magazine* (Mar. 1950): 51; Marion Faegre, John Anderson, and Dale Harris, *Child Care and Training* (Minneapolis, 1958), 38; Sidonie Gruenberg, *The Parents' Guide to Everyday Problems of Boys and Girls* (New York, 1958), 206; Marvin Gersh, M.D., "A Fitness Program for Overweight Teen-Agers," *Parents Magazine* (Aug. 1971): 50. On the notion that girls need clubs or groups of some sort and boys (implicitly) don't, Margaret B. Salmos, *Food Facts for Teenagers* (Springfield, IL, 1965). On the shift to greater gender neutrality, Waldo E. Nelson, ed., *Textbook of Pediatrics* (Philadelphia, 1969), 166.

10. Samuel Wishnik, M.D., *Feeding Your Child* (New York, 1958), 198.

11. Emily Post, *Etiquette* (New York, 1940), 208; Lulu G. Graves, "Coping," 63, citing comments by a doctor and a nutritionist from Nebraska; James S. McLester, "The Principles Involved in the Treatment of Obesity," *Journal of the American Medical Association* 82 (1924): 2103.

12. Alan Guttmacher, *Pregnancy and Birth* (New York, 1962); Barbara K. Rothman, *In Labor: Women and Power in the Birthplace* (New York, 1982); Ruth F. Wadsworth, "The Old Order Changeth," *Woman's Home Companion* (May 1923): 4.

13. *Random House Dictionary of American Slang,* I (New York, 1994), s.v. "broad," "slob."

14. Lelord Kordee, *Secrets for Staying Slim* (New York, 1971), 14.

15. Herman Taller, *Calories Don't Count* (New York, 1961), 47; John Yudkin, *This Slimming Business* (New York, 1959), 9.

16. Murray Siegel, *Think Thin* (New York, 1971), 28 and 103; Theodore Rubin, *The Thin Book* (New York, 1966), 11, 46, 54; Sidney Petrie, *The Lazy Lady's Easy Diet* (West Nyack, NY, 1968); Frank J. Wilson, *Glamour, Glucose and Glands* (New York, 1956).

17. Patricia Branca, *Silent Sisterhood: Middle-Class Women in the Victorian Home* (Pittsburgh, 1975), 99.

18. Peter N. Stearns, *American Cool: Creating a Twentieth-Century Emotional Culture* (New York, 1994), and "Girls, Boys and Emotions: Redefinitions and Historical Change," *Journal of American History* 80 (1993): 36–74.

19. Linda W. Rosenzweig, "The Anchor of My Life: Middle Class Mothers and College Educated Daughters, 1880–1920," *Journal of Social History* 25 (1991): 5–25; E. S. Martin, "Mothers and Daughters," *Good Housekeeping* 64 (May 1917): 27; Ruth Ashmore, "The Mother of My Girl," *LHJ* (Sept. 1894): 16; Charlotte Perkins Gilman, *The Home, Its Work and Influence* (New York, 1903); Jan Lewis, "The American Doctrine of Motherhood in the Nineteenth and Twentieth Centuries" (paper presented at the eighth Berkshire Conference on the History of Women, Douglass College, June 1990); Stearns, *American Cool*, 165–70; Regina Kunzel, "The Professionalization of Benevolence," *Journal of Social History* 22 (1988): 21–40; John B. Watson, chap. 3 in *Psychological Care of Infant and Child* (New York, 1928); Anna Wolf, *The Parents' Manual: A Guide to the Emotional Development of Young Children* (New York, 1941), 81; Lillian Gilbreth, *Living with Our Children* (New York, 1928), 106–7.

20. Steven Seidman, *Romantic Longings: Love in America, 1830–1980* (New York, 1991); Ben Lindsay and Wainwright Evans, *The Companionate Marriage* (New York, 1927), 65, 72–73; Beth L. Bailey, "Scientific Truth . . . and Love: The Marriage Education Movement in the United States," *Journal of Social History* (summer 1987): 711–32; William Robinson, *Woman: Her Sex and Love Life* (1917; reprint, New York, 1929), 363; Theodore Van de Velde, *Ideal Marriage: Its Physiognomy and Technique* (1930; reprint, Westport, CT, 1950), 6; Margaret Sanger, *Happiness in Marriage* (New York, 1926); on deviant girls, Mary Odem, *Delinquent Daughters* (Chapel Hill, NC, 1995).

21. Carol Z. Stearns and Peter N. Stearns, *Anger: The Struggle for Emotional Control in America's History* (Chicago, 1986), 87; "When I Love Him," *LHJ* (Mar. 1915): 18.

22. "Losing Weight with Soul," *Ebony* (July 1993): 62; "Burning Fat," *Ebony* (Jan. 1994): 76; "Shaping Up," *Ebony* (June 1987): 30. *Ebony* diet articles also suggested that African Americans' preference for food with some real taste and soul entered into reluctance to accept weight control norms. "Are We Overdoing the Diet Thing?" *Ebony* (Mar. 1978): 44. For the simple imbalance between diet articles and pieces on other beauty aids, see *Ebony*, 1943 ff.

23. "Big Can Be Beautiful," *Ebony* (Oct. 1978); "When Bigger is Better," *Ebony* (July 1994): 102–4; "Women Fight Back," *Ebony* (Mar. 1990): 27–31.

24. "When Bigger is Better," *Ebony*, 104.

25. Ali Mazrui, *The Africans: A Reader* (New York, 1980).

26. Jacqueline Jones, *Labor of Love, Labor of Sorrow: Black Women, Work and the Family from Slavery to the Present* (New York, 1986); Noralee Frankel, *Freedom's Women* (unpublished manuscript). On the ongoing contrast between black adolescent girls' pride in their bodies — "I know I'm fat; I don't care" — and white girls' obsessive concern about thinness, see "The Body of the Beholder," *Newsweek* (April 24, 1995): 66–7. There are indications, however, of growing of selective impact of white standards on black women: Maya Brown, "Dying to be Thin" (article ms., Western Psychiatric Institute, Pittsburgh). For continued evidence of confidence in attractiveness along with admitted overweight, S. K. Kumanyika, F. F. Wilson, and M. Guildford-Davenport, "Weight-Related Attitudes and Behaviors of Black Women," *Journal of the American Dietetic Association* 93 (1993): 416–22.

27. Stearns, *American Cool*; Warren Susman, *Culture as History: The Transformation of American Society in the Twentieth Century* (New York, 1985); Stanley Coben, *Rebellion against Victorianism: The Impetus for Cultural Change in 1920s America* (New York, 1991); White, *First Sexual Revolution*.

28. Leonard J. Moore, "Historical Interpretations of the 1920s Klan: The Traditional View and the Populist Revision," *Journal of Social History* 24 (1990): 341–58, and *Citizen Klansmen: The Ku Klux Klan in Indiana, 1921–1928* (Chapel Hill, NC, 1991).

29. Peter Laipson, "'Kiss without Shame, for She Desires It': Sexual Foreplay in American Marital Advice Literature, 1900–1925," *Journal of Social History* 29 (1996): 507–25.

30. Madhu Kishwar, "Love and Marriage," *Manushi: A Journal about Women and Society* 80 (1993): 13.

31. George D. Krupp, M. D., "My Mother Made Me Fat," *Redbook* (Jan. 1969): 53; Susan L. Johnson, "Effects of a Nonenergy Fat Substitute on Children's Energy," *American Journal of Clinical Nutrition* 58 (1993): 326–33; Wadsworth, "Old Order," 122.

32. Dear Abby column, *Pittsburgh Post-Gazette*, Oct. 27, 1994, section D; Mary Louise Roberts, "Samson and Delilah Revisited: The Politics of Women's Fashion in 1920s France," *American Historical Review* 98 (1993): 657–84.

33. Ann Landers column, *Pittsburgh Post Gazette*, Oct. 31, 1994. On the increasing fundamentalist pressure on heavy women, Shirley Cook, *The Exodus Diet Plan* (Old Tappan, NJ, 1986), and Marie Chapian and Neva Coyle, *Free to be Thin* (Minneapolis, 1979). For dramatic evidence of ongoing intensification's impact on adolescent girls, see the additional examples in Mary Pipher, *Reviving Ophelia: Saving the Selves of Adolescent Girls* (New York, 1996), 166–85.

NOTES TO CHAPTER FIVE

1. *Esquire* (Mar. 1936): 194; (Apr. 1957): 203; (June 1957): 91.

2. Quentin Miller, "There's a Handsome Man in the House," *LHJ* (Sept. 1955): 81.

3. Brandon Wertz, "Busting the Bullies," *Pittsburgh Post-Gazette*, Jan. 14, 1995, section D; Michael McGough, "Et tu, Baby Huey," *Pittsburgh Post-Gazette*, Sept. 20, 1994, section D; J. S. Hodgdon, P. I. Fitzgerald, and J. A. Vogel, "Relationships between Fat and Appearance Ratings of U. S. Soldiers," Naval Health Research Center, Report no. NHRC-90–1, 1984.

4. Hillel Schwartz, *Never Satisfied; A Cultural History of Diets, Fantasies, and Fat* (New York, 1983), 204 ff.

5. Peter N. Stearns, *American Cool: Constructing a Twentieth-Century Emotional Style* (New York, 1994), 224; Barbara Ehrenreich, *The Hearts of Men: American Dreams and the Flight from Commitment* (New York, 1983); Emma Wheeler, *The Fat Boy Goes Polyunsaturated* (New York, 1963); J. O. Leibowitz, *The History of Coronary Heart Disease* (Berkeley, 1970), 163–67.

6. Thomas Desmond, "Fat Men Can't Win," *Science Illustrated* (June 1948): 46–59; Elmer Wheeler, *The Fat Boy's Downfall, and How Elmer Learned to Keep It Off* (New York, 1952); Kay Barth, "From Man Mountain to the Mountain Climber," *Today's Health* (July 1954): 41–70.

7. Mary G. Winkler and Letha B. Cole, eds., *The Good Body* (New Haven, CT, 1994), 211.

8. *Harper's Weekly* (Nov. 7, 1908): 4; *Time* (Mar. 26, 1928); *Time* (Oct. 8, 1928); Charlotte Hays, "When the Clintons Come to Town," *National Review* (Nov. 2, 1992): 32.

9. Article by Marlene Cimons, *Los Angeles Times*, Dec. 20, 1994.

10. "Reduced 53 lbs. in Nine Weeks" (advertisement), *LHJ* (Jan. 1924): 108; Lois Banner, *American Beauty* (New York, 1983), 271; Schwartz, *Never Satisfied*, 165 ff; Kevin White, *The First Sexual Revolution: The Emergence of Male Heterosexuality in Modern America* (New York, 1993), esp. 29; "Weil Belt" advertisement, *Esquire* (Mar. 1936): 45.

11. H. A. Dunn, "The Dangers of Drugging for Fat," *Dearborn Independent*, June 12, 1926, 5–6; S. J. Cowell, "Recent Advances in Dietetics," *Practitioner* 135 (1935): 384; E. E. Cornwall, "Rules for the Treatment of Alimentary Obesity," *Medical Record* 150 (1939): 320.

12. Minneapolis Museum of Medical Quackery, various advertisements. I am grateful to Carol Stearns for these references.

13. Roberta Seid, *Never Too Thin: Why Women are at War with Their Bodies* (New York, 1989), 105–9; "Dieter's Clipboard," *Seventeen*, July 1962—this feature shifted to the name "Streamlines" in 1969; Jennifer Cross, *The Supermarket Trap: The Consumer and the Food Industry* (Bloomington, IN, 1970), 164–65; Kim Chernin, *The Obsession: Reflections on the Tyranny of Slenderness* (New York, 1981), 44.

14. M. B. Green and Max Beckman, "Supplement Protein in Weight Reduction," *American Practitioner and Digest of Treatment* 1 (1950): 1239; G. J. Warnshuis, "Individualizing the Treatment of Obesity," *Medical Review of Reviews* 37 (1931): 676; Schwartz, *Never Satisfied*, 200 ff; Chernin, *Obsession*, 44, passim.

15. *Deception and Fraud in the Dieting Industry: Hearing*, House Subcommittee on Regulations, Business Opportunities and Energy of the Committee on Small Business, 101st Cong., 2d sess., Mar. 26, 1990; Hilde Bruch, "Psychological Aspects of Reducing," *Psychosomatic Medicine* 14 (1952): 338. Bruch comments

further on how it was "hard to overestimate the intensity of the cultural rejection of even mild forms of overweight, particularly in the well-to-do urban population" and how doctors explicitly shared and furthered this moral judgment.

16. Abigail Wood, "Why Do I Make Myself Fat?" *Seventeen* (Mar. 1973): 28; "Dieting When You're Unhappy," *Seventeen* (May 1969): 43; Bruch, "Psychological Aspects," 337–48; Stanley W. Conrad, "The Problem of Weight Reduction in Obese Women," *American Practitioner and Digest of Treatment* 5 (1954): 38–39; John D. Comrie, "Advances in Dietetics," *Practitioner* 139 (1939): 368; Chernin, *Obsession*, 44; Robert Linn, *The Last Chance Diet Book* (New York, 1976); Peter Wyden, "Night Eating," *LHJ* (Apr. 1965): 38; "Ladies Home Journal Diet Club," *LHJ* (Apr. 1969): 98.

17. "Dieter's Clipboard," *Seventeen* (Dec. 1962): 123. In 1953 Mrs. Helen Fraley was the center of attention in the *LHJ* as a heroic dieter, with major emphasis on its impact on her romantic appeal. See also, for medical comment on slenderness and sexuality, Edward Weiss. "Psychosomatic Aspects of Dieting," *Journal of Clinical Nutrition* 1 (1953): 140.

18. For the standard medical approach of the interwar years, James M. Anders, "Obesity and its Treatment," *Atlantic Medical Journal* 26 (1923–24): 498–501; on cholesterol, E. Neige Todhunter, "The Food We Eat," *Journal of Health Education* 50 (1958): 512–13; Harvey Levenstein, *Paradox of Plenty, a social history of eating in modern America* (New York, 1993), 135–36.

19. Theodore Rubin, *The Thin Book* (New York, 1966), 11, 45.

20. Herman Taller, *Calories Don't Count* (New York, 1961); Comrie, "Advances," 368.

21. Emma Seifrit Weigly, "Average? Ideal? Desirable? A Brief Overview of Weight Tables in the United States," *Journal of the American Dietetic Association* (April 1984): 417–23; Artemis Simopoulos and Theodore B. Van Itallie, "Bad Weight, Health, and Longevity," *Annals of Internal Medicine* (Feb. 1984): 285–95; David F. Williamson, "Descriptive Epidemiology of Body Weight and Weight Change in U. S. Adults," *Annals of Internal Medicine* (1993): 646–49; "1983 Met Life Height & Weight Tables," *Statistical Bulletin of the Metropolitan Life Insurance Company,* (Jan.-June 1983): 3–9. On urging underweight, advice before 1920 by Braudreth Symonds continued to recommend slight overweight as healthier for younger age group, though it was noted that underweight was not bad and might be desirable after 30. It was in the 1930s and 1940s that life tables consistently favored underweight; this, of course, was a major pressure on the weight tables themselves. Weigly, "Average," 417–23.

22. Lelord Kordee, *Secrets for Staying Slim* (New York, 1971), 14.

23. Regina Herzlinger and David Calkine, "How Companies Tackle Health Care Costs," *Harvard Business Review* (1986): 70–80; Sharlene McEvoy, "Fat Chance: Employment Discrimination against the Overweight," *Labor Law Journal* 43 (1992): 3–19. As flight attendants aged, weight standards were eased in the 1980s, but except where gender distinctions were proved, most lawsuits failed on grounds that overweight was not a disability (though extreme obesity was). See also Gary Anthes and Kim Nash, "High-Tech Benefits Herald Brave New Office," *Computer World* 26 (1992): 1; Sibyl Bogardes, "Wellness Programs," *Benefits Quarterly* 9 (1993): 53–62; Stanley Siegelman, "Employers Fighting Battle of the Bulge," *Business and Health* 9 (1991): 62–63. See also *Prevention Magazine,* 1970s ff.

24. Jack Friedman, "Those Hidden Pounds: Executive Enemy No. 1," *Dun's Review and Modern Industry* (April 1961): 42–44; Quentin Miller, "There's a Handsomer Man in the House," *LHJ* (Sept. 1955): 81, 210–14, 211.

25. Jane Lincoln, "I'm to Blame That My Husband Died Young," *Cosmopolitan* (Aug. 1954): 84–89; "Obesity the Enemy," *Newsweek* (Oct. 20, 1947): 54; Arthur Snider, "The Progress of Medicine," *Science Digest* (Oct. 1938): 49–50; Bruch, "Psychological Aspects."

26. Stephen Whitfield, *The Culture of the Cold War* (Baltimore, 1991), 69–76; Jean Mayer, "Exercise Does Keep the Weight Down," *Atlantic* (July 1955): 63–66; Patricia Eisenman and C. Robert Barnett, "Physical Fitness in the 1950s and 1970s: Why Did One Fail and the Other Boom?" *Quest* 31 (1979): 117–18, 121; Curtis Mitchell, "Tennis, Everyone? Or Swimming, or —?" *New York Times Magazine* (April 23, 1961): 57.

27. Doctors' moralistic reactions promoted the sense among overweight patients that there must be something wrong with them if they could not live up to appropriate standards — see the *LHJ* (July 1958): 46, for a comment on Mrs. Fraley's relapse (regained 100 pounds) and the embarrassment and dejection this caused particularly in dealing with doctors. For a standard character flaw argument in popularized articles, Judy Shields (age nineteen, from Lincoln, Nebraska), "Problems of the Fad Diet Freak," *Seventeen* (June 1973): 116.

28. "Dieting When You're Unhappy," *LHJ* (1969): 62; "Young Living" *Seventeen* (Mar. 1973): 16 ff; Taller, *Calories Don't Count*; Robert Goodhart, *Teen Ager's Guide to Diet and Health* (Englewood Cliffs, NJ, 1964), 31; "Full-Figured Women Fight Back," *Ebony* (Mar. 1990): 50; Hilde Bruch, "Psychological Aspects," 338; Elizabeth Hayengor, "Dieting through the Decades: A Comparative Study of Weight Reduction in America as Depicted in Popular Literature and Books from 1940 to the late 1980s" (Ph.D. diss., University of Minnesota, 1989), 266; Robert Suczek, "The Personality of Obese Women," *Symposium on Nutrition and Behavior* (Minneapolis, 1956), 96.

29. "Size-Wise Diet," *Seventeen* (Oct. 1969): 26; Louise Paine Benjamin, "I Decide to Reduce," *LHJ* (Nov. 1935): 28; Max R. Tarnoff, "I Cut My Weight by 150 Pounds," *LHJ* (Oct. 1958): 146–47.

30. Dawn Norman, "100 Pounds Off," *LHJ* (July 1965): 83; Dawn Norman, "I Was a Hopeless Fatty," *LHJ* (Jan. 1955): 75; "16 and Slim — at last!" *LHJ* (Feb. 1953): 48; Kevin L. Jones, "Faith, Diet and Slam Dunks Help Pastor Lose 140 Pounds," *Ebony* (Oct. 1993): 68; Du Barry beauty advertisement, *LHJ* (Jan. 1942): 44; on Fraley, Dawn Norman, "The Diet that Launched a New Career," *LHJ* (Jan. 1953): 106.

31. On the evolution of major diet organizations, Schwartz, *Never Satisfied*; Marcia Millner, *Such a Pretty Face: Being Fat in America* (New York, 1980).

32. Frank A. Cummings, "Obesity and its Treatment," *New York Medical Journal* 102 (1915): 805; Dawn Norman, "I Was Too Fat to Have a Baby," *LHJ* (Mar. 1953): 176; Dawn Norman, "Dear Beauty Editor," *LHJ* (May 1949): 196; Elizabeth Scott Stearns diaries, 1936–42, in possession of Sarah Stearns Gipson, Indianapolis, IN; Tom Maloney, "Is Dieting Being Overdone?" *American Legion Magazine* (Aug. 1955): 20–21, 54–56.

33. Elizabeth Scott Stearns diaries, Sept. 1935-Feb. 1936 in possession of Sarah

Stearns Gipson, Indianapolis, IN. Hilde Bruch, *The Importance of Overweight* (New York, 1957), and "Psychological Aspects," 340.

34. Schwartz, *Never Satisfied*, 246; Ernest Havemann, "The Wasteful, Phony Crash Dieting Craze," *Life* (Jan. 19, 1959): 102.

35. Deborah Clark Stearns, "Easy Virtue and Immoral Appetites: Desire in the Impression of Moral Actors" (Ph.D. diss., University of Pennsylvania, 1959), 94–95; Peter Conrad, "Wellness is Virtue: Morality and the Pursuit of Health," *Culture, Medicine and Psychology* 18 (1994): 385–401; Richard Stein and Carol Nemeroff, "Moral Overtones of Food: Judgments of Others Based on What They Eat," *Personality and Social Psychology Bulletin* 21 (1995): 480–90; Molly O'Neill, "The Morality of Fat," *New York Times Magazine* (Mar. 10, 1996): 39.

NOTES TO CHAPTER SIX

1. Timothy Cuff, "The Body Mass Index Values of Mid Nineteenth-Century West Point Cadets," *Historical Methods* 26 (1993): 171–81; John Komlos and Peter Coclanis, "Nutrition and Economic Development in Post-Reconstruction South Carolina," *Social Science History* 19 (1995).

2. Hillel Schwartz, *Never Satisfied: A Cultural History of Diets, Fantasies, and Fat* (New York, 1983), 337–39.

3. David F. Williamson, "Descriptive Epidemiology of Body Weight and Weight Change in U. S. Adults," *Annals of Internal Medicine*, (1953): 646–49; "Trends in Average Weights, Insured Men and Women," *Statistical Bulletin of the Metropolitan Life Insurance Company* (1966): 1–3; "Trends in Average Weights and Heights of Men: An Insurance Experience," *Statistical Bulletin of the Metropolitan Life Insurance Company* (1970): 6–7. One important comment on recent trends is Robert Kuczmarski et al., "Increasing Prevalence of Overweight Among US Adults," *Journal of the American Medical Association* 272 (July 20, 1994): 205–211; Society of Actuaries and Association of Life Insurance Medical Directors of America, *Build Study 1979*, (New York, 1980); Edward A. Lew, "Mortality and Weight: Insured Lives and the American Cancer Society Studies," *Annals of Internal Medicine* (1989): 1024–29.

4. See advertisements juxtaposing diet products and fattening staples in *LHJ* (July 1958): 68–69; see also *LHJ* (Sept. 1962): 82.

5. Noting the failure of diet products, Peter Wyden, *The Overweight Society* (New York, 1965); Jennifer Cross, *The Supermarket Trap* (Bloomington, IN, 1970). On the 1890s-1920s' invention of new desserts and snacks (the sundae, 1890; Eskimo Pies, 1919), Waverly L. Root and Richard de Rochemont, *Eating in America: A History* (New York, 1976).

6. M. F. Najj and M. Rowland, *Anthropometric Reference Data and Prevalence of Overweight, 1976–80*, National Center for Health Statistics, Vital and Health Statistics Series, report no. DHH5/PUB/PHS-87–1688 (Hyattsville, MD, 1987); M. F. Najj and R. J. Kuczmarski, *Anthropometric Data and Prevalence of Overweight for Hispanics: 1982–84*, National Center for Health Statistics, Vital and Health Statistics Series, report no. DHH5/PUB/PHS-87–1689 (Hyattsville, MD, 1989).

7. Viviana Zelizer, *Pricing the Priceless Child* (New York, 1986); Peter N. Stearns, *American Cool: Constructing a Twentieth-Century Emotional Style* (New York, 1994).

8. Susan Householder Van Horn, *Women, Work, and Fertility, 1900–1986* (New York, 1988); Stearns, *American Cool*, 207–8; William Emerson, "The 'Weight Chart' Campaign," *Woman's Home Companion* (1921): 30.

9. Children's Bureau, *Infant Care* (Washington, DC, 1914); Herbert Loomis, Dorothy Reader, and Charles Catlin, "Methods of Treatment of Obesity," *Practitioner* 138 (1937): 95; James G. Hughes, *Pediatrics in General Practice* (New York, 1952), 144; L. E. Holt, Rustin McIntosh, and H. L. Barnett, *Pediatrics* (New York, 1953), 256, 258; I. N. Kugelmass, *Superior Children Through Modern Nutrition* (New York, 1942), 291; Mary S. Ross, *Feeding the Family* (New York, 1955), 185; Flanders Dunbar, *Your Child's Mind and Body* (New York, 1949), 386.

10. David Hull, D. I. Johnston, and L. Churchill, *Essential Pediatrics* (New York, 1987), 82; Monsen Ziai, *Pediatrics* (Boston, 1969), 67, 888–89.

11. Elizabeth Scott Stearns diary, Oct. 13, 1944, in possession of Sarah Stearns Gipson, Indianapolis, IN; Gladys O. Shultz, "Our Underfed Children," *LHJ* (Mar. 1951): 44–45; L. E. Holt. "The Reluctant Eater," *Good Housekeeping* (Nov. 1956): 132; Charles Aldrich, *Cultivating the Child's Appetite* (New York, 1931); Marion Farmer, "Between Meals," *Nation's School*, Jan. 1934, 256; Frank Richardson, "Your Underweight Child," *Good Housekeeping* (Jan. 1930): 35; Josephine Kenyon, "Thin Child," *Good Housekeeping* (Oct. 1933): 98; Lettie Gay, "Feeding the Under-weight Child," *Parents' Magazine* (Mar. 1936): 40.

12. Bruce Addington, *Your Growing Child* (New York, 1927), 290–99; Marion Faegre, J. E. Anderson, and Dale Harris, *Child Care and Training* (Minneapolis, 1958), 38–39. William Emerson, "The Over-Weight Child," *Women's Home Companion*, Apr. 1920, 31; Clara Taylor, "Boys Eat Too Much — or Do They?" *Parents' Magazine* (Aug. 1949): 65; Samuel Wishnik, *Feeding Your Child* (New York, 1925), 185; Josephine H. Kenyon, *Healthy Babies Are Happy Babies* (Boston, 1934), 252, 265; Benjamin Spock and M. E. Lowenberg, *Feeding Your Baby and Child* (New York, 1955), 68 and 206 ff.

13. Barbara Wyden, "The Fat Child is Father of the Man," *New York Times Magazine* (Sept. 13, 1970): 89–91; Hilde Bruch, "The Emotional Significance of Preferred Weight," *Symposium on Nutrition and Behavior* (Minneapolis, 1956), 91.

14. A. N. W. Evans and C. A. McCarthy, *Pediatrics* (Boston, 1986); Marvin J. Gersh and Iris F. Litt, "A Fitness Program for Overweight Teen-Agers," *Parents' Magazine* (Aug. 1971): 70; Janice T. Gibson, "Eating Right From the Start," *Parents' Magazine* (Jan. 1989): 122; David Hull and D. I. Johnson, *Essential Pediatrics* (New York, 1987); Michael Modell and Robert Boyd, *Pediatric Problems in General Practice* (Oxford, 1982); Donald Pinkel, "Editorial," *Parents' Magazine* (Oct. 1973): 26; Ziai, *Pediatrics*. It is important to note that actual medical judgments about the role of childhood fat in adult overweight are still in dispute, even as popular outlets like *Parents Magazine* now claim definite, even specific percentage relationships.

15. George Knapp, "My Mother Made Me Fat," *Redbook* (Jan. 1969): 53.

16. Winfred Van Atta, "Program for Overweight Teenagers," *Parents' Magazine* (Nov. 1968): 70.

17. Stearns, *American Cool*, 141–48; Carl Renz and Mildred Renz, *Big Problems on Little Shoulders* (New York, 1934), 84, 86–87; Robert I. Watson, *Psychology of the Child* (New York, 1959), 156; Ruth Benedict, *The Chrysanthemum and the Sword* (Boston, 1946).

18. Richard Klein, "Big Country: The Roots of American Obesity," *New Republic* (Sept. 19, 1994): 32, 34.

NOTES TO CHAPTER SEVEN

1. "Pourquoi les régimes ne marchent pas," *Biba* (Apr. 1994): 98.

2. Henri Feuillard and Maurice Feuillard, *Le Livre de l'obèse* (Paris, 1935), l; Guy Thuillier, *Aspects de l'économie nivernaise au XIXe siècle* (Paris, 1966); Jean-Anthelme Brillat-Savarin, *The Physiology of Taste, or Meditations on Transcendental Gastronomy* (1825; translation New York, 1860); see also chap. 9, below.

3. Paul Strauss, *Dépopulation et puériculture* (Paris, 1901); Louis Devraigne, *Vingt-cinq ans de puériculture et d'hygiène sociale* (Paris, 1928).

4. On French longevity interests, Gerald Gruman, "A History of Ideas about the Prolongation of Life," *American Philosophical Society Transactions* 56 (1966); P. Flourens, *De la longévité humaine* (Paris, 1854); M. A. Legrand, *La Longevité à travers les ages* (Paris, 1911); A. Quételet, *Sur l'homme et le développement de ses facultés* (Brussels, 1835), and *Essai sur le développement des facultés de l'homme* (Brussels, 1871); Charles Bouchard, *Traité de pathologie générale*, vol. III (Paris, 1900): Jacques Martinie, *Notes sur l'histoire de l'obésité*, (thesis, Paris Medical School, 1934), 661; E. D'Heilly, "Obésité," in *Nouveau dictionnaire de médecine et de chirurgie pratique* (Paris, 1877); Dancel, *Traite théorique et pratique de l'obésité* (Paris, 1863); Lucien Dubourg, *Recherches sur les causes de l'obésité* (Paris, 1863); Briquet, "Influence de la quantité de boisson sur la production de l'obésité," *Annales d'hygiène* (1898); Elisabeth Archer, *L'Obésité à travers les ages* (master's thesis, Clermont-Ferrand Medical School, 1978). For a discussion of the height and weight criteria for males, see Maurice Perrin and Paul Mathieu, *L'Obésité* (Paris, 1923), 1–16.

5. Geneviève Michel, *L'Enjeu des apparences* (master's thesis, University of Paris, 1987–8), 1; Baronne Stoffe, *Le Cabinet de toilette* (Paris, 1892); Edward Shorter, *Women's Bodies; A Social History of Women's Encounters with Health, Ill-health and Medicine* (New Brunswick, NJ, 1990); Vicomtesse de Lisle, "Élégance de femme," *Femme française* (1903): 1183.

6. Marie-Pierre Jolly, *Les Femmes et la consommation de vêtements à partir des années 50* (Paris, 1991); Philippe Perrot, *Le Travail des apparences, ou les transformations du corps féminin XVIIIe-XIXe siècles* (Paris, 1987).

7. Rudolph Binion, "Fiction as Social Fantasy: Europe's Domestic Crisis of 1879–1914," *Journal of Social History* 27 (1994): 679–99.

8. *Journal de la beauté* (1896); Perrot, *Travail des apparences*.

9. Marylene Delbourg-Delphis, *Le Chic et le look: Histoire de la mode féminine et des moeurs, de 1890 à nos jours* (Paris, 1981); Perrin and Mathieu, *Obésité*.

10. Bibliothèque historique de la ville de Paris, document series under the heading Actualités: Diététique, Culture Physique.

11. M. Labbé, "Dangers de la suralimentation habituelle," *Revue médicale* (Feb. 1907); LeNoir, *L'Obésité et son traitement* (Paris, 1909); Francis Heckel, *Grandes et petites obésités* (Paris, 1920); Archer, *Obésité à travers les ages*; P. Oulmont and F. Rainard, *L'Obésité* (Paris, 1907); A. Gautier, *L'Alimentation et les régimes* (Paris, 1908); Albert Mathieu, *L'Hygiène de l'obèse* (Paris, 1906).

12. Labbé, "Dangers," 37.

13. Gaston Durville, *L'Art de vivre longtemps* (Paris, 1903); H. Collière, *Végétarisme et longue vie* (Paris, 1904); Barnay, *Comment on se defend de la vieillesse* (Paris, 1909).

14. On the nineteenth-century French medical establishment, Olivier Faure, *Maladies et médecins* (Lyons, 1993); Jacques Leonard, *La France médicale au 19e siècle* (Paris, 1978), and *La Médicine entre les savoirs et les pouvoirs; histoire intellectuelle et politique de la médicine française au XIXe siècle* (Paris, 1981).

15. Heckel, *Grandes et petites obésités*; *Journal de la beauté*, 1896.

16. Heckel, *Grandes et petites obésités*, 65; Vicomtesse de Lisle, "Élégance," 1183; "Comment on doit s'habiller," *La Femme française* (May 22, 1903).

17. Comtesse de Tramar, *Le Bréviaire de la femme* (Paris, 1903), 164, 167–68; *Journal de la beauté*, 1896.

18. Françoise Héritier-Auge, "Older Women, Stout-Hearted Women, Women of Substance," in Michel Feher, ed., *Fragments for a History of the Human Body* (New York, 1990).

19. Dubourg-Delphis, *Le Chic et le look*; Mary Louise Roberts, "Samson and Delilah Revisited: The Politics of Women's Fashions in 1920s France," *American Historical Review* (1993): 679–81.

20. Karen Offen, "Body Politics: Women, Work and the Politics of Motherhood in France, 1920–1950," in Gisela Bock and Pat Thane, eds., *Maternity and Gender Policies* (London, 1991); James McMillan, *Housewife or Harlot: The Place of Woman in French Society, 1870–1940* (New York, 1981); Rene Bizet, *La Mode* (Paris, 1925); Anne-Marie Sohn, *Chrysalides: femmes dans la vie privée (XIXe-XXe siècles*, 2v. (Paris, 1996).

21. *Votre beauté* (Apr. 1934): 14.

22. Dr. Ruffier, *Le Traitement de l'obésité par la culture physique* (Paris, n.d. [1930s]), 19; Paul Mathieu, *Pourquoi on engraisse: Comment on maigrit* (Paris, 1931), 12, 21.

23. Ellen Furlough, "Selling the American Way in Interwar France," *Journal of Social History* 24 (1991): 237–54; "Traité de la silhouette féminine," *Vogue* (Nov. 1924): 48; *Vogue* (1936 and June 1937): 130; "La Beauté facile," *L'Illustration* (Apr. 22, 1933); Roberts, "Samson and Delilah," 659.

24. *Votre beauté* (Jan. 1934); "Maigrir, Premiers conseils," *Votre beauté* (Jan. 1934): 32; "Maigrir et bien manger," *Votre beauté* (Mar. 1934): 13; Gilbert-Dreyfus, *Hygiène et régimes des obèses* (Paris, 1934).

25. Perrin and Mathieu, *Obésité*.

26. Jean Leray, *Embonpoint et obésité* (Paris, 1931), 23–25; Leven, *L'Obésité et son traitement* (Paris, 1934); J. Frumusan, *La Cure de l'obésité* (Paris, 1922), 28, 55; Comité national de l'enfance, *L'Alimentation de l'enfant à l'adulte* (Paris, 1936); P. Mathieu, *Pourquoi on engraisse*. On children, see chap. 8, below.

27. Paul Deboux, *Nouveaux régimes* (Paris, 1931); Martinie, *Notes sur l' histoire de l'obésité*, 661; Gilbert-Dreyfus, *Hygiène et régimes*.

28. Henri Béraud, *La Martyre de l'obèse* (Paris, 1923), 12, 14, 54, 78, 145.

29. *La Femme chez elle* (Jan.-Feb. 1935) (dossier "régime," Bibliothèque Marguerite Durand); Susan B. Whitney, "Embracing the Status Quo: French Communists, Young Women and the Popular Front," *Journal of Social History* 29 (1996): 29–54; Gilbert-Dreyfus, *Hygiène et régimes*.

30. *Vogue* (1936) (dossier "régime," Bibliothèque Marguerite Durand); L. Lonjon-Raynaud, *Maigrir par l'éléctricite* (Paris, 1937); dossier "sport," Bibliothèque Marguerite Durand; *Figaro* (June 1927); *Eve* (1929); *Fémina* (1924) (dossier "régime," Bibliothèque Marguerite Durand).

31. J. A. Huet and Guy Godlewski, *Obésité maigreur: régimes rationnels* (Paris, 1939).

32. Michel Albeaux-Fernet, *Comment traiter l'obésité* (Paris, 1953); Claude Petit, *Maigrir en vous amusant* (Paris, 1955); Marguerite Duvel, *Je veux maigrir, je veux grossir* (Paris, 1956), 16; Georges Decormeille, *Maigrir sans larmes* (Paris, 1952); Roger Rivallard, *Quelques considérations sur l'attitude du médecin practicien face à l'obèse* (master's thesis, Paris Medical School, 1963); Elie Azaral, *Lettres à un ami obèse* (Paris, 1970).

33. *Marie-France*, 1946–47; Josette Lyon, "Les 10 Enemies de votre jeunesse," *Marie Claire* (Jan. 1954): 62, and "Vous allez vaincre les 2 enemies de votre ligne, embonpoint et cellulite," *Marie Claire* (May 1954): 39.

34. Elmer Wheeler, *Le Manuel de l'obèse repenti* (Paris, 1953); Georges Decormeille, *Maigrir sans larmes* (Paris, 1952); *Marie Claire* (Mar. 1957): 71–72; Pascale Pinson, *La France à table, 1960–1986* (Paris, 1987), 135, 163. For general comments on the complex Americanization context, see Richard Kuisel, *Seducing the French: The Dilemma of Americanization* (Berkeley, 1953).

35. Jolly, *Les Femmes et la consommation de vêtements*.

36. Jolly, *Les Femmes et la consommation de vêtements*, 11.

37. Jean Petit, *Maigrir et bien manger* (Paris, 1972); Olivier Roujansky, *Comment maigrir en mangeant 400 grammes de pain par jour* (Paris, 1976); Claude Fischler, *L'Omnivore* (Paris, 1990), which particularly highlights — and laments — the innovation of the past three decades.

38. Jacques Moron, *La Clef du poids* (Paris, 1974); Léone Bérard, *Pour Maigrir* (Paris, 1977); A. D. Herschberg, *Maigrir et rester mince* (Paris, 1977); Albert Francis Creff and Léone Bérard, *Les Kilos de trop* (Paris, 1977); Gérard Debuigne, *Vivre mince et belle* (Paris, 1978); Gilbert-Dreyfus, *Pourquoi l'on grossit et comment mincir* (Paris, 1977); Jean Trémolières, *Diététique et art de vivre* (Paris, 1975).

39. Jolly, *Les Femmes et la consommation des vêtements*; *Marie Claire* (Mar. 1956) (dossier "régime," Bibliothèque Marguerite Durand); "Les Conseils de Josette Lyon," *Marie Claire* (Jan 1956); Josette Lyon, "Voici un plan de beauté au soleil," *Marie Claire* (May 1957): 53–54.

40. Y. Thiery, *Le Conseiller de la femme* (Brussels, 1963), 655; L. Pernaud, *J'attends un enfant* (Paris, 1966), 49–70; J.-P. Cohen and R. Goirand, *Mon bébé* (Paris, 1976); Geneviève Delaincle Parseval and Suzanne Lallemand, *L'Art d'accommoder les bébés* (Paris, 1980).

41. Duvel, *Je veux maigrir*, 7–8; Marcel Rouet, *Plaire* (Paris, 1949), 26.

42. Rouet, *Plaire*; Moron, *La Clef du poids*, 225–28 particularly drives home the *culotte de cheval*, claiming interestingly that the condition has increased as a result of widespread use of birth control pills (which can alter fat distribution). For other early emphases of the term, Herschberg, *Maigrir*, 154; Creff and Bérard, *Kilos*, 179.

43. *La Vie* (Aug. 1982) (dossier "régime," Bibliothèque Marguerite Durand); "La Folie des kilos," *Marie Claire* (July 1994); "Enquête," *Marie Claire* (Jan. 1995): 68; *Le Monde* (Oct. 1980); *Le Monde* (Jan. 26, 1995); *Figaro Madame*, "Spécial minceur" (Mar. 1995): 98.

44. Josette Lyon, "Il n'y a plus de grosses femmes," *Marie Claire* (Sept. 1959): 110.

45. "Questions de poids," *Elle* (Aug. 15, 1994): 56–57.

46. Lyon, "Il n'y a plus de grosses femmes," 110.

NOTES TO CHAPTER EIGHT

1. Michel Perin, *Contributions à l'étude des obésités* (master's thesis, Paris Medical School, 1954), #375; Gilbert-Dreyfus, *Pourquoi l'on grossit et comment mincir* (Paris, 1977).

2. Henri Béraud, *Le Martyre de l'obèse* (Paris, 1933); Pascale Pinson, *La France à table, 1960–1986* (Paris, 1987), 236.

3. Jean Trémolières, *Diététique et art de vivre* (Paris, 1975), 117.

4. Mary Louise Roberts, "Samson and Delilah Revisited: The Politics of Women's Fashion in 1920s France," *American Historical Review* 98 (1993): 679–81.

5. See, for example, a woman's reaction to turn-of-the-century American feminism, "Woman, American or other, is like a child. . . . Power, liberty are dangerous instruments in her hands." Charlotte Chabrier-Rieder, "Ce que les américains pensent de leurs femmes et du féminisme," *Mercure de France* 49 (1904): 348.

6. Maurice Perrin and Paul Mathieu, *L'Obésité* (Paris, 1923); Paul Irlinger, Catherine Couveau, and Michele Metoudi, "L'Activité physique, une manière de soigner l'apparence" *Données sociales* (1990): 269–72.

7. *Modes et travaux* (1950–1989); Pinson, *La France à table*, 249.

8. "Les Miracles du régime," *Information* (July 4, 1995): 7; "Alimentation: mangez sain," *Voici* (July 3–9, 1995): 13; see also diet advertisements in the issue; "Maigrir: les trucs de l'été," *Ton Santé* (July 1995): 1.

9. Albert-François Creff and Léone Bérard, *Les Kilos de trop* (Paris, 1977).

10. I was able to find no relevant publication for French of African origin that dealt with weight issues. Simple observation on the street suggests a commitment by French of African or West Indian origin to considerable slenderness, whether according to French or African standards or both.

11. Comité national de l'enfance, *L'Alimentation de l'enfant à l'adulte* (Paris, 1936), 6; Marie-Joseph P. A. Maynadier, *L'Obésité chez l'enfant* (master's thesis, Paris Medical School), 1934, #635; Louis Devraigne, *Vingt-cinq ans de puériculture et d'hygiène sociale* (Paris, 1928).

12. Paul Strauss, *Dépopulation et puériculture* (Paris, 1901); Tony Blanche, *L'Enfant: Causeries sur la manière d'élever les enfants* (Paris, 1892); Dr. Bonniot,

Notions d'hygiène pratique à l'école primaire (Paris, n. d.); H. Rouèche, *Hygiène social de l'enfance* (Paris, 1948); E. C. Aviragnet and J. Peignaux, *Soins à donner aux enfants* (Paris, 1932).

13. René Martial, *Principes d'hygiène* (Paris, 1920); G. Demirleau, *Catéchisme de puériculture pratique et modern* (Paris, 1932); J. L. Montangé and A. Jacquot, *Notions d'hygiène à l'usage des écoles* (Paris, 1914); E. C. Aviragnet and J. Peignaux, *Soins à donner aux enfants* (Paris, 1932).

14. J. Renault and C. de Tannenberg, *Alimentation des enfants* (Paris, 1923); Comité national de l'enfance, *Cours de puériculture en dix leçons* (Paris, 1939), 45; Raoul Mercier, *Conférences d'hygiène et de puériculture* (Paris, 1908); Augusta Moll-Weiss, *L'Alimentation de la jeunesse française* (Paris, 1931); Comité national de l'enfance, *Problèmes et aspects de la puériculture moderne* (Paris, 1942), 110; Dr. Rocaz, *L'Hygiène de l'enfant* (Paris, 1935), 85.

15. Simonne Lacapère, *Le Métier des parents* (Paris, 1982).

16. Augusta Moll-Weiss, *Nos tout petits* (Paris, 1906); Geneviève Delaincle Parseval and Suzanne Lallemand, *L'Art d'accommoder les bébés* (Paris, 1980); Leon Kriesler, *Guide de la jeune mère* (Paris, 1975); Dr. Champendal, *Le Petit manuel des mères* (Mulhouse, n.d.).

17. Dr. Galtier-Boissières, *Pour elever les nourissons* (Paris, 1906), 74.

18. Fernand Lagrange, *L'Hygiène de l'exercice chez les enfants et les jeunes gens* (Paris, 1910); Moll-Weiss, *Alimentation de la jeunesse française*, 125; Rocaz, *Hygiène de l'enfant*, 118.

19. Kriesler, *Guide de la jeune mère*, 61; M. Manciaux, *Abrégé de pédiatrie préventive et sociale* (Paris, 1971); Simonne Lacapère, *Le Métier des parents* (Paris, 1982), 31; Simone Benjamin and Roger Benjamin, *Le Jeune enfant et ses besoins fondamentaux* (Paris, 1975), 57.

20. Champendal, *Petit manuel des mères*, 50.

21. On the overall dimensions of the puériculture campaign and its social outreach, H. Rouèche, *Hygiène social de l'enfance* (Paris, 1948); Louis Devraigne, *Vingt-cinq ans de puériculture et d'hygiène sociale* (Paris, 1928). For a critique of traditional strictness with children, and a claim that times are changing, Parseval and Lallemand, *Art d'accommoder les bébés*.

22. Claudine Marence, *Manières de tables, modèles de moeurs, 17ème-20ème siècle* (Paris, 1992), 226–29; Berthe Foumier, *Nos Enfants*, (Paris, 1935), 35.

23. Moll-Weiss, *Alimentation de la jeunesse française*; Jean-Paul Aron, *Le Mangeur du XIXe siècle* (Paris, 1973), 230.

24. Trémolières, *Diététique et art de vivre*, 114, 149; Gilbert-Dreyfus, *Pourquoi l'on grossit*, 13

25. Trémolières, *Diététique et art de vivre*, 114

26. Paul Mathieu, *Pourquoi on engraisse: Comment on maigrit* (Paris, 1931), 12; Paul Deboux, *Nouveaux régimes* (Paris, 1931); A. D. Herschberg, *Maigrir et rester mince* (Paris, 1977).

27. Colaude Canot, *L'Obésité: Apport de la psychologie* (master's thesis, Paris Medical School, 1961), #554; Gilbert-Dreyfus, *Pourquoi l'on grossit*.

28. Gilbert-Dreyfus, *Pourquoi l'on grossit*, 105; Herschberg, *Maigrir*, 204; Creff and Bérard, *Kilos*, 133; Francis Heckel, *Grandes et petites obésités* (Paris, 1920), 459.

29. Gilbert-Dreyfus, *Pourquoi l'on grossit*, 240, 249.

30. *Eve* (1929) (dossier "régime," Bibliothèque Marguerite Durand); Josette Lyon, "Vous allez vaincre les 2 enemies de votre ligne, embonpoint et cellulite," *Marie Claire* (May 1954); Marie-Pierre Jolly, *Les Femmes et la consommation de vêtements à partir des annees 50* (Paris, 1991); Josette Lyon, "Il n'y a plus de grosses femmes," *Marie Claire* (Sept. 1959): 110; Gerard Débuigne, *Vivre mince et belle* (Paris, 1978); "La Beauté facile," *L'Illustration* (Apr. 22, 1933) (dossier "régime," Bibliothèque Marguerite Durand).

31. Creff and Bérard, *Kilos*, 73, 133.

32. Jacques Decourt and Michel Perin, *L'Obésité* (Paris, 1962), 63–65; Marguerite Duvel, *Je veux maigrir, je veux grossir* (Paris, 1956), 15–16; Elie Azaral, *Lettres à un ami obèse* (Paris, 1970), 7–8, 45, 55–57.

33. Herschberg, *Maigrir*, 154; *Elle* (Mar. 14, 1994): 117.

34. Gilbert-Dreyfus, *Pourquoi l'on grossit*, 29

35. Annick Peinge, "Nous maigrirons ensemble," *Le Temps des femmes* (1988): 14–16; *Le Monde* (June 25, 1995) (dossier "régime," Bibliothèque Marguerite Durand); Creff and Bérard, *Kilos*, 133 ff.; on different jealousy reactions in France and the United States, see Peter Salovey, ed., *The Psychology of Jealousy and Envy* (New York, 1991).

36. Robert W. Fogel, "New Sources and New Techniques for the Study of Secular Trends in Nutritional Status, Health, Mortality and the Process of Aging," *Historical Methods* (1993): 5–43; A. Quetelet, *Essai sur le développement des facultés de l'homme* (Brussels, 1871); A. Quetelet, *Sur l'homme et le développement des ses facultés* (Paris, 1835), 325–26; LeNoir, *L'Obésité et son traitement* (Paris, 1909).

37. Quetelet, *Sur l'homme*; A. Charraud and H. Valdelièvre, "Le Taille et le poids du français," *Economie et statistique* #132 (1981): 23–38.

38. Charraud and Valdelièvre, "Le Taille et le poids du français," 23–38; Corrine Postel, *Poids et taille des français en 1970* (master's thesis, Paris V Medical School, 1970), #38; Marceline Bocher, "Le Corps change, son image aussi," *INSEE Première* (Institut national de la statistique et des études économiques) (Jan. 1995): 356; S. M. Retchin et al., "Health Behavior Changes in the United States, United Kingdom, and France," *Journal of General Internal Medicine* (Nov.-Dec. 1992): 615–22; Dominique Laurier et al., "Prevalence of Obesity: A Comparative Survey in France, the United Kingdom, and the United States," *International Journal of Obesity* 16 (1992): 568; M. F. Rolland-Cachera et al., "Body Mass Index Variations: Centiles from Birth to 87 years," *European Journal of Clinical Nutrition* 45 (1991): 13–21; J. Delarue et al., "Anthropometric Values in an Elderly French Population," *British Journal of Nutrition* (1994): 295–302; C. Bonithon-Kopp et al., "Relationships between three-year longitudinal changes in body mass index, waist-to-hip ratio, and metabolic variables in active French female population," *American Journal of Clinical Nutrition* (1992): 475–82.

39. Pinson, *La France à table*, 82; Trémolières, *Diététique et art de vivre*, 59; A. Basdevant, C. Craplet, and B. Guy-Grand, "Snacking Patterns in Obese French Women," *Appetite* 21 (1993): 17–23.

40. A. Randrianjohany et al., "The Relationship between Behavioural Patterns, Overall and Central Adiposity in a Population of Healthy French Men," *International Journal of Obesity and Related Metabolic Disorders* 17 (1993): 651–55; on

emotional concealment, Shula Summers, "Adults Evaluating Their Emotions: A Cross-Cultural Perspective," in *Emotions in Adult Development,* Carol Zander Malatesta, and Carroll E. Izard, eds. (Beverly Hills, 1984); Peter N. Stearns, *American Cool: Constructing a Twentieth Century Emotional Style* (New York, 1994).

41. Stewart Toy, "Guiltless Gorging in the French Fashion," *Business Week* (Dec. 30, 1991): 46; Daryn Eller, "How Frenchwomen Stay That Thin," *Mademoiselle* (Jan. 1992): 35; Laura Shapiro, "Eat, Drink and Be Wary," *Newsweek* (Mar. 2, 1992): 68; Richard Klein, "Big Country: The Roots of American Obesity," *New Republic* (Sept. 19, 1994): 32.

42. Marcia Millner, *Such a Pretty Face: Being Fat in America* (New York, 1980); *Le Monde* (Jan. 26, 1995) (dossier "régime," Bibliothèque Marguerite Durand).

NOTES TO CHAPTER NINE

1. Pascale Pinson, *La France à table, 1960–1986* (Paris, 1987), 17–32, 259. MacDonald's started in France in 1972. By 1983, 45 percent of all French restaurant meals were rapidly cooked, one-course offerings of some sort, with actual fast foods a growing portion of this total.

2. Marylène Delbourg-Delphis, *Le Chic et le look: Histoire de la mode féminine et des moeurs de 1850 à nos jours* (Paris, 1989), 39, 108; Lois Banner, *American Beauty* (New York, 1983).

3. Gerald Mendelsohn, Françoise de la Tour, Geneviève Coudin, and François Baveau, "A Comparative Study of the Adaptation to Breast Cancer and Its Treatment in French and American Women," *Cahiers d'Anthropologie et Biométrie Humaine* 2 (1984): 71–96.

4. John Ardagh, *France in the 1980s* (London, 1982). For reasonably precise comparison of leisure and sexuality, Michel Forsé et al., *Recent Social Trends in France, 1960–1990* (Frankfort/Main, 1993), 274, 290; and Theodore Caplow et al., *Recent Social Trends in the United States* (Frankfort/Main, 1991), 435.

5. Jean-François Revel, *Un Festin en paroles* (Paris, 1979); Jean-Paul Aron, *Essai sur la sensibilité alimentaire à Paris au 19e siècle* (Paris, 1967); Jean-Louis Flandrin, *Chronique de plantine: pour une gastronomie historique* (Paris, 1922); *Le Cuisinier français* (Paris, 1983).

6. Jean-Anthelme Brillat-Savarin, *The Physiology of Taste, or Meditations on Transcendental Gastronomy* (1825; translation, New York, 1860), 3–4. French re-editions have appeared every decade or so into the 1960s.

7. Ibid., 8, 42, 107, 173, 273.

8. Flandrin, *Chronique,* 95.

9. Reay Tannahill, *Food in History* (New York, 1973); A. Tavenat, *L'Art culinaire,* 2 vols. (Paris, 1863); Philéas Gilbert, *L'Art culinaire,* 2 vols. (Paris, 1884); Stephen Menell, *All Manners of Food: Eating and Taste in England and France from the Middle Ages to the Present* (New York, 1983), 34 ff.

10. Jean-Paul Aron, *Le Mangeur du XIXe siècle* (Paris, 1973), 230; for the contrast with British banquets, John Burnett, *Plenty and Want: A Social History of Diet in England* (London, 1979), 218–30; on American banquets, Betty Watson, *Cooks, Gluttons and Gourmets* (New York, 1962), 297.

11. Anne Audier, *Le Temps écoute: Comme on glane la mémoire paysanne* (Saintonge, 1994), 46, 86, 105. Thanks to Eugen Weber for this reference.

12. Pinson, *La France à table.*

13. Aron, *Le Mangeur,* 83, 230, 280.

14. Richard Cummings, *The American and His Food* (Chicago, 1940); Howard Jones, *American and French Culture, 1750–1848* (Chapel Hill, NC, 1917), 92–94; Harvey A. Levenstein, *Revolution at the Table* (New York, 1988), 11–14; Yves Grosrichard, *L'Amérique insolite* (Paris, 1958), 31.

15. Waverley Root and Richard de Rochemont, *Eating Well in America* (New York, 1976), 124, 125; Constantin Volney, *View of the Soul and Climate of the United States of America* (London, 1804), 323.

16. John C. Super, *Food, Conquest and Colonization in Sixteenth-Century Spanish America* (Albuquerque, 1988), 84–85; thanks to Erick Langer for this reference; Leon Baritz, *The Good Life: The Meaning of Success for the American Middle-Class* (New York, 1982); Eleanor Arnold, *Voices of American Homemaker* (Bloomington, 1985); David M. Potter, *People of Plenty: Economic Abundance and American Character* (Chicago, 1954), 191–93; Tannahill, *Food*; Watson, *Cooks,* 297.

17. Root and de Rochemont, *Eating,* 314; Volney, *View,* 323; Cummings, *American,* 10–11. On haste, convenience trends, and other recent habits, Sidney Mintz, *Tasting Food, Tasting Freedom* (Boston, 1996), esp. chap. 8.

18. On the evolution of snacks, see *LHJ* (Dec. 1889-Jan. 1930), esp. (Dec. 1889): 16, (Feb. 1900): 71, (July 1900): 42, (Nov. 1914): 48, (Aug. 1920): 129, (Jan. 1927): 78, (Jan. 1930): 108; Levenstein, *Revolution,* 35–41. Oddly, the unique role of American snacking has not previously been envisioned.

19. Maureen Greenwald, "Mealtime over Time" (paper presented to the Organization of American Historians, Apr. 1994), my thanks to Professor Greenwald; Richard Klein, "Big Country: The Roots of American Obesity," *New Republic* (Sept. 19, 1994): 32.

20. Root and de Rochemont, *Eating,* 138, Jo Ann Cassall, *Carry the Flame: The History of the American Dietetic Association* (Washington, DC, 1990); Mary I. Barber, *History of the American Dietetic Association* (Philadelphia, 1959).

21. On the importance of implanting abundance in children, Potter, *People of Plenty,* 191–93; Paul Rozin et al., "Attitudes to Food and the Role of Food in Life," unpublished ms. I am most grateful to Professor Rozin for letting me consult this important study.

22. *Gourmet, Connoisseur in Eating and Drinking,* 1941–1958; Rozin et al., "Attitudes," 17.

23. Rozin et al., 17.

24. It is important to note that definitive histories of consumerism, much less comparisons, are few and far between. This book uses some major findings about overall consumerism patterns and anxieties — the rising tide of the latter has been well studied for France — while seeking to advance the field in the comparative direction.

25. Elaine S. Abelson, *When Ladies Go A-Thieving: Middle-Class Shoppers in the Victorian Department Store* (New York, 1989), 46, 58; Patricia O'Brien, "The Kleptomania Diagnosis: Bourgeois Women and Theft in Late Nineteenth-Century France," in Peter N. Stearns, *Expanding the Past: A Reader in Social History*

(New York, 1988), 105–16; Alexandre Lacassagne, "Les Vols à étalage et dans les grands magasins," *Revue de l' hypnotisme et de la psychologie physiologique* 2 (1896): 77.

26. Emile Zola, *Au Bonheur des dames* (Paris, 1871); Michael Miller, *The Bon Marché: Bourgeois Culture and the Department Store, 1869–1920* (Princeton, 1981), 204 ff.; Mary Louise Roberts, "Samson and Delilah Revisited: The Politics of Women's Fashion in 1920s France," *American Historical Review* (1993): 657–81.

27. Rosalind H. Williams, *Dream Worlds: Mass Consumption in Late Nineteenth-Century France* (Berkeley, 1982), 173, 263, 323; Robert F. Byrnes, *Anti-Semitism in Modern France* (New Brunswick, NJ, 1950), 261–63.

28. Georges Duhamel, *Scènes de la vie future* (Paris, 1929); Ellen Furlough, "Selling the American Way in Interwar France," *Journal of Social History* 26 (1993): 501–20.

29. Warren G. Breckman, "Disciplining Consumption: The Debate about Luxury in Wilhelmine Germany, 1890–1914," *Journal of Social History* 24 (1991): 237–54.

30. Bonnie G. Smith, *Ladies of the Leisure Class: The Bourgeoises of Northern France in the Nineteenth Century* (Princeton, 1981), 71.

31. R. W. Fox and T. J. Jackson Lears, eds., *The Culture of Consumption* (New York, 1983). In their introduction, the editors attribute new consumerism to the new, more boring corporate structure of middle-class work, along with the sheer abundance of goods.

32. Seth Koven and Sonya Michel, eds., *Mothers of a New World: Maternalist Politics and the Origins of Welfare States* (New York, 1993).

33. Albert Mathieu, *L'Hygiène de l'obèse* (Paris, 1906), 83–84: Jean Trémolières, *Diététique et art de vivre* (Paris, 1975).

34. Julius H. Ruben, *Religious Melancholy and Protestant Experience in America* (New York, 1994).

NOTES TO CHAPTER TEN

1. Norbert Elias, *The Civilizing Process* (New York, 1978): Mary Lindemann, s.v. "Body," in Peter N. Stearns, ed., *Encyclopedia of Social History* (New York, 1994), 80–82; Michel Forsé et al., *Recent Social Trends in France, 1960–1990* (Frankfurt/Main, 1993), 274.

2. For a convenient summary, Geoffrey Growley, "The Biology of Beauty," *Newsweek* (1996): 60–67.

3. Peter N. Stearns, *American Cool: Constructing a Twentieth-Century Emotional Style* (New York, 1994).

4. Hillel Schwartz, *Never Satisfied: A Cultural History of Diets, Fantasies, and Fat* (New York, 1983); Roberta Seid, *Never Too Thin: Why Women Are at War With Their Bodies* (New York, 1989); Claude Fischler, *L'Omnivore* (Paris, 1990), 372.

This is the approach taken in the recent book by Richard Klein—*Eat Fat* (New York, 1996)—which offers a highly selective history of worthy fat, brushes aside much serious inquiry into modern culture (though correctly if oversimply commenting on extensive diet failure) and, in what is essentially an extended editorial, urges contemporary people to loosen their belts.

5. The current culture of biological science, with its passion for genetics, may obfuscate causation, confusing genetic predispositions with the shifts in culture and economic context that primarily prompt change. For a recent comment on genetics and obesity, with some recognition of this dilemma amid great enthusiasm for the proposition that genetics may explain everything, see "Hormone is Clue to Control of Weight," *New York Times*, Aug. 1, 1995, Science section, 8.

6. Leon Kass, *The Hungry Soul: Eating and the Perfecting of Our Nature* (New York, 1994).

INDEX